ideas number thirteen
ideas number fourteen
ideas number fifteen
ideas number sixteen

Four Complete Volumes of Ideas in One

Edited by Wayne Rice and Mike Yaconelli.
Previously published as four separate books.

table of contents

CHAPTER FOUR: SPECIAL EVENTS 160

CHAPTER FIVE: CAMPING 183

HOW TO GET MORE GREAT IDEAS

There are many other outstanding books like this one in the complete **Ideas** library, each with a different assortment of great youth programming ideas. Since 1968, Youth Specialties has collected more than three thousand tried and tested ideas from America's most creative youth workers and has published them in **Ideas,** with several new books being published each year.

All 35 volumes of **Ideas** are still available from Youth Specialties by using the order form below. Each book is different and contains dozens of ideas that you can use right now. The first twenty-four volumes have been updated and re-published as six "combo" books, with four complete volumes in each book. These books are $17.95 each and are a real bargain. The other books (volumes 25 through 35) are available at the single volume price of $6.95 each, as is the **Ideas Index,** a handy guide to the first thirty volumes. The entire **Ideas** library (six "combo" books, eleven single volumes, plus the **Index**) may be purchased for a total of $150.00, a savings of over $40.00 off the regular prices.

HOW TO KEEP IDEAS COMING

A brand new volume of **Ideas** is published every three months, and you may automatically receive each of the next four books by ordering a subscription to **Ideas** for $24.95. It's the best way to make sure you always have plenty of the latest youth programming ideas available anywhere. To start your subscription to **Ideas,** use the order form below.

IDEAS ORDER FORM

Check desired books below:

☐ Ideas 1-4 ($17.95)
☐ Ideas 5-8 ($17.95)
☐ Ideas 9-12 ($17.95)
☐ Ideas 13-16 ($17.95)
☐ Ideas 17-20 ($17.95)
☐ Ideas 21-24 ($17.95)
☐ Ideas Index ($7.95)

Single volumes of Ideas at $6.95 each:

☐ Ideas #25 ☐ Ideas #29 ☐ Ideas #33
☐ Ideas #26 ☐ Ideas #30 ☐ Ideas #34
☐ Ideas #27 ☐ Ideas #31 ☐ Ideas #35
☐ Ideas #28 ☐ Ideas #32

☐ Subscription to Ideas (four volumes for $24.95)
☐ Entire Ideas Library (35 volumes for $150.00)

☐ **Check or money order enclosed.** (We pay shipping. California residents add 6% sales tax.)
☐ **Please Bill Me.** (Shipping charges plus a 5% billing charge will be added to the total amount.)

Name _____

Address _____

City _____ State _____ Zip code _____

Church or Organization _____

Have you ever ordered from Youth Specialties before?   ☐ Yes   ☐ No

Clip and mail to: Youth Specialties, 1224 Greenfield Dr., El Cajon, CA 92021

Your Idea May Be Worth $100

It's worth at least $10.00 if we publish it in a future volume of **Ideas**. And it's worth $100.00 if it is chosen as the outstanding idea of the book it appears in.

It's not really a contest. It's just our way of saying "thanks" for sharing your creativity with us. If you have a good idea that worked well with your group, send it in. We'll look it over and decide whether or not we can include it in a future **Ideas** book. If we do, we'll send you at least ten bucks!

In addition to that, our **Ideas** editors will select one especially creative idea from each new book as the outstanding idea of that particular book. To its contributor, we'll send a check for $100.00

So don't let your good ideas go to waste. Write them down and send them to us along with this card. When you do, try to explain your ideas as completely as you can (without getting ridiculous), and include any sample materials, illustrations, diagrams, or photos that might be helpful.

FILL OUT BELOW

Name _____

Address _____ State_____ Zip _____

City _____

I hereby submit the attached idea(s) to Youth Specialties for publication in IDEAS, and guarantee that to my knowledge the publication of these ideas by Youth Specialties does not violate any copyright belonging to another party. I also understand that I will receive payment for these ideas, the exact amount to be determined by Youth Specialties, payable on publication in IDEAS.

Signature _____

Write or type out your idea(s) and attach to this form or a copy of this form. Put your name somewhere on the idea(s) as well. Mail to Youth Specialties, 1224 Greenfield Drive, El Cajon, CA 92021. Ideas submitted to Youth Specialties cannot be returned.

Chapter One

Crowd Breakers

BASKETBALL AWARDS

The following "awards" can be awarded to members of the school or church basketball team at a "fifth quarter" social event, or youth meeting. The "trophies" can be mounted on wooden bases and the "plaques" on 6 x 12 inch pieces of plywood. All should be sanded, varnished, and made to look as much like the real thing as possible. Names can be done with one of those plastic label-making devices.

1. *Player with the greatest offense:* Bottle of mouthwash on base.
2. *Player who smiles the most:* Tube of toothpaste on a plaque.
3. *Player who plays the dirtiest:* Bar of soap on base.
4. *Player with the most fouls:* A chicken (dead or alive) or free dinner at "Kentucky Fried Chicken"
5. *Most energetic player:* Vitamin pill on base.
6. *Best substitute player:* Book to read while sitting on the bench.
7. *Toughest Player:* Bottle of "Brut" aftershave lotion on base.
8. *Most injured player:* First-aid kit on base.
9. *Player with most baskets:* Easter basket full of candy eggs.
10. *Best dribbler:* Baby bib on a plaque.
11. *Best Jumper:* Frog (real or phony) on base.
12. *Best "clutch" player:* Old clutch or brake pedal on a base.

You can add more to this list with a little creativity. A "serious" trophy or award to outstanding players can also be added to end with a positive note. (Contributed by Ron Allchin, Gary, Indiana)

CHARACTER ANALYSIS

This is good when members of a group don't know each other very well. Have everyone write down some information about themselves, on a sheet of paper, without their names. Suggested information could include:

1. Favorite food
2. Middle name
3. Hobby
4. Favorite T. V. Show
5. Age when first kissed
6. Most embarrassing moment

After these are filled out, the kids pass them in. They are shuffled, redistributed and each person reads the slip of paper he received to the rest of the group (one at a time). The group then tries to guess who the person is described by the information. This is a fun way to have kids get better acquainted. (Contributed by Roger Paige, Columbia Missouri)

CHRISTMAS CAROLS TO SHOP BY

The following "carols" are great fun to sing during the holiday season. The message of each rings through loud and clear. They were written by Mike Royko and appeared originally in the Chicago Daily News and are reprinted here with permission.

Tune: SANTA CLAUS IS COMING TO TOWN

Y'better not mope, Y'better not frown
Y'better not keep expenditures down,
Santa Claus is coming to town.
Y'better not scrimp, Y'better not save,
Ya gotta give more than the other guy gave,
Santa Claus is coming to town.

So load up all your charge accounts
And let the payments wait
And send expensive Christmas cards
To people that you hate, hate, hate!

Y'better not whine, Y'better not cry,
Everything's fine just as long as you buy;
Santa Claus is coming to town.

Tune: DECK THE HALLS

Deck the streets with phony holly
Fa-la-la-la-la-la-la-la-la
Christmas makes the merchants jolly,
Fa-la-la-la-la-la-la-la-la!
Windows full of gifts to please us,
Fa-la-la-la-la-la-la-la-la!
Happy Birthday, little Jesus
Fa-la-la-la-la-la-la-la-la-la-la-la!

Tune: O, LITTLE TOWN OF BETHLEHEM

O, little town on Christmas Eve
How busy art thou tonight!
Thy stores won't close 'til 10 o'clock,
Thy streets are thronged and bright.
The clerks are tired and cranky,
The merchandise is junk.
The little dears are all in tears,
And Santa Claus is drunk.

Tune: GOOD KING WENCESLAUS

Good King Wenceslaus went out,
'ere the Feast of Stephen:
Merchandise lay all about,
Priced beyond believin'.
"Gee," said Good King Wenceslaus,
"Such expensive presents!
"Isn't it a lucky thing
"I can tax the pea-a-sants?"

Tune: COME ALL YE FAITHFUL

Oh come all you buyers,
How 'bout some radial tires?
Or maybe you want to give
A mink to your love.
Come sign at the bottom,
You don't need no cash, chum;
O come and let us sell you,
O come and let us dun you,
O come and let us sue you-hoo,
Welcome aboard!

Tune: JINGLE BELLS

Dashing through the streets,
Snarling as you go;
if someone's in your way,
Shove the so-and-so.
Whizzing through the doors,
Charging down the aisles,
All the Christmas faces wreathed
In tense and nervous smiles.

(Chorus) Oh, buy our stuff!
Buy our stuff!
Empty out your purse!
Christmas is a spending time
That steadily grows worse.
Oh, we have got . . . lovely gifts
For each Him and Her.
If we're out of frankincense,
Buy our dandy myrrh!

(Contributed by Mark Senter, Wheaton, Illinois)

CONFUSION

This is a great crowd breaker for parties or socials. Type up a copy of the list below for everyone in the group; however, no two lists should be in the same order unless the group is very large. The idea is to have everyone doing something different at the same time. Also, you are not able to tell who is winning until the game is over. The winner is the first one to complete all ten things on their list *in order.* Anyone who will not do what someone asks him to do is automatically disqualified.

1. Get ten different autographs. First, Middle, and Last names. (On the back of this sheet.)
2. Unlace someone's shoe, lace it and tie again. (Not your own.)
3. Get a hair from someone's head over six inches long. (Let them remove it.)
4. Get a girl to roll a somersault and sign her name here. _____
5. Have a boy do five pushups for you and sign his name here. ___
6. Play "Ring around the Rosy" with someone and sing out loud.
7. Do twenty-five "jumping jacks" and have someone count them off for you. Have that person sign here when you have done them. _____
8. Say the "Pledge of Allegiance" to the flag as loudly as you can.
9. Leap-frog over someone five times.
10. You were given a piece of bubble gum at the beginning of the race. Chew it up and blow ten bubbles. Find someone who will

watch you do it and sign here when you have finished. _____

(Contributed by Marcie Stockin, West Valley, New York)

CRAZY QUIZ

Print up the following "I. Q. Test" and give your group ten minutes to complete it. Award a prize to anyone who can answer all 20 questions correctly. Exchange papers and give them the correct answers which follow the test. It's good for a few laughs (as well as groans).

I. Q. TEST

1. If you went to bed at 8 o'clock a.m. and set the alarm to get up at 9 o'clock the next morning, how many hours of sleep would you get?_____
2. Does England have a Fourth of July? _____
3. Why can't a man living in Winston-Salem, North Carolina, be buried west of the Mississippi River?_____
4. If you had a match and entered a room in which there were a kerosene lamp, an oil heater, and a wood-burning stove, which would you light first? _____
5. Some months have 30 days, some have 31 days, how many months have 28 days?
6. A man builds a house with four sides to it and it is rectangular in shape. Each side has a southern exposure. A big bear came wandering by, what color is the bear?____
7. How far can a dog run into the woods? _____
8. What four words appear on every denomination of U. S. coin? _____
9. What is the minimum of baseball players on the field during any part of an inning in a regular game? _____ How many outs in an inning?_____
10. I have in my hand two U. S. coins which total 55 cents in value. One is not a nickel. What are the two coins?_____
11. A farmer had 17 sheep; all but nine died. How many does he have left? _____
12. Divide 30 by one-half and add 10. What is the answer?_____
13. Take two apples from three apples and what do you have?_____
14. An archeologist claimed he found some gold coins dated 46 B.C. Do you think he did? _____ Explain: _____
15. A woman gives a beggar 50 cents. The woman is the beggar's sister but the beggar is not the woman's brother. How come? _____
16. How many animals of each species did Moses take aboard the Ark with him? _____
17. Is it legal in North Carolina for a man to marry his widow's sister? _____
Why? _____
18. What word in this test is mispelled? _____
19. From what animal do we get whale bones? _____
20. Where was Paul going on the road to Damascus? _____

Answers:

1. One hour
2. Yes
3. Because he's not dead
4. The match
5. They all do
6. White
7. Halfway. The other half, he's running *out*
8. "United States of America" or "In God We Trust"
9. Ten—nine outfielders and a batter; six outs per inning
10. 50¢ and 5¢. One is not a nickel but the other is
11. Nine
12. Seventy
13. Two
14. No
15. They are sisters
16. None. *Noah* took the animals, not Moses
17. No. He is dead
18. Misspelled
19. Whale
20. Damascus

(Contributed by Charles Easley, Denver City, Texas)

DOOR SUR-PRIZES

Give away a door prize at every party. Here are some suggestions:

1. *Digital Computer:* Two gloves with the digits one to ten pinned on the fingers. It adds, subtracts, multiplies, and divides with a minimum of effort and guesswork.
2. *The Perfect Gift to Take Care of All your Hang-ups:* Two clothes hangers. Also keeps your room clean.
3. *Fourteen Carrot Gold Ring:* Fourteen carrots with greens secured together in a giant ring, sprayed with gold paint. Hang around winner's neck.
4. *California Wet Suit:* One pair of baby's plastic pants. A vacation "must." Stops the water, but not the sun.
5. *Tickets to a Free Dinner:* Give two blank tickets. Dinner follows the floor show which begins at 7:30. Courtesy of the San Francisco (any glamorous city) gospel mission.
6. *Motorized Brick for Lazy Radicals:* Attach wings, engine, and propeller from inexpensive toy plane to a brick. Eliminates effort, personal involvement, and risk of incarceration. Just aim brick on a long, smooth surface and start the engine.
7. *A Couple of Dates Lined Up for Two Guys:* Two attractive girls come out, hold up a long string threaded through two dates (fruit).
8. *Free Chicken Dinner:* One Baggie full of birdseed, a dinner to delight any chicken.
9. *Automatic Egg Beater:* We couldn't afford the giant-sized maxi-stir or the medium sized midi-stir, so we are giving you the inexpensive mini-stir. Pastor Jones, would you please say a few words appropriate to the occasion? Pastor could respond with, "When the time's up, just pull my plug. Actually, Joe's afraid I'll get you all mixed up."
10. *Vacuum Cleaner or Dishwasher:* Introduce the suprise clean-up committee or K.P. crew to be "run" by the winner.

(Contributed by Dave Cassel, Springfield, Oregon)

DUMMY BAG

This idea is a variation of the old "Take Off What You Don't Need" gag (See *Ideas Number Three*). Get the group in a circle and give each a grocery bag. The group is seated in chairs. The instructions are that you are going to have an endurance test to see who can last the longest. Each person is then told to place the bag over their head to minimize embarrassment. Then they are told to take off something that they didn't wear to bed the night before. Some will catch on immediately, others will take off an article of clothing or piece of jewelry, etc. Then they are instructed to take off something else that they didn't wear to bed the previous evening. Just to watch someone sitting with a paper bag on his head undressing is hilarious. Before the slow ones take off too much, you yell at them, "Take off the bag, dummy. Or did you wear it to bed last night?" (Contributed by Richard Ginn, Elizabethton, Tennessee)

FLOUR POWER

Select three girls and three boys for this event. The guys are sent out of the room. While they are out, one girl gets a mouthful of flour. One of the boys are brought in and told to try and guess each girl's favorite flower. If he is correct, he wins a kiss from that girl. Of course, whatever he guesses for the girl with the flour in her mouth is correct. She starts to kiss him, but instead spits flour all over his face. Do the same with the next two guys. (Contributed by Joe Wright, Archer City, Texas)

FRACTURED FLICKERS

Contact the parents of the kids in your group and see how many short segments of home movie film you can get of the kids when they were very young. Assure the parents that the film will be returned. Splice it all together and show it to the group at a party or social event. Have the kids try to guess each person when they appear on the film. Old home movies are great fun to watch, especially if you get some embarrassing shots of each kid in the group, as a baby or toddler. Some film will be super-eight and some will be regular-eight, so you may need to make two reels. Only a short segment is needed for each kid. (Contributed by Joe Wright, Archer City, Texas)

I'M DREAMING OF A WHITE CHRISTMAS

Choose two volunteers from the crowd. Give to one a Kazoo, and to the other a Slide-a-phone (available in most any music store). Have the crowd sing ''I'm Dreaming of a White Christmas'' in their best Bing Crosby style, and then have an instrumental duet by your two volunteers. The results are hilarious. (Contributed by Dallas Elder, Portland, Oregon)

JINGLE BELLS

This is a great way to put new life into an old song next Christmas. Divide into six groups and assign each group a phrase of the first verse of ''Jingle Bells'':

1. Dashing through the snow . . .
2. In a one horse open sleigh . . .
3. O'er the fields we go . . .
4. Laughing all the way . . .
5. Bells on bobsled ring . . .
6. Making spirits bright . . .

Each group is instructed to decide upon words, actions, or both to be done by their group when their phrase is sung. For example, the group that has ''Laughing all the way'' might hold their stomachs and say ''HO,HO,HO.'' The entire group sings the chorus (Jingle Bells, Jingle Bells, etc.'') together and then the first verse. As each phrase in the verse is sung, the assigned group stands, does its thing, and sits down. Do it several times, getting a little faster each time through. (Contributed by Dallas Elder, Portland, Oregon)

LETTER FROM GRANDMA

The following is a fun letter that can be read for laughs. Read it slow and pause after each period. If you use it at a camp, you can read it during mail-call. Just introduce it by explaining that ''There wasn't a name on the envelope, so we couldn't figure out who this letter was to. Maybe you will recognize it if we read it. It's from your grandma . . .''

Dear _____

Since I have time because I am not busy, I thought I would write you a few lines and let you know the up-to-date news. We are all as well as can be expected, for the condition we are in. We ain't sick, we just don't feel good. I am feeling fine: Aunt Martha is dead. I hope this letter finds you the same. I suppose you will want to hear about us moving from Illinois to Hollywood. We never started until we left. It didn't take us any longer than from the time we started until the time we arrived. The trip was the best part of all. If you ever come out here, don't miss that.

They didn't expect to see us until we arrived and most of the people we were acquainted with, we knew: and the people we didn't know seemed like strangers. We still live at the same place we moved to last, which is beside our nearest neighbors across the road from the other side. Randy says he thinks we will stay here until we move or go somewhere else.

We are very busy farming. Eggs are a good price; that's the reason they are so high. Some of the ground here is so poor you can't raise an umbrella on it; but we have a fine

---

crop of potatoes. Some of them are the size of a hickory nut, some the size of a pea, and then there are a whole lot of little ones.

Pete was taking the cows to water and when they went across the bridge one fell through and strained her milk. Now she has the hiccups once a week and churns her own butter.

Sharon fell through the back porch. It bruised her somewhat and skinned her elsewhere.

Everytime Bill gets sick, he starts feeling bad. The doctor gave him some medicine and said if he got better it might help him, and if he didn't get any worse, he would stay about the same.

I would have sent you the five dollars I owe you, but I already had this letter sealed before I thought of it. I sent your overcoat, but I cut the buttons off so it wouldn't be so heavy. You can find them in the left-hand pocket.

We were out of jelly, so Bob went to New York to get some of the traffic jam. Well, I think I must close now. It took me three days to write this letter because you are a slow reader.

P.S. We now live in Hollywood where everything is modern. We have a kitchen, living room, dining room, and two bedrooms. And then there is one little room upstairs to water the horses out of, only more fancy. Then there is a little white thing about three feet tall with hot and cold water. It wasn't any good, though, 'cause there was a hole in it. Then there is another thing over in the corner that is the handiest thing in the house. You can put one foot down in it and wash it all over and press a little lever and you can have clean water for the other foot. It has two lids on it. We took the solid lid off and we roll pie dough on it; and the other lid had a hole in it, so we framed Grandpa's picture in it. Everybody said it looked just as natural as if he were sitting there.

All my love, Grandma.

(Contributed by Eugene Gross, Seattle, Washington)

LOOPING THE LOOP

Give each person a strip of paper about 1 ½ inches wide and a foot or so long. Also, provide scissors and Scotch tape. Have them make the strip into a loop, and twist it once, joining the two ends carefully with the tape. (If you use gift-wrap paper, the colored side of the strip meets the white side at the junction where they are taped.)

You have now created a "Mobious Strip," a one-sided geometrical figure discovered in the 1800's by a famous German mathematician named Mobius. Draw a line down the center of the strip continuously, and you will mark the entire strip on both sides without ever lifting your pencil, and you end up where you began. This proves that the figure has only one side.

Next, if you use a pair of scissors to cut along your center dividing line all the way around, the loop becomes suddenly twice as big, but it is no longer a "Mobius Strip." It has two sides again. Finally, try cutting this longer, thinner loop of paper right down the middle all the way around. What do you get? Not a longer loop this time, but two linked loops.

What all this proves has not yet been determined, but with a little creativity it can undoubtedly be applied to something. (Contributed by Kathryn Lindskoog, Orange, Calif.)

MATCH MIXER

This is a great way to help kids in a youth group get to know each other better. Give each person three slips of paper or 3 X 5 cards. Have everyone write one thing about themselves on each slip of paper. Suggested items could be:

1. The most embarrassing thing that ever happened to me.
2. My secret ambition.
3. The person I admire most.
4. My biggest hang up.
5. If I had a million dollars, I would . . .

All the cards are collected and redistributed three to each person. No one should have one that they wrote themselves. On a signal, everyone then tries to match each card with a person in the room. They circulate around the room and ask each other questions to determine whose cards they have. The first to do so is the winner. All the kids may be allowed to finish, and then share their findings with the rest of the group. (Contributed by Cecelia Bevan, Overland Park, Kansas)

MIND BLOWERS

The following stories are great fun at camps and other casual get togethers to test the group's problem solving ability. Read each story to the group. The kids become detectives and attempt to solve the problem by asking you questions which may be answered "yes" or "no." Solutions are given in parentheses at the end of each story.

To make a contest out of it, have two "sharp" kids try to solve one of the problems by bringing each kid in one at a time. They ask questions and whoever can "get it" by asking the fewest questions is the winner. The audience can be "clued-in."

Horror Movie: A man took his wife to a horror movie. As he had planned to do, when the audience screamed at a particularly scary point in the show, the man stabbed his wife to death. The noise of the audience muffled any cry from the wife. He took her out the regular exit at the close of the movie, and nothing unusual was noticed by others who were leaving. How did he manage to get her out? (Drive in movie)

Swiss Alps: A man in New York City happened to read a small article in the paper about a mid-western man who had taken a cruise to Europe with his wife. The article stated that while skiing in the Swiss Alps, the wife had had an accident and died. The man in New York immediately phoned the police and told them that he had proof that the woman's death was not an accident. Later that evidence was instrumental in the conviction of the husband for premeditated murder. Who was the man in New York and upon what did he base his action? (Travel agent had sold the man one round-trip ticket and one one-way ticket.)

Guillotine: A man and his wife were sitting on a sofa in the den of their home watching television. He fell asleep in a sitting position with his head bowed. In his sleep, he dreamed that he was in the French Revolution, was captured and imprisoned in the Bastille, and sentenced to have his head cut off. He was taken to the guillotine and placed in position for the knife to cut off his head. At this point in the dream, the wife noticed he was asleep and hit him on the back of the neck with her fan. He immediately fell over dead. What is wrong with the story? (How would we know what the man dreamed if he never awakened?)

Watchman: Once there was a night watchman who had been caught several times sleeping on the job. The boss issued the final ultimatum and the very next night he was caught again at his desk with his head in his hands, elbows resting on the desk. "Ah, ha, I've caught you again," exclaimed the boss. The watchman's eyes popped open immediately and he knew what had happened. Being a quick thinking man, he said one word before looking up at the boss. The boss apologized profusely and went home. What was the one word? (Amen)

Elevator Ride: Once there was a bachelor who lived on the 10th floor of a swank apartment building. Each morning he would leave his room, walk down the corridor to the self-service elevator, get on when it arrived, push the first floor button, ride down, get off, and go to work. Each afternoon he would return to the building, get on the elevator, push the 6th button, ride to the 6th floor, get off, and climb the 4 flights of stairs to the 10th floor. Each day this procedure would take place. Why? (The man was a midget and couldn't reach beyond the 6th button.)

Hardware Store: A man went into a Hardware store and was looking for an item when the clerk walked up and asked, "Yes sir, may I help you?" "Yes," said the man. "How much are these?""They are 25 cents each, but you can get 25 for 50 cents and 114 for 75 cents." What were the items? (House numbers)

Elevator Operator: Picture this...it is summer-time. You do not have a job. You go downtown and try to get on at numerous places, but find that the positions are all filled. As a last resort, you inquire at an old office building. The manager tells you that he does need an elevator operator and although the salary is small, you take the job because it is the best you can find. Well, everything goes all right for three weeks and then, one day, the elevator operator gets a call from the 10th floor. At the 10th floor a 212 pound woman gets on carrying a 25 pound typewriter and a 7 pound briefcase. The elevator was quite old, and as it moved down past the 6th floor, the cable slipped. You can imagine how frightened they were, but how thankful when the falling elevator slowed down and stopped smoothly at the ground floor. Now, tell me, how old was the elevator operator and what was the elevator operator's mother's maiden name? (Notice the word "you" at the begining of the story. You, the listener, are the elevator operator.)

One Dead—No Charge: There was a wreck. It was the fault of a man in a small foreign car, who had darted out in front of a big car causing it to crash through a store window. The people in the foreign car were unhurt. In the other car there was one injured and one dead. A manslaughter charge was never filed against the driver of the foreign car. Why? (The big car was a hearse.)

(Contributed by Bob Fakkema, Greensboro, North Carolina)

MONSTER MAD LIB

Here's a "Mad Lib" that would be great for your next Halloween Party. It's simply a story with key words left out. Without letting the kids in on the story, have them (orally) supply the missing words as you tell them the type of word needed (noun, part of body, adjective, etc.). Tell them to be as creative and wild as possible while thinking up words. Then read back the story after all the missing words are filled in.

"Once upon a time, _____ years ago, in that fiendish place Tran-
                    number
sylvania (which is now known as _____), the _____
                                 local high school   adjective
Count Dracula _____-ed. Our story finds him just after he has
               verb
finished his dinner, which tonight included _____. Since he
                                            person in group
was still a little hungry and a full moon was out, he decided to catch
the next _____ to _____'s house and peek
         means of transportation   girl in group
into her _____ to see if she was _____-ing. By chance she
         room   verb
was, which brought a _____ smile to his _____ face. Without
                     adjective   adjective
wasting a second, he _____-ed into her _____, startling her
                     verb   noun
so much that she broke her _____. "_____" spake Count
                           toy   greeting
Dracula. "I have come to drink your blood!" "_____" she re-
                                              exclamation
plied, whereupon she kicked Dracula in the _____ and fled.
                                           part of body
Not to be deterred, Dracula chased her as far as _____
                                                 place
where he finally tackled her. It looked like the end for _____
                                                         same girl

but just before Dracula could sink his _____ fangs into her
adjective
_____ neck, _____ arrived on the scene. Quickly sizing
adjective   boy in group
up the situation, he grabbed the nearest _____ and smote Dra-
noun
cula so hard it was heard in _____. "_____", sighed
place   mushy line
_____. "Aw, it was nothing," replied _____ as he
same girl   same boy
flexed his _____ for her. "By the way," he asked. "What's a
part of body
nice girl like you doing in the _____ high school group???"
your church
(Contributed by Jim Berkley, Los Angeles, Calif.)

MOOING CONTEST

Send two people out of the room after telling them that they are to
be judges in a "mooing contest." After they are both out of ear-
shot, take the entire group into confidence and explain that this is a
trick to be played on one of the two volunteers (person number
one). The object is to get him to "moo" loudly all by himself after his
turn at judging. Go through the entire instructions beforehand,
even to the point of rehearsing the moos. The steps are as follows:

1. Person number one comes back in the room and stands in the
   center of the circle where he is told that he is to judge which
   member of the group is the loudest after the group moos three
   times. He is told the group has chosen a mooer to be the one
   and he must try to guess who he is. The group then moos once,
   then a second time, then a third time and person number one is
   asked who the loudest mooer is. By common consent whoever
   he picks is wrong and another is offered (usually a quieter person) as the real loudest mooer. So person number one loses.

2. Then person number one rejoins the group (sits down in the
   audience). The leader says the group must now pick another
   loudest mooer. After suggesting several (they all decline) the
   leader fakes that he has a novel idea and asks person number
   one to be the loudest mooer — for person number two would
   never guess him. Others join in support of idea and person
   number one is rehearsed several times as the loudest mooer of
   the group (until he's really bellowing).

3. Here's the trick. When person number two comes into the circle, he's told to listen for the loudest mooer. The leaders count
   1, 2, 3 and all moo once. He counts again and all moo the second time. He counts again and all take a deep breath, but *don't
   moo* — and you will then hear a great solo moo from person
   number one. He is then awarded the Bull-calling award.

(Contributed by Richard C. Boyd, New Orleans, Lousiana)

19

MUSICAL PIES

Kids get in a circle. A "crazy foam pie" is passed around the circle, until the music stops (or a whistle is blown, etc.) Whoever is holding the pie at that time, may hit the person on either side of him in the face with it. He is then eliminated (the person who was caught holding the pie) and the game continues, with a new pie brought in. The last person left is the winner. Note: "Crazy Foam" may be purchased at most toy stores and is excellent for making "pies." (Contributed by Dave Gilliam, Henryetta, Oklahoma)

NAME RIDDLES

This game requires an unusual dose of creativity on your part, but can be well worth the extra effort. Make a list of the names of kids in your group, and then try to make up a "riddle" or clue about each name. Most names can be used in some kind of a riddle if you think about it long enough. Then print the riddles up on pieces of paper and the kids mill about and try to fill in all the blanks, matching riddles with names. Below are some sample riddles to give you an idea of what can be done:

A. What does a good mother do when her son comes to her, crying with a skinned knee? *(Pat-ter-son)*

B. The tongue-tied sports announcer called the famous race between the rabbit and the _____! *(Tuttle)*

C. Two things you do with coffee! *(Brew-ster)*

D. What the man from Boston said he was going to do with his leaves. *(Reich, pronounced Rike).*

E. When he talks about his fishing exploits, you know he is _____. *(Lyon)*

F. What the hippie said when he was asked what was wrong with his lips! *(Chap-man)*

G. The last streaker I saw was _____! *(Baird)*

H. A past tense male. *(Boyd)*

(Contributed by Charles W. Stokes, Amory, Mississippi)

PARK BENCH

Send three or four people out of the room, either boys or girls. While they are out, have a boy and girl sit side by side on a park bench (or two chairs). Bring in one of the people waiting outside the room. Tell him that the people on the park bench like each other a lot, have just been out on a date, etc. (big build-up). Then ask him to arrange the two people in a position to make them look more romantic (such as holding hands, embracing, etc.). After doing this, he must take the place of either the boy or girl, doing what he suggested. (That's when the fun begins). Bring in the next person and repeat the process and continue until you feel it is time to stop. (Contributed by Lynne Surft, Trafford, Pennsylvania)

SING SONG SORTING

This game is similar to "Barnyard" *(Ideas Number One)* and is great as a way to divide a crowd into teams or small groups. Prepare ahead of time on small slips of paper an equal number of four (or however many groups you want) different song titles. As each person enters the room, they receive (at random) one of these song titles. In other words, if you had 100 kids and you wanted four teams, there would be 25 each of the four different songs. On a signal, the lights go out (if you do this at night) and each kid starts singing the song he received as loudly as possible. No talking or yelling, only singing. Each person tries to locate others singing the same song, and the first team to get together is the winner. Song titles should be well-known. (Contributed by Arthur R. Homer, Tioga Center, New York)

SQUIRM RACE

Place a volleyball (or ball of similar size) between the foreheads of a boy and a girl couple. Without using their hands, they must work the ball down to their knees and back up again. Their hands must be kept behind their backs and the two must start over if they drop the ball. Couples do not have to be of the opposite sex. Two guys or two girls will work fine but a boy-girl couple usually adds to the fun of this event. (Contributed by Bryan Pearce, Jr., Elmhurst, Illinois)

STRAW MUMBLE

Have three guys come to the front of the room. Each gets a plastic drinking straw. The idea is to get the entire straw inside your mouth by chewing. No hands allowed. It is harder than you think. First person to do so, wins. (Contributed by Roger Copeland, Hurst, Texas)

WHIRLING HIGH JUMP

Get three volunteers to come forward and try this simple game. Give each a stick about 18 inches long. Tell him (or her) to hold it straight out at arm's length with both hands so that he can watch it while turning around 50 times. He then must drop the stick and jump over it. Whoever jumps the farthest is the winner. Of course, most kids get so dizzy they can't even *see* the stick when they drop it, let alone jump over it. It's fun to watch. Have the rest of the group count as the person turns around. (Contributed by Kent Johnson, St. Paul, Minnesota)

WHY AND BECAUSE

Give everyone in the group a pencil and a 3x5 card. Have them write out a question beginning with the word "why." Collect them. Now have everyone write out answers on cards that begin with "because." Collect them. Redistribute them at random and have kids read the questions they receive along with the answer. The results will be hilarious. (Contributed by Johnn Powell, Albany, Georgia)

Chapter Two

Games

APPLE CIDER RELAY

Divide into teams and give each team member a straw. The object is to see which team can consume a gallon of apple cider first. You control the contest with a whistle. Each time you blow the whistle, the kids run to the jugs and drink as much cider as possible, using the straw. (One kid from each team at a time.) Make sure that teams stay in line so that every youth has a turn. Also make sure that your group smartalec doesn't lift the jug and chug half of it while you're scratching your ear. For hilarious results, give the kids that like apple cider a short time to drink and give the ones that can't stand it a long turn. (Contributed by Larry Jansen, Indianapolis, Indiana)

BALLOON BAT RELAY

Teams line up, single file, with kids as close together as possible. There should be a space between the legs to "bat" a balloon down the line, through the legs, with the hands. This is not easy if all the kids are standing close together. The person at the front of the line starts the balloon back and when it reaches the last person, he takes it to the front and continues until the team is once again in starting order. (Contributed by David Parke, Minneapolis, Minnesota)

BALLOON GOLF

This game is great in a small game room, and can also be played outdoors when there is no wind. First, drop a penny or smooth rock into each round balloon. Then blow the balloon up to about a 5 or 6 inch diameter. Golf clubs can be made by rolling a full sheet of newspaper into a stick. Cardboard boxes are used as the holes, with the par for each hole written on the side of the box. The weight inside the balloon creates a kind of Mexican jumping bean effect, causing both difficulty and hilarity for the participants. (Contributed by Wayne Mathias, San Diego, California)

BARREL OF FUN

Line up two teams. Each is given a 55 gallon drum with one side removed. Have each team pair off in twos (kids about the same size). One person goes inside the barrel and the other pushes. When the signal is given, the barrels are pushed to a half way point and then the one in the barrel changes places with the pusher. The first team to get its team through wins. The barrel, if possible, should have two garage door handles welded or bolted inside it. This will give the person inside something to brace himself to. It also helps the tall guys from being mangled. (Contributed by Roger Disque, Chicago, Illinois)

BASKETBALL DERBY

Play a game of basketball on roller skates. It is extremely funny to watch as well as play. There is no out-of-bounds or dribbling, but the other regular rules apply. Other games (such as softball, football, etc.) can be played on roller skates as well with excellent results. (Contributed by Joe Wright, Archer City, Texas)

BATTLE FOR THE SAHARA

This is a game for two or more teams in an outdoor setting. Each team has a water container and must transport water across the ''Sahara'' (playing field), to fill the container. The first to do so wins. Each team should consist of (1) a ''general,'' (2) a ''bomb,'' (3) three "colonels," (4) four "majors," (5) five or six "privates." For a smaller or greater number of players, more majors, colonels and privates are added with perhaps lieutenants as well. Each player (except the general) has a water cup and each team has a water jug (container of a gallon or so).

There is a specified area where water may be obtained (which may be neutralized so players can not get caught while filling up). There is also a specified neutral area around the water jugs which are located at a fair distance away from the water supply. This distance could be 1000-2000 feet.

Each player (except the general) travels to the water supply area with his cup and gets it full of water. He then travels to the water jug and pours it in. While en route, he may be tagged by a player of one of the opposing teams. A tagging person must also have a cup full of water in order to make him eligible to tag. If a person tagged is of a lower rank, he must empty his cup. If two equal ranks are tagged, they part friends with their cups still full. If of a higher rank, the tagger must tip his out. Each person has an identity card with his rank marked on it. These can be written out in their team color.

All may tag except the bomb (although the private has no use for tagging, being the lowest rank). The bomb carries water but may tag no one. Anyone tagging the bomb is automatically demoted to private and has his cup emptied. Anyone demoted to private must give up his card to the bomb, who then turns it in to one of the referees at the earliest opportunity. (This keeps people in the game).

Any accidental emptying by an opponent gets the offended player a free escort with a full cup to his jug by the offending player. A general may tag without carrying a cup of water. He doesn't have one and is free to tag others at any time.

It is wise to set a time limit and the winning team is the one who either has the most water in their jug at the end of the time or who fills it up first. It is wise also to have referees along the route to make sure no foul play ensues and that offences get free escorts properly. (Contributed by Brett Cane, Montreal, Quebec, Canada)

BEAN-BAG BALL

This is a wild game that is great for camps and can be set up like a championship "football" game. Divide the crowd into two large groups and give them names of schools (make them up). Each "school" is then provided plenty of newspapers, tape, magic markers, crepe paper, scissors, poster paint, etc. They then have thirty minutes or so to do the following:
a) Prepare a band, complete with uniforms (make them), instru-

25

ments (anything you can find), drum major, majorettes, etc., plus a march or two that can be hummed (waxed paper on combs help here). One band should be prepared to play the "Star Spangled Banner."

b) Prepare cheerleaders (usually boys dressed like girls), complete with costumes, cheers, etc.

c) Prepare a Homecoming Queen with Court (could be boys or girls, or mixed). Fix up costumes.

d) Prepare a team for "Bean-Bag-Ball" (see following rules). Ordinarily a team of seven plus a coach will do.

e) Prepare a half-time program and a crowning of the Homecoming Queen and court.

After each school has done all this, then begin the action as follows:

a) School A Marching Band marches onto the field followed by the team and cheerleaders. An announcer introduces the team. The cheerleaders do their stuff.

b) School B does the same.

c) Leaders ask one band to play the "Star Spangled Banner."

d) First half of the game (5 to 7 minutes), cheerleaders and bands do stuff.

e) Half-time program:
   -School A's program and crowning of Queen.
   -School B's program and crowning of Queen.

f) Second half of the game.

g) Victory celebration by the winning team.

Here's how "Bean-Bag-Ball" is played: Two referees are needed with whistles. The playing field can vary in size, but anything larger than a volleyball court will do. There should be a half-way line and at each end of the field a folding chair is placed three feet beyond the goal line. The rules are similar to basketball except the bag-holder may only take three steps with the bean bag, then he must pass it. Goals are scored by tossing the bean bag between the seat and the seatback of the chair. A good P.A. system and announcer will add a great deal. (Contributed by Richard Boyd, New Orleans, Lousiana)

BIBLE PAIRS

Here's a mixer that works well as a way to get everybody paired off. Have everyone put on a "name tag" which has a Bible name or event written on it. (These are prepared in advance). Each tag has a "match" somewhere in the crowd. (For example, "Noah" and "The Ark"). On a signal, those pairs are to find each other and sit down. The last to do so is the "loser." For added fun, throw in one that doesn't have a match. Following are some sample "pairs":

Abraham and Sarah
Adam and Eve
Samson and Delilah
Noah and The Ark
David and Goliath
Daniel and Lion's Den
Jacob and Esau
Joseph and Coat of Many Colors
Moses and Ten Commandments
Joshua and Walls of Jericho
Prodigal Son and Fatted Calf
Zacchaeus and Sycamore Tree
Matthew and Tax Gatherer
Jonah and Whale
Paul and Barnabas
Peter and Rock

Sermon on Mount and Beatitudes
Mary and Martha
Mary and Joseph
Cain and Abel
Amos and Hosea
Easter and Resurrection
Garden and Eden
Angel and Gabriel
Isaac and Sacrifice
Jacob and Ladder
Ruth and Boaz
Moses and Bullrushes
Luke and Physician
Methuselah and 966 years old
Solomon and Wisdom
Wisemen and Star

(Contributed by John T. Dunham, Batavia, New York)

BIRTHDAY TURNOVER

This game is similar to the old game "Fruit Basket Turnover." Have everyone sit in a circle with the same number of chairs as there are people. "It" stands in the center, without a chair. He calls out any *three* months of the year. After the last month is called, everyone who has a birthday during one of those three months gets up and tries to take another seat. "It" also tries to find a vacant seat. Whoever is left without a seat becomes "it." The big move is when "It" calls "Leap Year." *Everyone* has to get up and find another seat. (Contributed by Scotty Shows, Jackson, Mississippi)

BLOODY MARSHMALLOW

Have the kids pair off. Partners stand about ten feet apart facing each other. Each gets five marshmallows and a paper cup full of catsup. One at a time, each person dips a marshmallow in the catsup and tries to toss it in his partner's mouth. The partner tries to catch it in his mouth. The couple that catches the most out of all ten marshmallows, wins. (Contributed by Steven Kjorvestad, Bonsall, California)

CAPTURE THE FOOTBALL

This, of course, is based on capture the flag—however, it can be played by smaller groups with less room as well as large groups. Also, it doesn't have to be completely dark. Instead of using flags— use footballs. These are placed on each team's territory. You must get the other team's football over to your team's territory. You may pass the ball over the line to win, or run it over. If you are tagged, you must remain a prisoner until a teammate tags you. If you pass the ball to a teammate over the line which separates the team territories and your teammate drops it—you both become prisoners. If the ''pass'' is ''complete,'' your team wins. You must adopt the capture the flag rules to your group and setting for the best results. (Contributed by Larry Jansen, Indianapolis, Indiana)

CASTOR RACE

Get several mechanic's castors (the type they lay on and slide under cars with). Line teams up and have races. Kids lay on the castors and race by propelling with hands only, feet only, on their backs, etc. This is best on cement floors only. (Contributed by Roger Disque, Chicago, Illinois)

CHAOS-VS-CONTROL

This is an outdoor spy game that is best played at a camp where there is plenty of room and good hiding places. It should be played at night and preferably in an area with a lot of trees, high grass, and the like. Divide into two teams: the ''Chaos'' agents and the ''Control'' agents. (You can name the teams anything. The names are not important to the game.) The Chaos agents try to leave the U.S. by reaching a landing strip where their planes are to pick them up. The Control agents try to capture or eliminate the Chaos agents by hitting them with a stocking full of flour. The set up should look like this:

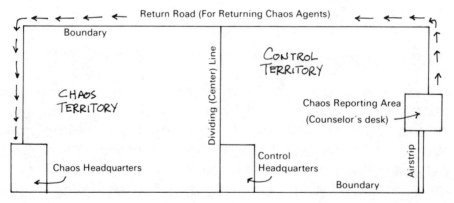

The Chaos agents are safe when in their own territory. They simply have to sneak through Control territory to get to the ''airstrip'' located behind Control territory. If they manage to get through, they report to a counselor sitting at a desk on the airstrip. They are safe once they get to the airstrip. When they arrive there, they turn over to the counselor a set of ''secret plans'' (an envelope marked ''SST'' or APOLLO,'' etc.). The Chaos team gets 1000 points for each envelope delivered to the airstrip counselor. Chaos agents may then return to their own headquarters via a path around Control territory to get a new set of plans and try to sneak through again. Control agents may patrol that path to make sure Chaos people are only going back and not coming to the airstrip.

Control agents can only be in their own territory and they must try to spot and club a Chaos agent with their nylon (or newspaper, water balloon, paper bag full of mud, or whatever.) If they hit a Chaos agent, the Control agent takes his prisoner to Control headquarters and the Chaos agent must give up his plans. The Control team gets 2000 points for each set of plans seized. The Chaos agent is then set free to try again. Adult Counselors should keep score, hand out the plans, etc.

You can use several large flashlights (controlled by counselors) to sweep the entire area to give a "searchlight" effect to the game. The two teams should wear different colored armbands to distinguish them. (Contributed by Neil Graham, Edmonton, Alberta, Canada)

CHURCH TRIVIA

Divide the group into teams (or kids may compete individually) and give each a list of unusual things in the church to identify. Here's a sample list:

1. The name of the company that manufactured the church's fire extinguisher.
2. The number of steps in the baptistry.
3. The number of fuses in the fuse box.
4. The location of the first-aid kit.
5. The last word in (A certain book in the church library).
6. The number of yellow lines painted on the parking lot.

Your list should include twenty or so items such as these. On "go", everyone tries to locate the various information required as quickly as possible. With teams, the questions can be assigned to the different team members. The first to finish, or the most questions correctly answered, wins. (Contributed by Don Snider, Elgin, Illinois)

CINDERELLA

Arrange chairs in a circle. All the Cinderellas (girls) in the group select a chair. The Prince Charmings (guys) each pick a Cinderella and kneel down in front of her. He removes her shoes and holds them in his hand. The leader calls for the shoes and they are thrown to the middle of the circle. Then the Cinderellas blindfold their Prince Charmings. After each prince is blindfolded, the leader rearranges

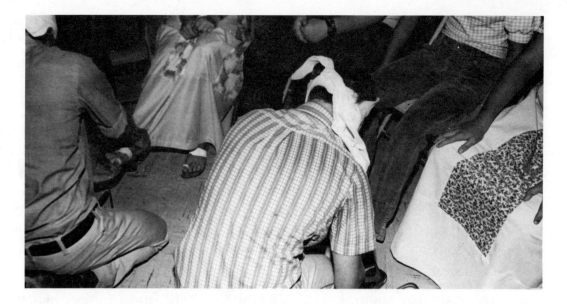

and mixes the shoes in the middle.

On a signal, all the Prince Charmings crawl to the circle and attempt to find their Cinderella's shoes. The Cinderellas can help only verbally, shouting out instructions to their men. After finding the shoes, the Princes crawl back to their girls (again guided only by verbal instructions). They place the shoes (right one on right foot, etc.) on the girls and then remove their blindfolds. The game continues until the last contestant succeeds. (Contributed by Carol Wennerholm, San Diego, California)

CIRCLE SOCCER

Two teams get into one circle, half on one side and half on the other.

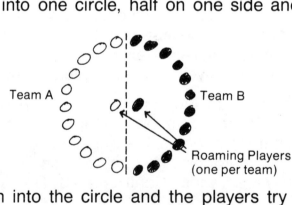

Team A   Team B

Roaming Players
(one per team)

A ball is thrown into the circle and the players try to kick it out through the other team's side. If the ball is kicked out over the heads of the players, the point goes to the nonkicking team. If the ball is kicked out below the heads of the players, the kicking team gets the point. Hands may not be used at all, only feet and bodies. No one may move out of position except one player per team who may kick the ball to his teammates if the ball gets stuck in the center. He may not score, however, or cross into the other team's teritory. If the roaming player gets hit with the ball (when kicked by the other team), the kicking team gets a point. (Contributed by Ellis

Meuser, McMinnville, Oregon)

CLOTHESPIN CHALLENGE

Two contestants are selected and seated in chairs facing each other with their knees touching. Each is shown a large pile of clothespins at the right of their chairs. Each is blindfolded and given 2 minutes to pin as many clothespins as possible on the pant legs of the other contestant. (Contributed by William Moore, Brainerd, Minnesota)

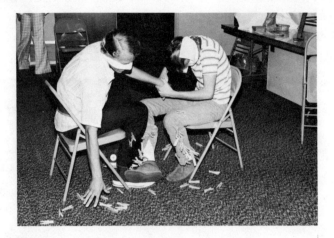

COTTONTAIL TAG

Have all the kids in the group bring a can of shaving cream to the meeting. When the kids show up you give a "Bull's-eye Belt" to each kid. This consists of a square foot of cardboard with a circle drawn on it and a string strung through it big enough to go around a kid's waist. Each kid ties it on his belt with the cardboard around back in the general area that a tail would go. You split the kids into two teams and explain that the object of the game is to try and squirt a glob of shaving cream into the "Bull's-Eye" worn by members of the opposing team, while protecting yours at the same time. You may not touch your own or sit down on it. The shaving cream must stick to the cardboard and be inside the circle. The team that has successfully put the most "cotton tails" on the other team within the time limit is the winner. (Contributed by Andrea Sutton, Ipswich, Massachusetts)

CRAB BALL

This is an active game for groups of twenty or more. All that is needed is a playground ball. Divide into four teams of equal size, and form a square with each team forming one side of the square. Players should then sit down on the floor, and number off from one to however many players are on each team. To begin the game the leader places ball in the center and calls a number. All four persons of that number "crab walk" out to the ball. "Crab Walking" is bending over backwards and then walking on all fours. The object is to kick the ball over the heads of one of the other teams (other than one's own). When a crab walker succeeds in kicking it over the heads of another team, the team over whose head it went, gets a point. The remaining members of the team must stay in place with their seats on the floor. They may block the balls coming at them either by kicking, using their bodies, or using their heads. They may never use their hands or arms. They also may try to kick it over the heads of an opposing team. Either way the team over whose head the ball goes gets the point. When the first team reaches ten points, the game is ended and the *lowest* score wins. (Contributed by Richard Boyd, New Orleans, Lousiana)

CRAZY CANOE

Two people get in a canoe facing each other. Each has a paddle. One paddles one direction the other paddles the other way. The winner is the one who can paddle the canoe across his goal line about 20 feet away. It is very difficult and hilarious to watch. The canoe tends to just go around in circles. This can be done in a large swimming pool. In a larger canoe, four or six people can play, with the two teams on each end of the canoe. (Contributed by Tom Barwick, Shelton, Washington)

CRAZY VOLLEYBALL

If you don't have quite enough kids to get up a ''real'' volleyball game, or if you have several inept players, here's a fun version of the game with a few new rules:
1. Each team may hit the ball four times before hitting it over the net.
2. A ball hitting the floor counts as one hit.
3. A ball cannot hit the floor two bounces in succession.
These rules keep the ball in play over a much longer period of time. (Contributed by Dallas Elder, Portland, Oregon)

CROWS AND CRANES

Divide the group into two teams. One side is the "Crows," the other is the "Cranes." The two teams are lined up facing each other on two lines four or five feet apart. The leader flips a coin (heads — "Crows," tails — "Cranes") and yells out the name of the team which won the toss. If he yells "Crows," the "Crows" must turn around and run, with the "Cranes" in hot pursuit. If any of the "Cranes" succeed in touching a member (or members) of the "Crows" before he crosses a given line (20 to 60 feet away), he is considered a captive of the "Cranes" and must aid the "Cranes" when play continues. The team which captures all the members of the other team is the winner. (Contributed by David Parke, Minneapolis, Minnesota)

FAMILY GAME

This game is great for camps, retreats and special events and is best with a larger group (say 80 or so kids) in an indoor setting, such as a gymnasium or recreation hall.

Divide the group into "families" (8 families of 10, for example). Each family should represent a family immigrating to this country from another. In honor of their immigration to their new home, this game can begin with a banquet (sponsored by the Immigration Department), in which all the families are invited. Each family selects a mother and father and the rest of the children have to have some resemblance to the mother and father, i.e., all exceptionally fat, freckles, hats alike, or something. Each family must also prepare a native dance or native song from the country they come from to perform at the banquet and also they must introduce their family by their full names to everyone else. The banquet can feature a variety of international dishes to make everyone feel at home.

At the conclusion of the banquet, the "Minister of Immigration" gives a little speech and presents each family with $2,000.00 in cash (play money made up of packets of $50, $100, $500 and $1,000 denominations) and gives "jobs" to about 6 members of each family. A "job" can be an old computer card with a particular occupation written down on it with the salary stated at the bottom. For example, a card might say "This certifies that you are a qualified PLUMBER. Salary: $8,000 per year." Each family is told by the Minister of Immigration that the Government would keep close watch on them and that only those families that really succeeded in their jobs would be allowed to remain in the country. After the banquet is cleared away, the game begins.

In the course of the game, 15 minutes represents a year. At the end of each year, the families meet together in a specified place to discuss what happened. At the beginning of each year (indicated by a

33

whistle or bell) each member of the family with a job goes to an area of the room marked with their appropriate job description. For instance, there should be a medical center (for doctors), a trade center, a funeral home, etc. Also, at the beginning of each year, the father goes to the government desk and picks up his family's list of "problems" (see sample "problem card" below), which must be solved in that year. At this time he also gives the government a list of which members of his family have what jobs. In the first year, the problems are not many, but as the years go by, the problems get heavier and heavier. The list might contain from 5 to 12 problems per family that the father has to solve. For example, his house might have plumbing problems—he might need to build a new bathroom. He might have a leaky roof, need new furniture or need the services of a doctor. There can be deaths in the family; grandmothers, uncles, aunts, children and a funeral director would have to be consulted, along with a minister, perhaps a doctor, hospital, lawyer about the will, etc., etc.

"Problem Cards" may look like this:

Year One Obtain a place to live Get a job Obtain for personal use form of transportation	*Year Two* Pay rent if you do not own a house. Succeed at job. Wheels need balancing —see mechanic Buy color TV—see Furniture store Electrician Girlfriend gets sick— See florist mother bank

For every problem that is listed, there must be an appropriate "job" to solve the problem. Thus the father may either assign someone else or go himself to the various job areas and have the problem solved by a person who is qualified to do so. To get a problem solved you have to have a qualified plumber, for instance, sign that all the plumbing work has been done in your house and he may charge you according to how difficult the problem seems to be to him. The father then "pays" for the plumber to sign and the signature is put on the problem and at the end of each "year," the Government examines the problem list of each father to see that everything has been taken care of and only people who have a certain job have signed for the work done. If everything is in order, he is given the next year's list; if he does not have everything done, he may be fined several thousand dollars, maybe even up to $10 or $20 thousand dollars because of the seriousness of not getting certain things done. Then he may be given next year's list and he must go and solve the new problems.

There can also be a Government Employment Centre where new jobs are for sale and occasionally it can be announced that there is severe unemployment and everyone has to turn in several jobs. This keeps the job market floating around, thus making it possible for families to improve their position—or to get wiped out, as the case may be. The Employment Centre also sells B.A.'s, M.A.'s and Ph.D.'s for fairly high sums. If you are a plumber and have a B.A., you would get 25% more on your salary each year—the B.A. would be stamped by the Government on your job card. If you got an M.A., you'd get 50% more on your salary and if it was a Ph.D., you would get 100% more.

If you have, say, 80 people, you would need almost 60 jobs, thus leaving some members of each family who are free to solve problems. Each "year" lasts approximately 15 minutes, with a 5-minute break in between before the next year begins, when the family may plan for the next year, look at the next year's list of problems and work out who is going to solve them. This is also time for counting money and for going to the bank where all salaries are paid. Thus, the bank has to have a great supply of play money. Occasionally, you may hit the families with taxes as well and they have to pay the Government a certain amount, a percentage of their income, or something for taxes. You can run the game for 5-15 minute "years" and the family that comes out economically the best is the winner.

It is important to be fair when you are handing out the jobs at the beginning of the game, to make sure that the higher-paying jobs such as doctors and lawyers and dentists are spread evenly among the families so that no family has a tremendous advantage to begin with. Normally there should be 3 or 4 doctor jobs, 3 or 4 dentists, etc., so that there will be a good deal of competition in bidding between members of a profession to solve problems. This keeps the prices down and provides a lot of entertainment, however, you may have several professions where there are only 1 or 2 jobs available, such as garbage collectors, funeral directors and ministers and this almost creates a monopoly for certain families, with prices sky-rocketing. You may want to do this, as it makes the game much more entertaining. This game can fit well into a later discussion on the family and enable you to talk about exclusive and inclusive families and the whole problem of competition in our society. "Do unto others as you would have them do unto you" becomes a very real principle when you realize that what you charge for your plumbing job, you may also get charged for when you are burying a loved one. (Contributed by Neil Graham, Edmonton, Alberta, Canada)

FEET-BALL

This is a good indoor game which is very active and requires real team work. Divide the group into two teams and seat them (in chairs) in two lines, facing each other. The object is for the teams to move the ball (a volleyball) toward and through their goal (at the end of the line) by using their feet only. Players must keep their arms behind the chairs to keep from touching the ball, which is a penalty. To begin the game, drop the ball between the two teams in the middle. The game can be any length desired. To avoid injuries to feet, shoes can be removed. Also, make sure the two teams are just far enough apart that their feet barely touch when legs are extended on both sides. (Contributed by Mike Weaver, Panama City, Florida)

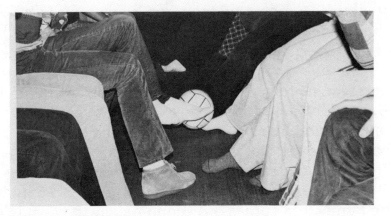

FILL MY POCKETS RELAY

One guy puts a coke bottle in his back pocket (if it will fit). Girls (or the rest of the team) line up and get dixie cups). The guy stands at one end of the line and a pail of water is at the other end. The idea is to transport the water, passing it from cup to cup, from the pail to the coke bottle. First group to do so wins. The guy's pants usually get soaked. (Contributed by Roger Copeland, Hurst, Texas)

FLAGS

Since many youth groups are beginning to take trips by bus or car, this is a good game to pass the time on a long trip. The idea is simply to divide into two teams, one on each side of the bus or car. Each team tries to find a church on their side of the road. This must be verified by someone on the other team. The side with the most churches wins. The game becomes more interesting when the opposing team spots an American flag on their side of the road. This cancels out three churches from the other team's score. Have someone act as "scorekeeper." (Contributed by Larry D. Bennett, Mitchell, Indiana)

FLY SWATTER

This is a good little game taken from "Pin the Tail on the Donkey."

Blindfold a kid, give him a fly swatter (the type with holes in it) and spin him around a few times. Place a glob of shaving cream on the wall and have the kid try to swat it. On impact the "swatter" usually gets hit with flying shaving cream. Wipe it up and position a new glob in a different spot for the next contestant. The winner is whoever can swat the glob in the fastest time. (Contributed by Andrea Sutton, Ipswich, Massachusetts)

FRISBEE RELAY

Divide the group into equally sized teams of 5 or 6 per team. Any number of teams can play at once. Each team will need a frisbee. The playing area should have plenty of length, such as a road (without traffic) or a large open field. Each team should spread out in a line with players about 50 feet apart or so. The first person throws the frisbee to the second, who allows the frisbee to land. That person then stands where the frisbee landed and throws it towards the third person, who throws it to the fourth, and so on. The object is to see which team can throw it the greatest distance in the shortest time. Award points for throwing it the farthest, and points for finishing first. For added fun, have the guys throw left-handed (or right-handed if they are left-handed). Footballs can be substituted for frisbees if they are easier to get. (Contributed by Scotty Shows, Jackson, Mississippi)

GEIGER COUNTER

This is a great party game. Everyone is seated in the room. The leader selects a "volunteer" to leave the room. While he is away, the group agrees on a hiding place for a random object, which the leader hides. The person returns and tries to find the object, not knowing what it is. The rest of the group, much like a geiger-counter "tick-tick-tick-ticks" slower as he moves away from the object and faster as he moves closer, until he finds it. Volunteers may compete for the fastest time. (Contributed by Steve Illum, San Diego, California)

GIFT GRABBER

Here is a different way to "open gifts" at this year's Christmas Party. It can be used anytime of the year, actually, but it would seem most appropriate at Christmas. It works best with 15 to 20 people. Everyone gets a wrapped gift to begin with. (they should be joke gifts and absolutely worthless, if possible, like an old shoe, an old motel key, etc.) After the gifts are distributed, deal out an entire deck of playing cards, so that everyone has an equal number of cards. The leader should have a second deck of cards that he keeps. When everyone has a gift and some cards, the leader shuffles his deck, draws one card and announces what it is. Whoever has that card (from the first deck) gives the leader that identical card and then gets to help himself to any other person's gift that he'd like. Then, the next card is announced by the leader and the possessor of that identical card gets his turn to help himself to someone else's gift, and so on until the whole deck of cards is used up. It is a scream to see how the gifts go back and forth. One person at first might accumulate several but as his cards are exhausted, the momentum shifts. Of course, whoever has the gifts at the end of the game gets to unwrap them and keep them. Sometimes seeing what actually was the content of some of the packages that were most furiously sought after produces as much fun as the game itself. (Contributed by Douglas Whallon, South Hamilton, Massachusetts)

GRAPE TOSS

Teams appoint one kid who is the "tosser." He gets a bag of grapes. The rest of the team gets in a circle around him. The tosser is in the middle. He must toss grapes to everyone on his team, one at a time, and each team member must catch the grape in his or her mouth. The first team to go around their circle (the whole team), wins. (Contributed by Richard Reynolds, Cheyenne, Wyoming)

GREAT SPAGHETTI RELAY

Divide the group into teams. Each person gets a potato chip (the larger, the better). Each team lines up, and the first person in line holds his potato chip in his mouth. A wet spaghetti noodle is then draped over the chip and the person must run to a set point and back without dropping the noodle or breaking the potato chip. On returning, he passes the noodle on to the next person, who does the same thing. The game continues, and the first team to finish is the winner. The rules: (1) No hands are allowed. (2) If the noodle drops off, breaks, or becomes mutilated, the player must return to the line, get

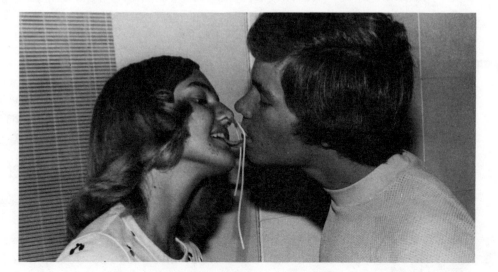

a new one and start over. (3) If the potato chip breaks or becomes too soggy, the player must get a new chip. (Contributed by Keith Geckeler, Escondido, California)

HAND-IN-GLOVE RELAY

This is a relay game in which the teams stand in line and pass a pair of gloves from one end to the other. The first person puts the gloves on, then the next person takes them off and puts them on himself. Each person takes the gloves off the person in front of him and puts them on himself. All fingers of the hand must fit in the fingers of the gloves. Options: Use rubber kitchen gloves or large work gloves. (Contributed by Lee Weems, Newport News, Virginia)

HIP CHARADES

This is a great game for casual get-togethers. It is played just like charades, except that team members spell out words with their *hips* instead of using pantomine or hand signals. Each contestant tries to get their team to guess the words they are spelling out by standing with their *back* to the team and moving their hips to form (or "write") the letters in the air. The team shouts out each letter as they recognize it and attempt to guess the correct title in the fastest time possible. The results are hilarious. (Contributed by Lorne H. Belden, Louisville, Kentucky)

JERUSALEM SQUARES

This is a takeoff on the television program "Hollywood Squares." It's an entertaining way to learn little known facts in the Bible. To begin, select nine of your youth (include sponsors, too) to be your "Tic Tac Toe" board celebrities. . Place three chairs side by side facing all non-participating youth. Three celebrities sit on these chairs, three stand behind them, and three sit on the floor in front of them. Each of the nine celebrities receive two medium-size pieces of poster board, one with an "X" on it and the other with an "O" which can be held up at the appropriate times. (Biblical names or famous names can be given to each celebrity to add to the fun.)

Two other kids are then selected to be the first contestants. One is assigned to be X and the other is O. They sit facing the "board of celebrities." Prior to the game, someone prepares a list of questions to be asked. That person then acts as emcee, asking the questions.

Toss a coin to determine who begins. The winner selects one of the "squares" (celebrities). The emcee asks his first question of the celebrity occupying that square. The celebrity gives an answer (the correct one or one that he has made up as a bluff.) The contestant then must either agree or disagree with the celebrity's answer. If he is correct in agreeing or disagreeing with the answer given, the celebrity holds up the contestant's letter (either X or O). If the contestant was wrong, the celebrity holds up the opponent's letter. (All rules are the same as the TV program.) The winner is the first to receive three X's or O's in a row.

A good book to give you ideas for questions to ask is a fascinating book called, *Is That In The Bible?* It is a paperback published by Fawcett World Library, 67 West 44th Street, New York, New York 10036. Some sample questions that could be used:

I. What book in the Bible does not contain the name of God? *Answer: Esther*
2. Within 10 pounds either way, what is the weight of the largest hailstones mentioned in the Bible? *Answer: 110 pounds (Rev. 16:21)*
3. True or False: The fish, whales, and all in the sea did not die in the flood of Noah's time. *Answer: True (Gen. 7:22)*
4. How many different men named Jesus are mentioned in the Bible in the King James Version? *Answer: 4*
5. True or False: There is actually a verse in the Bible where raisins and apples are recommended for the lovesick. *Answer: True (Song of Solomon)*
6. What famous Bible character had bad breath, B.O., and bad teeth? *Answer: Job (Job 19:27-30)*

(Contributed by Alan Sheldon, Austin, Minnesota)

KAMIKAZE

This is an outdoor game, good for camps or with any group of thirty or more kids. Divide the group into two teams. One team will be identified by blue and the other by gold. These colors can be made with arm bands. Each team has a "president" who can only be assassinated by a water balloon. The president is seated in a chair which is inside a four foot circle, which is in the center of a larger circle, some 30 or 40 feet in diameter.

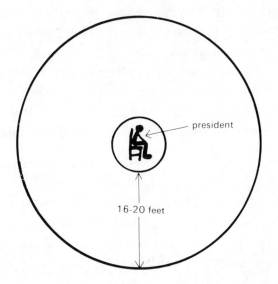

Each team has the same set-up for their own president in two different locations. Both teams have offensive and defensive players. The offensive players each get two water balloons and may move in any part of the boundaries except for the area which composes the two circles with the president in the center. No person (offensive or defensive), may enter or pass through the two circles which surround the president.

The offensive players try to assassinate the president of the opposite team. He does this by tossing underhanded, a water bomb (balloon), from the edge of the outer circle. The toss must have an arch in it. If the balloon hits below the waist of the president, he is merely wounded and it takes three ''wound'' shots to assassinate him. A balloon hitting on target (above the waist), kills the president and the game is over (or if not over, points scored and the team elects a new president . . .) An adult ''judge'' should be on hand to determine the legality of shots.

Defensive players are armed with a small paper bag of flour. Obviously, their job is to defend the president. They can ''kill'' the other teams offensive players by breaking the bag of flour on them, thus getting flour all over them. Offensive players cannot kill defensive players. They simply must run back into their own territory. Defensive players are not allowed into the other team's territory. (The playing area should be divided in half, with each team's president located in their own half of the total playing area.) When a defensive player kills an offensive player, he takes his armband and the dead offensive player must go to the graveyard and is out of the game. When all of the offensive players of a team are killed, they automatically lose the game.

The game is over either after a time limit or when the president is assassinated. However, to prevent the game from being over too soon, it might be best to simply call a time-out when the president is assassinated and the teams have five minutes or so to re-organize, elect a new president, get their dead players back in the game and then the game resumes. Also, during the break, scores are taken by the scorekeeper. Assassination of the president is worth 200 points and armbands of enemy players are killed are worth 50 points each. New water balloons and flour sacks are passed out during each break (if any), which follows a president's assassination.

There should be at least four adult judges. One judge each for the team play areas and one judge to watch each president. Another person should be on hand to pass out flour sacks and balloons. (If a player uses up his supply at any time, he can go and get more.) This ammo area is ''safe'' and no fighting can be done there. (Contributed by Lewis E. Trotter, Lakeland, Florida)

LAWN SKIING

For those who long for the mountain slopes or whose lakes and rivers may be dry, try this. Acquire several pair of water skis and remove the fins from the undersides. Get the necessary number of tow ropes or just plain rope (you'll need at least 40 feet), and begin your races. Local school or park lawns (just watered) provide a slick surface and kids pulling the ropes provide the power. Many variations are possible using slalom skis, skim boards, inner tubes, etc, and other surfaces besides grass are suitable. Events can range from slaloms to marathons. (Contributed by Gary Liddle, Camarillo, California)

LEMON GOLF

Kids get a broom and a lemon. They must hit the lemon with the stick end of the broom onto a piece of paper some distance away. It must stop on the piece of paper. Count the strokes as in regular golf. (Contributed by Richard Reynolds, Cheyenne, Wyoming)

MAD RELAY

This is a different kind of relay race in which each contestant does something different. What the contestants do is determined by the directions in a bag at the other end of the relay course.

At the beginning of the race, each team is lined up single file as usual. On a signal, the first person on each team runs to the other end of the course to a chair. On the chair is a bag containing instructions written on separate pieces of paper. The contestant draws one of the instructions, reads it, and follows it as quickly as possible. Before returning to the team, the contestant must tag the chair. The contestant then runs back and tags the next runner. The relay proceeds in this manner and the team that uses all of its instructions first is the winner. Below are a few examples of directions:

1. Run around the chair 5 times while continously yelling, "The British are coming, the British are coming."
2. Run to the nearest person on another team and scratch their head.
3. Run to the nearest adult in the room and whisper, "You're no spring chicken."
4. Stand on one foot while holding the other in your hand, tilt your head back, and count, "l0, 9, 8, 7, 6, 5, 4, 3, 2, 1, Blast off!"
5. Take your shoes off, put them on the wrong foot, and then tag your nearest opponent.
6. Sit on the floor, cross your legs, and sing the following: "Mary had a little lamb, little lamb, little lamb, Mary had a little lamb, its fleece was white as snow."
7. Go to the last person on your team and make 3 different "funny-face" expressions, then return to the chair before tagging your next runner.
8. Put your hands over your eyes and snort like a pig 5 times and meow like a cat 5 times.
9. Sit in the chair, fold your arms, and laugh hard and loud for 5 seconds.
10. Run around the chair backwards 5 times while clapping your hands.
11. Go to a blond-headed person and keep asking, "Do blonds really have more fun?", until they answer.
12. Run to someone not on your team and kiss their hand and gently pinch their cheek.

(Contributed by Larry Bennett, Mitchell, Indiana)

MATCH GAME

This is an indoor game that is quite simple and easy to play. Distribute a list similar to the following sample to each person:

1. A letter from home
2. The colonel
3. A famous band
4. Looks like a foot
5. Headquarters
6. A stirring event
7. The end of winter
8. A pair of slippers
9. Pig's retreat
10. An old beau of mine
11. The peace maker
12. There love is found
13. Cause of the Revolution
14. An absorbing article
15. A place for reflection
16. The reigning favorite
17. A morning caller
18. Seen at the ball game

19.	Messenger	23.	Life of China
20.	Fire when ready	24.	Peacemaker
21.	Drive through the wood	25.	My native land
22.	Bound to shine		

Next, place various articles on a table or around the room that will match the "clues" given in the first list. For example, the corresponding items for the preceding list would be:

1.	The letter "o" on a card	14.	Blotter or sponge
2.	Kernel of corn	15.	Mirror
3.	Rubber band	16.	Umbrella
4.	Ruler	17.	Alarm clock
5.	Pillow	18.	Pitcher
6.	Spoon	19.	Penny (one sent)
7.	Letter "r"	20.	Match
8.	Two banana peels	21.	Nail
9.	Writing pen	22.	Shoe polish
10.	Old ribbon bow	23.	Rice
11.	Pair of scissors	24.	Scissors
12.	Dictionary	25.	Dirt
13.	Tacks on tea bags		

Of course, you can think of many more besides these. The winner is the person who can correctly match up all the items in the fastest time. To make the game harder, place twice as many items on the table than you have clues for. (Contributed by Steve Stricklen, Birmingham, Alabama and Bob Fakkema, Greensboro, North Carolina)

MATH SCRAMBLE

Divide into teams. Each person is given a number on a piece of paper which is to be worn. (Numbers should begin at 0 and go up to 10 or the number of kids on the team.) The leader stands an equal distance away from each team and yells out a "math problem" such as "2 times 8 minus 4 divided by 3" and the team must send the person with the correct answer (the person wearing the number "4" in this case) to the leader. No talking is allowed on the team. The correct person must simply get up and run. The first correct answer to get to the leader wins 100 points. The first team to reach 1,000 (or whatever) wins. (Contributed by J. C. Heneisen, Louisville, Kentucky)

MARSHMALLOW WAR

Many "tag" games can be played by using marshmallows as weapons. Kids get three or four marshmallows and may throw them. If you get hit by one, you have been "shot." They are soft and the white powder on them usually leaves a mark. They may be dipped in flour to make this more so. Wet ones leave a mark also. (Contributed by Robert Wilson, Redondo Beach, California)

MESSAGE RELAY

The following is a good team game. Teams divide in half and stand a distance away. Type out a crazy message on a piece of paper (one for each team) and give it to the first member who opens it, reads it, wads it up and throws it on the ground. He *runs* to the next person at the other side and whispers it in his ear. Then he runs back and tells it to the next person and so on until the last person runs to the supervisor and whispers it to him. The team closest to the original message wins. Accuracy, not time, is most important, but they must run. Sample message, "Mrs. Sarah Sahara sells extraordinary information to very enterprising executives." (Contributed by Richard Reynolds, Cheyenne, Wyoming)

"MOUNTED MEDIC" SNOWBALL WAR

Here's a new version of one of the oldest games in existence, the old fashioned snowball fight. Divide the group into two teams and play by the following rules:

1. Anyone hitting an opponent on the head is automatically out, even if it was done accidentally.
2. If you are hit by a snowball, you must fall to the ground and remain there until your "mounted medic" comes and "heals" you.
3. Each team is allowed one "mounted medic." This person must be a girl. Her "horse" must be a guy.
4. The "mounted medic" must stay on her horse at all times. She may get off only when she must "heal" a soldier. She "heals" a guy by kissing him on the forehead. A girl is "healed" by being kissed by the medic's horse.
5. You may only be healed by your own "mounted medic."
6. Anyone hitting either a medic or her horse is automatically out, even if it was done accidentally.
7. Each team chooses one King.
8. The War is won by assassinating the opposing King, that is, by hitting him on the body, not limbs or head. If the King is hit on the limbs, he must fall to the ground and be healed by the "mounted medic." The King may be assassinated while wounded. Anyone hitting the King on the head is automatically out, even if it was done accidentally.
9. Option: Kissing may be replaced by wrapping the "wounded" part with toilet paper.

(Contributed by Ron White, Lake Villa, Illinois)

PAGE SCRAMBLE

Give each team a children's story book with titles such as "Waldo the Jumping Dragon" or "Big Albert Moves into Town." The dumber the better. You must also make sure each book has the same number of pages. Before passing them out, however, carefully remove the pages from each book cover, and mix them up so that each team has a book with the correct number of pages . . . but not the correct pages. On a signal, the teams distribute the pages among team members and they begin trading page for page with other teams. The whole place becomes a giant trading floor. The first team with a completed book, with pages in the correct order, wins. (Contributed by Lee Bracey, Corunna, Indiana)

PILLOW BALANCE-BEAM BLAST

Take an old railroad tie or make your own narrow, raised playing area. The two players stand at either end of the beam. Each is given a pillow. At the signal "go," they try to knock their opponent off the beam. The first one to touch the floor loses. However, the winner must remain standing after the other person falls. (Contributed by Ron Wells, Oregon City, Oregon)

POLISH BASEBALL

This is a great game for groups of 50 or more. (25 per team). There are only 2 bases: home plate and first base (located approximately 120 feet from home). A regular baseball bat is used with a volley ball slightly mushy. There is no out of bounds. The ball can be hit in any direction. The pitcher is always from the team that is up. Each batter gets only one pitch. The batter does not have to accept the pitch but if he does swing, it counts as one pitch. Outs are made in the following manner:

1. A missed swing.
2. A fly ball that is caught.
3. A force out at first base. (You cannot be forced out at home.)
4. Being touched by the ball. (A runner can be hit by a thrown ball or tagged out.)

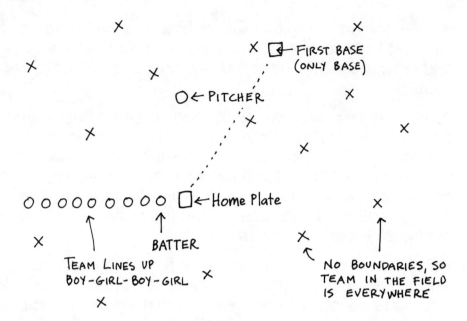

Once a runner reaches the first base, he does not have to leave, until it's safe to. (Any amount of players can be on first base at the same time.) As soon as the team at bat has three outs, the team immediately runs to the field and the fielding team immediately lines up and starts playing. They do not have to wait for the fielding team to get in position as long as all of their players are lined up behind home. You can have up to four games going at once, on the same field but on different sides of the field, which can be very confusing, but a lot of fun. Each game needs a neutral umpire who judges "outs." The team with the most runs wins. Any amount of innings can be played.

POLISH PING-PONG

This game requires the same equipment as regulation ping-pong, and the game begins in the same way. But after the ball crosses the net on the serve, it must bounce at least once on the table and once on the floor before it can be returned. On the return serve, the ball has to hit the table once (it does not have to cross the net) and then bounce on the floor once before it can be returned. The ball on any return serve (once it is across the net in the beginning serve), and on all other returns, may bounce from 1 to 12 (or more) times on the table, but can only be hit after it has bounced once on the floor.

The fun begins, for example, when a returned serve hits the table on the return side, takes a quick bounce off to the left or right side of the table, and bounces on the floor. It's now up to the server to get to the ball and hit it back up on the table (anywhere) after the first bounce. Here, surprise shots can cause quite a mad scramble for the ball.

Fun also enters in when the table is in a room with close walls and a low ceiling. Then combination shots off the walls and ceiling add to

47

the excitement. Here, the rule of one bounce is altered, as the ball can first bounce against the walls or ceiling before hitting the floor and after bouncing off the table, and it is still considered a "fair shot."

Also, a return server can hit the ball (after the floor bounce) against the wall, carrom it off the ceiling, hit the table on one or more bounces, and then continue to another wall or floor. It's then up to the other person to get that ball as soon as it leaves the first bounce on the floor. Again, quickness and practice pay off. There are some games in which all one does is run from one end of the table to the other just to keep in the game.

Score is kept in the same way as in regulation ping-pong: each server serves until 5 points are made (total) and after a total of 10 points the people switch sides. This is done since some room combinations favor one side or the other.

Increased fun can be added when teams play with mandatory alternate shots on both teams. This causes real excitement as one team member is always in the other's way, or the person who is to return the serve is always on the wrong side of the table. Again, fast footwork and expert combination shots are the keys to success.

If in any game, after the first serve, the ball bounces on the table, hits the net and then goes off to the floor, it constitutes a "fair shot." Also any "net" ball on a return shot which causes the ball to stop dead on the table, can be blown off the table by the person who's next to hit it. However, he must wait till it bounces once off the floor before hitting it. A team member can blow it off for you to add suspense in team competition. (Contributed by The Polish Team at Covenant Theological Seminary, St. Louis, Missouri)

Typical Polish Ping-Pong Game

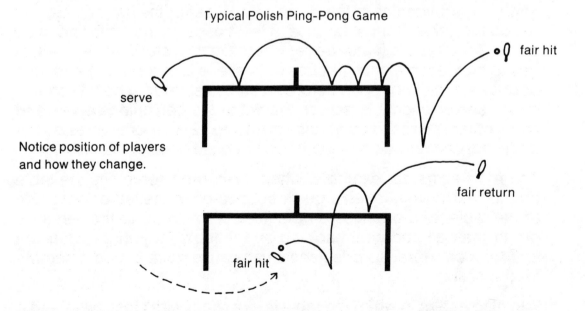

serve

fair hit

Notice position of players
and how they change.

fair return

fair hit

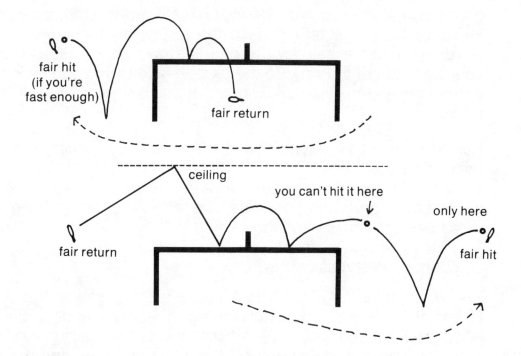

fair hit
(if you're
fast enough)

fair return

ceiling

you can't hit it here

only here

fair return

fair hit

RATTLESNAKE

For this game of stealth and skill, you will need two blindfolds, a small plastic bottle (a Rx bottle works fine) with a rock in it, and a defined area for play. This can be done on large mats (of the wrestling variety) or on a carpeted floor. The referee blindfolds both people. One is designated the rattlesnake and the other is the hunter. The hunter is spun in circles several times so he loses his sense of direction. We are now ready to begin play. It is essential that everyone remains absolutely quiet (everyone not playing is seated around the edges of the playing area). The referee says, ''rattlesnake.'' The rattlesnake must shake his ''rattler'' and then try to escape capture by the hunter. The game continues with the referee periodically saying ''rattlesnake'' until the hunter captures the rattlesnake. (Contributed by Ron Wells, Oregon City, Oregon)

ROLLING PIN THROW

This is a hilarious idea for church picnics, adult recreation or youth. Have a contest to see which women can throw a wooden rolling pin the longest distance. Results are side-splitting! (Contributed by Roger Copeland, Hurst, Texas)

ROUND BUZZARD

"Round Buzzard" is played with the same rules and the same way as a game called "round robin." In round robin, everyone stands in a circle around a ping-pong table. There is one ping-pong paddle on each end of the table and one ping-pong ball used in the game. It begins with one person serving the ball just like in a ping-pong game. But after he serves, he must rotate around the table and let the person next to him receive the return of his serve. In other words, you hit the ball, lay the paddle down on the table, move to your right, out of the way, so the person next to you can pick up the paddle and return the ball from someone on the other end of the table.

Round Buzzard is played the exact same way, except for a few minor changes.
1. Instead of a ping-pong ball, use a tennis ball.
2. Instead of ping-pong paddles, use tennis rackets. (Old ones because they take a beating.)
3. Instead of playing on a ping-pong table, you play on a tennis court, or volleyball court.

The other rules for Round Buzzard are the same as for Round Robin, there is just a lot more running, especially near the end, when each person who either misses the ball (or fails to return the serve or keep the volley going) is *out of the game,* and there are only three or four people left. It requires a lot of hustle. (Contributed by Gary Armes, Cincinnati, Ohio)

SHUFFLE YOUR BUNS

Arrange chairs in a circle so that everyone has a chair. There should be two extra chairs in the circle. Each person sits in a chair except for two people in the middle who try to sit in the two vacant chairs. The persons sitting in the chairs keep moving around from chair to chair to prevent the two in the middle from sitting down. If one or both of the two in the middle manage to sit in a chair, the person on their right replaces them in the middle of the circle and then tries to sit in an empty chair. (Contributed by Mary McKemy, Lincoln, Nebraska)

SILLY SOCCER

Divide your group into two teams. In a large open field, place two pylons 100 to 150 feet apart. The object is to hit the opposing teams pylon with the ball. There are no boundaries, and the pylon may be hit from any direction. All other soccer rules apply. For added confusion with a large group, throw in a second ball. (Contributed by Ron Elliott, Simi Valley, California)

SKUNK

This is a game of strength and agility. You need a defined padded area, either a carpeted floor or a large mat. In the center of the playing area a skunk skin is placed (be creative with your substitutes!). The two players stand on either side of the skunk skin and lock arms over the skin. At the signal ''go,'' each tries to force the other to touch the skunk skin with some part of their body. The first one to touch the skin loses. Have the other people sit around the playing area to keep the sprawling players on the mat. (Contributed by Ron Wells, Oregon City, Oregon)

SLIDE STORIES

Divide the group into teams of five to ten each. Provide each team with twenty or more slides of various things: people, objects, travel, nature, whatever you can throw in. Each team must make up a story using as many of the slides as possible. Set a time limit and have each team project their "slide story" for the rest of the group. The most creative, funny, longest, etc. wins. (Contributed by Don Snider, Elgin, Illinois)

SOCK TAIL RELAY

Make several ''sock tails,'' one for each team. A sock tail consists of a belt with a sock tied onto it, with an orange in the end of the sock,

51

as a weight. The first person on each team puts on the tail with the sock hanging down from his rear. Another orange is placed on the floor. On the signal, the player must push the orange on the floor to a goal and back, with the sock tail. If he touches it with his feet or hands, he must start over. First team to have all team members complete this task wins. (Contributed by John Simmons, Warminster, Pennsylvania)

SOUND-OFF

Here's a fun game that requires some audio-visual equipment. Obtain two home movie projectors, two cassette recorders, and either two different cartoons (that can be shown on the home movie projectors) or two copies of the same cartoon. Divide the crowd into teams.

First, show the two cartoons (or comedies) to both teams. They should, of course, be silent films with titles written on the screen. Then give each team one of the projectors, one of the films, and one of the cassette recorders (with a blank tape) and have them record a "soundtrack" for their film. If the same cartoon is used for both teams, then a contest can be had to see which team can do the best job. Any sound effects, music, or dialogue can be used. Allow 20 minutes for this, then have each team show their film with sound. The results are a lot of fun. (Contributed by Chuck Prestwood, Brookhaven, Mississippi)

STACK 'EM UP

Have everyone sit in chairs in a circle. Prepare a list of qualifying characteristics such as those found in the "Sit Down Game" (See IDEAS NUMBER TWO). Here are a few examples:

1. If you forgot to use a deodorant today . . .
2. IF you got a traffic ticket this year . . .
3. If you have a hole in your sock . . .
4. If you are afraid of the dark . . .

Then read them one at a time and add " . . . move three chairs to the right" or "move one chair to the left," etc. In other words, you might say, "If you forgot to use a deodorant today, *move three chairs to the right,* and all those who "qualify" move as instructed and sit in that chair, regardless of whether or not it's occupied by one or more persons. As the game progresses, kids begin "stacking up" on certain chairs. (Contributed by Mary McKemy, Lincoln, Nebraska)

STAFF STUMPERS

Here's a fun game that will really help kids to get to know the staff (youth director, youth sponsors, advisors, teachers, etc.) a lot better. In advance of the game have each staff member answer a list of questions (with short answers) similar to these:

1. Why are you on the staff?
2. What has been your most embarrassing moment while "on the job" with the youth?
3. If you could go anywhere in the world, where would it be?
4. What makes you happy?
5. Who has had the most influence on your life?
6. Who is your favorite performer?
7. If you had a million dollars, what would you do with it?
8. My dream is to....(complete sentence).
9. What has been the best book that you have read recently (excluding the Bible)?
10. What is your favorite scripture verse?

After each staff member has filled out the questionnaire, print up their answers along with the questions, in a multiple choice type of quiz. For example, question number three might look like this:

3. If you could go anywhere in the world, where would it be?
   _____1. The French Riviera
   _____2. The Holy Land
   _____3. Home
   _____4. Butte, Montana
   _____5. Hawaii

The answers are the actual answers that were given by the staff, and the object is for each kid to try and guess which staff-member gave which answer. The answers should be jumbled (in a different order) for each question.

After the kids have made their guesses, the staff-members can come to the front and each answer the questions correctly. The kids can then check their papers to see just how well they know their staff. (Contributed by Stanley Jewell, Elmhurst, Illinois)

STEAL THE BACON IN-THE-ROUND

Draw a large circle with lines for line-up which are separate from the circle. Locate the center. (Circle diameter, approximately 15 feet. Lime works well in field or paint on black top.) By curving the line-up line, all the kids can see the activity without interfering with the action of the game.

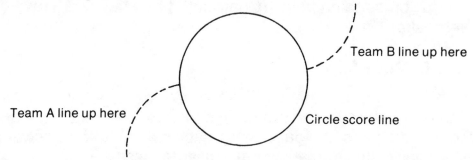

Team B line up here

Team A line up here

Circle score line

Place the "bacon" (an old shirt, a sponge, or small ball) in the center. The players line up. The first person on each team, on the blow of a whistle, runs to the center and takes the bacon over the circle score line. If the person possessing the bacon is tagged, then the tagging person receives the point. If, after a pre-determined time (say, 30 seconds) no one picks up the bacon, blow the whistle and the next two players may join the two in the circle. When two team members are working together, they may pass the bacon between themselves.

Advantages:

1. The circle allows for a person to run in any direction to score.
2. The teams do not have to be equal, in fact, it is better if they are not equal, so that the players never compete against the same person on future turns.
3. You do not have to number off players or call out numbers.
4. The game handles large numbers of players and all get a turn.

(Contributed by Norman Jones, Sebastopol, California)

STILTS RELAY

Have someone who is handy with wood make up four pairs of stilts out of 2 x 2's (two pairs for each team). The foot-mount only needs to be 12-18 inches off the ground. Most kids will be able to walk on them with ease. Just line the teams up relay style and let 'em go. The first team to go to the goal and back on stilts (one at a time) wins. (Contributed by Roger Disque, Chicago, Illinois)

STILTS STEAL THE BACON

This works best with four teams. Have the teams line up forming a square (each team on one side of the square). The teams need to be numbered from one to however many are on each team (equal number on each team). A pair of stilts are given to each team and placed about six feet centered and in front of each team. When the leader calls a number, those with that number from each team run to the stilts, mount them and try to go after the "bacon" on stilts and also try to get the bacon back across their side. A volleyball will make the best "bacon" and should be placed in the middle. The team with the highest score wins. (Contributed by Roger Disque, Chicago, Illinois)

STORY LINE

The group is divided into two or more teams. Each team elects a "spokesperson" for their group. Each group then gets a card with a daffy sentence typed on it (create your own; the daffier the better. Example: "Fourteen yellow elephants driving polka-dotted Volkswagens converged on the Halloween party.") The spokesperson from each group then comes forward with their card. The leader then explains that he/she will begin telling a story; at a certain point, he/she will stop and point to one of the "spokespersons" who will have to pick up the story line and keep it going. Every minute or so, a whistle will sound and that person must stop talking and the next "spokesperson" must pick up the story line. This continues for about 10 minutes. The object is to work the story line around so that you get the sentence you have been given into the story in such a way that the other groups cannot tell that you have done so. At the end of the story, each group must decide whether the "spokesperson" for the other groups were able to get their sentence into the story—and if so, what it was. Points may be awarded for getting sentence, guessing whether or not it got it and what the sentence was. (Example of beginning story line: "Dudley Do-Right and Priscilla Pure were rowing in the middle of the lake one fine summer day. Dudley had a passionate crush on Priscilla and longed to hold her fair soft hand. When no one was around, he pulled his oar in and reached out for Priscilla's smooth tender fingers. He was inches away when suddenly . . .") (Contributed by Keith Geckeler, San Diego, California)

SUCKER RELAY

Teams line up. Each person has a paper straw. A piece of paper (about 4 inches square) is picked up by sucking on the straw and is carried around a goal and back. If you drop the paper, you must start over. Each person on the team must do it. First team to finish wins.

TARGET PRACTICE

Place a table against a wall. On the table place many "targets" made from paper folded in half. These targets should be various sizes from two inches to about six inches. Put point values on each one (10, 25, 50, 100) depending on how big the target is. Each team gets an "arsenal" of rubber bands and tries to shoot as many targets over in one minute as possible. All players must stand behind a line 15 feet (or so) away from the table. Points are scored each time a target is knocked over. Team with the most points wins. (Contributed by J. C. Heneisen, Louisville, Kentucky)

TASTE TEST

Here's a fun little quiz that might be appropriate at your next banquet or perhaps to kick off a discussion on world hunger. The answers are at the end.

Fill in each blank with the name of a food item:

1. "Hurry, dear. _____ be going."
2. Istanbul is in _____.
3. "Say, I'm broke, man. Can you loan me a little _____?"
4. . The _____achian mountains are beautiful in the fall.
5. The Parthenon is in _____.
6. I have a _____ on my big toe.
7. Some prizefighters have _____ ears.

56

8. The 20th letter of the alphabet: _____
9. Some people just don't _____ all about the environment.
10. It's found in the area of a circle: _____
11. "You are the _____ of the earth."
12. Two of a kind: _____
13. She wanted to buy it, _____ husband said, "no."
14. If you step on a tomato, you might _____ it.
15. "I'll _____ you at 6:30 sharp."
16. "She's been a little sluggish, so I tried to _____ up."
17. "_____ on earth, goodwill toward men."
18. "Okay, just what is your _____?"
19. Kids always _____ their noses at foods that they don't like.
20. At Waikiki, you'll find many people _____ in the sun.
21. Adam and Eve were busy _____ Cain.
22. Every year, good gardeners will _____ their trees.

Answers: 1. Lettuce 2. Turkey 3. Bread 4. Apple 5. Grease 6. Corn 7. Cauliflower 8. Tea 9. Carrot 10. Pie (R-squared) 11. Salt 12. Pear 13. Butter 14. Squash 15. Meat 16. Pepper 17. Peas 18. Beef 19. Turnip 20. Bacon 21. Raisin 22. Prune

(Contributed by Walter Kukkonen, Joliet, Illinois)

THE TEAM DIVISION GAME

The following is a good game that can be used as a method for randomly assigning kids to a team for further team competition or discussion groups. Here is how it works:

Each team is assigned a two-color combination (use construction paper), distinct from any other (for team identification). The same color can be used twice but each time with a different color. For each color combination (hence, each team to play), place two sheets of paper on each other and cut out two circles of equal size, using the entire sheet. Then cut each set of circles into any number of random-shaped pieces. Each set of circles cut into three pieces yields 6 pieces of each color. (12 pieces)

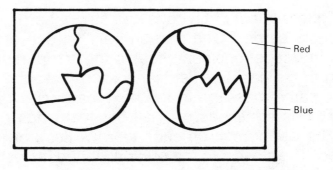

Then discard half of the 12 pieces so that you are left with 2 circles composed of pieces of the two basic colors.

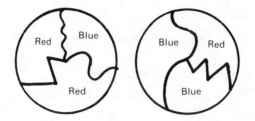

Note that you are left with six pieces which match into circles but not necessarily of the same color. This allows up to 6 members per team. For 7 or 8 per team, cut circles into 4 pieces each; for any number less than 6, simply discard some from above diagram leaving one circle only partially complete. Paper clip the combinations together in a stack so that at the last minute, you can discard enough to result in the exact amount to be on each team. Repeat this process for *each* team's color combination and place them in a paper bag for drawing.

To begin with, everyone draws one piece out of the paper bag. They must then match their piece to the others who have the matching portions to their circle. To explain that:
  1. Colors do not necessarily match.
  2. Once you match with someone, stick together.
  3. Do not exchange pieces with anyone.
  4. After all are matched (this will take some time, but help out if it takes more than 15 minutes), there will be many groups of 3 standing around together (or 2 or 4, in some cases, if that's how you set it up). Then combine all of the groups with the color combinations chosen for each team into that team, e.g., all those with circles of red and blue (will be two groups) gather together and become Team A and so on.

You may make signs for each team, using the color combinations that can be hung on the wall, or that the kids can wear around their necks, or whatever. (Contributed by Richard Reynolds, Cheyenne, Wyoming)

TELEPHONE GOSSIP RELAY

Make "phones" out of tin cans and string (see illustration) and play the "gossip game." One person gets on one end of the line and gives a message (one sentence) to the first person who listens with the can at his ear. The listener then runs to the other phone and tells the same message to the next team member who is now the listener. This continues until all the team has received the message. The last person on each team writes down the message he received. The closest to the original (in the fastest time) wins. (Contributed by Dave Gilliam, Henryetta, Oklahoma)

Hole punched in the end of each can   String pulled taut (about 40 feet)

Knot should be tied in each end of string

TETHERBALL JUMP

Here's an old game that kids really go for. Have ten to twenty kids form a circle. You get in the center of the circle with a tether ball (a ball attached to a rope about eight feet long). You take the rope in your hand and begin making circles with the ball, about six inches off the ground. The circle of kids then move in closer and each person must jump over the ball as it passes by. You keep going around and around, getting faster and faster until someone goofs. That person is then out, and the game continues. The last person in is the winner. As the game progresses, you can make the ball go faster and/or higher off the ground. Two leaders (ball twirlers) are recommended to take shifts in the center if you get dizzy easily. (Contributed by Rich Read, Los Angeles, California)

TIN PAN BANG BANG

This game is similar to "Clumps." The leader stands on a chair in the middle of the room with a stainless steel pot in his hand and a metal spoon. The crowd begins milling around the room. Everybody

has to keep moving. The leader then bangs on the pot with the spoon a certain number of times and then stops. The players count the number of beats and then get in a circle holding hands with the same number of persons as the number of beats. Those who are not in a circle with the right number of people when a whistle blows are eliminated from the game. This is continued with a varied number of beats each time, until all are eliminated except for one person. (Contributed by Dallas Elder, Portland, Oregon)

TOILET PAPER RACE

Guys (or girls) race to see who can unroll a roll of toilet paper by pushing it along the ground with their *noses*. The first person to unroll the entire roll, or cross the finish line wins. For a switch, have other contestants do it in reverse, that is, roll it back up in the fastest time. (Contributed by Andy Hansen, Lansing, Michigan)

TOSS THE RAG

Tie a rag or sock into a tight knot. Everyone is seated in a circle with "it" in the middle. He tosses the rag to someone and shouts some category (like soft drinks, washing machines, presidents, birds, theologians, books of the Bible, etc.) He then counts to ten rapidly. If he reaches ten before the other person names an example of that category (Coke, Kenmore, Lincoln, Sapsucker, Kierkegaard, Ezekiel, etc.), then that person takes his place in the center. The category named should be a "common noun," while the examples given are normally "proper nouns." (Contributed by Richard Bond, New Orleans, Lousiana)

TRIVIA TIC-TAC-TOE

This game is played sort of like the TV game show, "Hollywood Squares." Two people play at a time. A game board should be constructed out of poster board or cork (bulletin) board like the one below:

Old Testament	Sports	Morning Sermon
Riddles	Little Known Facts	Movies
Current Events	Saintly Secrets (Gossip)	New Testament

Prepare plenty of questions for each category (semi-hard). Contestants try to get their "X's" or "O's" three in a row, up, down, or diagonally. This is done by correctly answering the question in the appropriate category. If the "X" person misses, then the "O" person gets to try it. Or, for a faster version, if one person misses, the opponent automatically wins that spot. "X's" and "O's" can be hung up with thumbtacks. (Contributed by Ellis Meuser, McMinnville, Oregon)

TRUST TAG

This is the usual game of "tag," except that the players play in partners, or groups of two. One partner must wear a blindfold while his teammate must guide him by keeping his hands on his blindfolded partner's waist and shouting out directions. The object is for the blindfolded "it" player to tag another blindfolded player. To make it even more difficult, the un-blindfolded player must give his partner directions without talking, just pushing or pulling him around. (Contributed by Dick Babington, Ontario, California)

TUG-O-WAR IN THE ROUND

Get a large rope about 24 feet in length and tie (or splice) the two ends together, making one round rope. Four teams line up on four sides of a square. In the center of the square, the rope is placed opened out into a circle. The teams should be equal in size and each team should number off from one on up. The leader then calls out a number and the four kids (one from each team) with that number grab one side of the rope and try to get back across their team's line. As soon as a player crosses the line (pulling the rope), he is declared the winner. Continue until everyone has had a try. (Contributed by Roger Disque, Chicago, Illinois)

TURKEY

This can be done at Thanksgiving. In commemoration of the holiday, you can have a little *competition* to see which group can do the best job of "decorating a turkey." Divide into three or four groups . . . Give each group a paper sack full of goodies . . . an old pair of nylons, a roll of toilet paper, scissors, scotch tape, crepe or tissue paper, newspaper or anything else you might be able to think of that will contribute to making a person look like a turkey. Set a time limit. You explain to the kids what they are to do, then divide the room up. Have the group select one person to be the "turkey." Give them three or four minutes to do the decorating and then have the whole group be judges and decide the winner by applause. (Contributed by Ron Wilburn, El Paso, Texas)

TURTLE RACE

Cut a number of turtle shapes out of thin plywood similar to the diagram below. Make sure that all the shapes are identical. Drill a hole in the neck. Thread a heavy string through the hole and tie one end to a fixed object.

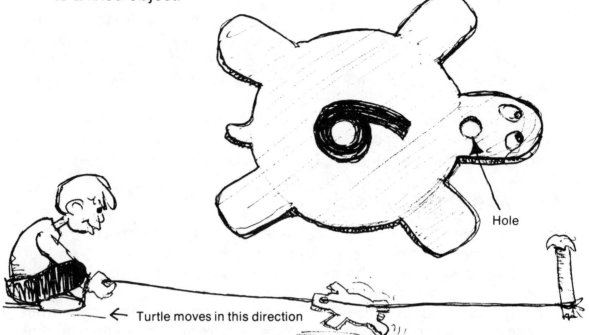

Hole

← Turtle moves in this direction

When the string is pulled upward, the turtle lifts up and scoots forward. The legs must always stay touching the floor. The higher the turtle is lifted, the further it will scoot. But look out!....you are liable to flip him over and lose ground while your opponents are in hot pursuit. For relays, have someone at each end of the string (one holding and one pulling). When the turtle reaches a certain finish line, flip him over and the other teammate takes him back. This game is great with all age groups. (Contributed by Tracy Guthrie, Houston, Texas)

UNDERDOG

Choose one player to be "it." "It" tags the free players, who must "freeze" when tagged. Frozen players must obtain freedom by spreading their legs apart, allowing a free player to pass between their open legs. "It" must freeze all the free players and the game is over. Spice the game up by making two or three players "it." (Contributed by Steve Illum, San Diego, California)

WATER-BUCKET RACE

Use either a gallon paint can or a half gallon milk carton, or a gallon plastic milk carton. Put this object, empty, on a wire or thin rope that is tied at both ends to something solid. Do this over an open space. Then choose up two teams. Give each one a water hose with water running through them. The object is to see who can push the container to the opponent's end first. The water from the hoses just happens to come falling down on everyone involved. (Contributed by Paul Enns, Lancaster, California)

THE WATERGATE GAME

This game has been named after the famous Washington scandal, but may be re-named if used after the Watergate event has vanished from the American scene or if it is considered to be in poor taste. The important thing is the fun of playing the game. However, the play can become more intense when associated with a famous event such as Watergate. The game can be played with any number of kids (over 20 or so) and is designed as an indoor game, utilizing several rooms.

The basic theme of the game is this: certain security agents of the FBI are allowed to see and hear a number of tapes connected with Watergate. They are only allowed to see and hear these in a top secret room in the White House, off the White House Library. Any top secret FBI man is allowed into the White House Library and into the special room where they can hear tapes. However, they are not allowed to leave the White House without being searched by security police. The security police are not allowed to go out of the White House Library into the special room where the tapes are heard by the FBI agents. The FBI are under instructions to obtain a certain number of these tapes containing certain conversations that the Watergate Committee wishes to hear and the Dept. of Justice wishes to obtain. They must then systematically examine all of the tapes from the library in this special room and decide which ones they wish to try to smuggle out of the White House. If they wish to smuggle a tape out of the White House, they take it out of its envelope or box, whichever is being used, and replace it with something of the same size and shape and weight, seal the box once more and turn it back in at the library and they take the tape itself and place it in a suitcase or bag or knapsack or whatever, in amongst clothes or whatever people want to carry in the bags and then seek to leave the White House by one of say, 5 or 6 different doors. The White House security police are allowed to search half of the luggage of a person leaving the White House. This means that you have every FBI agent either carrying two or four pieces of luggage and only 1 or 2 pieces can be searched as they leave. The other half of their luggage represents their person and can only be searched if the person is first arrested and taken to the special police station room off the White House Library. Thus, if a White House security agent decided that a person is really suspicious and should have all of his luggage checked, then they can place their hand upon that person's shoulder and put them under arrest and take them to a police station right within the White House, where the agent is turned in and must admit whether or not he has a tape on him. If he does, he must turn it in and the White House security police collects 35,000 points for having seized the tape. If, on the other hand, the FBI man does not have a tape in his possession, the White House security police lose 10,000 points for falsely arresting an agent. In either case, the agent is set free as soon as he has been questioned by police. It becomes obvious, then, that once an FBI agent is turned in to the police station, he must tell the truth or the whole game breaks down.

If the security police manage to find a tape in a suitcase, as someone is leaving, they don't bother arresting the fellow, they just seize the tape and turn it in at the police station, thus receiving another 35,000 points for their vigilance.

You will need a great deal of "tapes" in the White House Library. One group used empty cassettes with empty tapes, another used home movies and home movies boxes and another used small plastic pill bottles in brown paper bags. There should be a number on the bag or box on the outside and the same number on a piece of masking tape on the actual tape, film or pill bottle. There should also be a note stuck on the tape stating the contents of that particular tape, i.e., "Meeting between Nixon and Dean, Nov. 21, 1972," etc. The FBI is given a list of about 40 tapes that they are to seize, that is given a list of the contents of 40 meetings that they are to get ahold of. The game runs for about 30 to 35 minutes and then breaks for 10 minutes in the middle, where you may re-organize and the people who were the security police become the FBI agents and the FBI agents become security police for the second half.

One group threw a wrinkle into the whole game, which made it much more interesting. They had approximately 80 people playing the game, 40 on each team. They therefore made up 40 pieces of paper for each half, neatly folded over and on about 6 of them wrote down a combination password, for instance a statement that an FBI agent would make, like: "It's been a lousy day, hasn't it?," with a reply by the White House security police to the effect that: "It's been lousy ever since Nov. 1st." They had each White House security policeman draw one piece of paper, keep it to himself and get a chance to look at it as soon as he could without anyone else around. If he found, on his piece of paper, a set of statements to be used as a password, he knew that he was a collaborator, a double agent, who was actually working for the FBI although he was on the White House security police staff.

Every collaborator was to seek to try to help the FBI get tapes out of the White House. The main way of doing this, of course, was simply to be stationed at one of the doors, to somehow contact the FBI and let them know that they were a collaborator and then to help them go through their station by searching their suitcases and letting them go through if they did find a tape. The collaborators' main problem was that they did not know who else was a collaborator and who was not. Therefore, they had to be very careful lest they be caught by their own security force. Their situation was made even more difficult by the fact that every time the FBI was able to use a collaborator, they had to pay them and we gave every FBI agent some phony $1,000 bills that they were to give to a collaborator who helped them. The money had to be given to the collaborator within 3 minutes of his helping an agent. Thus, every collaborator had to be very careful that he was not spotted receiving cash from the FBI. If a White House security policeman suspected that one of his colleagues was a collaborator, he could arrest him and turn him in at the police station. At the police station, they were interviewed and if they were collaborators, they went over and started working for the FBI and the White House security police received 100,000 points for catching a collaborator. If, on the other hand, he was not a collaborator, they would lose 10,000 points for falsely arresting one of their own men, and that man would be back to work for them.

Further pressure was put on the collaborators by saying that, if, at half time, when they were asked to confess whether or not they were collaborators, they admitted to being collaborators but had not received any money from the FBI, then the FBI would lose 50,000 points. Thus, every collaborator, if he really wanted to help his team, had to get a contact with them, and had to be of some use to them and get paid for it.

This game can be run with one team simply the FBI and one team as the White House security police, but generally the kids like to play both sides.

This game can be used in conjunction with a discussion on ''Honesty,'' in which you may consider much wider issues of both public and private honesty, particularly ''Why am I afraid to be honest?'' ''Do I wish really I could be honest about myself with others?'' ''What is my reaction to the fact that God knows all about me and that I can only be honest with HIM?'' Tie this theme into a study of Psalm 139 and also I John 1. The game may be played just as a sort of comic relief from the theme of honesty and yet also heighten the whole sense of the terrible temptation to be dishonest and how you have to cover up once you have been. It may lead into an excellent discussion of forgiveness as well. (Contributed by Neil Graham, Edmonton, Alberta, Canada)

WATERMELON GAMES

Next time you serve watermelon to your group, try these fun games.

1. *Seed Spit-off:* See who can spit their seeds the farthest.

2. *Seed Race:* Give each kid an equal size slice and race to see who can dig out the most seeds in the time limit or out of his piece.

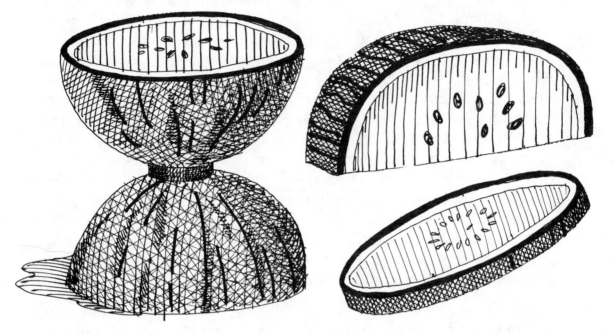

3. *Watermelon Carving:* Kids carve creative designs with a knife out of the watermelon rind.

(Contributed by Jim Elliott, Fort Wayne, Indiana)

WET SPONGE

This is a fun get-acquainted game that works best with a group of at least 30. Have the group make a fairly large circle (about an arm's length from each other). In the center, place a large bucket of water. Have about 5 people start out as "it" (in a camp situation, have the staff start as "it.") Each person who is "it" gets a sponge soaked with water and runs up to a different person in the circle and says, "Wet Sponge," and that person answers "Take a plunge," which is responded to with, "Who's a grunge?" and the person in the circle names another person in the circle. The person with the sponge then runs up to that person and hits them with the soaked sponge. That person is now "it." The game goes very rapidly and ends when everyone is soaked or water is gone. (Contributed by the camp staff of Susquehanna Valley Presbytery and Susquehanna Association of the U.C.C.)

WHEELBARROW

Get a six-inch wheel and place a 12 inch length of pipe through it. One guy grabs both sides of the pipe and another guy lifts the first guy's legs and pushes him like a wheelbarrow to a goal. (Contributed by Roger Disque, Chicago, Illinois)

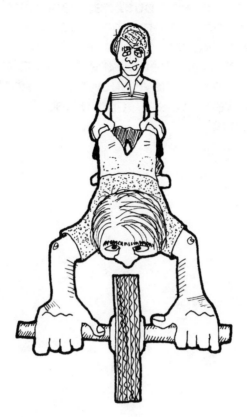

WINK

Chairs are arranged in a circle, facing inward. One boy stands behind each chair with his hands behind his back. Girls sit in the chairs, except for one chair that is left vacant. The boy behind that particular chair is "it." He must get a girl into that chair. He does this by winking at any one of the girls seated in the other chairs. She then tries to get out of the chair that she is sitting in without the boy behind her tagging her on the back. If she is tagged, she must remain in her chair and "it" tries again, either by winking at another girl or the same one. If the girl winked at can get out of her chair without being tagged, she takes the chair in front of "it" and the boy with the vacant chair is now "it." The game proceeds in this manner and anyone who can avoid becoming "it" is declared the winner. Halfway through the game, have the boys switch places with the girls. (Contributed by Larry Bennett, Mitchell, Indiana)

WRIST WATCHERS

All the girls leave the room. The guys stay and are given a list of all the girls participating in the game. A sheet is placed in the doorway with a slit in which a hand can be placed. (The doorway must be completely covered for best results.) One at a time, each girl comes to the doorway and puts her hand through the slit so that only her hand can be seen by the boys. The guys may touch the hand, look at the hand, etc. Then they try to guess who contestant #1 was by writing the number on the list next to a girl's name. This continues until all the girls have shown their wrists. The guy with the most correct answers wins. (Contributed by Carol Wennerholm, San Diego, California)

Chapter Three

Creative Communication

ABC BIBLE STUDY

Here's a creative way to get kids more actively involved in Bible Study. Give them a passage of Scripture (several verses or an entire chapter if you are working your way through a book of the Bible) and have them locate the following:

A. The theme of the passage.
B. The *BEST* verse.
C. The most *CHALLENGING* verse.
D. The most *DIFFICULT* verse to do or understand.
E. The most *ENCOURAGING* verse.
F. Your *FAVORITE* verse.
G. A *GIFT* from God.
H. The most *HELPFUL* verse.
I. The most *INFORMATIVE* verse.

Have the kids share their answers with each other, discuss, and close with conversational prayer. (Contributed by Marsha Dealey, St. Clair Shores, Michigan)

ALL TIED UP

At the beginning of the meeting or lesson time, seat the kids around a table(s). Tie their hands behind their backs. (Be sure that they are tied securely enough so that they cannot get loose.) Before tying them, give them these instructions:

1. They are being tied for a deliberate reason.
2. They are to try to remember how they feel while tied.
3. They are not to try to untie themselves or get loose until they are told to do so.
4. They must remain seated at all times, with feet flat on the floor.

Then read passages of Scripture that describe people who had positive attitudes in negative situations. (example: Acts 12, 14, 16, etc.) After reading these passages and commenting on positive attitudes in negative circumstances, give the group the task of handing you a dollar bill. Put a dollar on the table with a paper weight on it. (Give them a time limit of 30 seconds). If you have tied them securely, it is an impossible job. After they have finished trying, untie the ropes. (Collect the ropes if you want their attention during the rest of the time). Ask them how they felt when tied and yet given a job (feelings of frustration, helplessness, etc.) Make the application that negative attitudes tie up God when He wants to do good things for us. Positive attitudes free Him to really do great and exciting things in our lives. (Contributed by Peter Torrey, Manito, Illinois)

ALLEGIANCE

This is a "table-top" discussion game which requires the construction of the game board (about 24 x 36 inches on cardboard) and the discussion cards shown below.

The object of Allegiance is to get the players to examine the teachings of Jesus concerning the state and related topics in light of American government and individual attitudes. The only winner is the one who responds honestly and attempts to apply the teachings of Jesus and their consequences.

Each player rolls dice to determine the amount of spaces he moves his marker (any small object) around the board. He then responds according to the space he lands on:

a. On a black space, the player takes a card and responds.
b. On a red space he may respond to another player's response, or make comment concerning Jesus and government.
c. On the other squares, the player moves as directed. (Note: the losing or gaining of a turn does not imply judgment concerning that issue, but is merely meant to add variety.)

Players may go around the board as many times as time and interest allow. Sample discussion questions for the cards are printed below:

1. Does "Render unto Caesar" include military service?
2. Could you have been a tax-collector for Rome? Why or why Not? (Luke 19:2-10)
3. Would you be willing to go to jail because your convictions were not compatible with the government? (Matt. 5:10)
4. Is politics a legitimate means of achieving the goals of the Kingdom of Heaven? (Matt. 11:12)
5. Was Jesus a "politician" in any sense of the word?
6. Name something you could *not* render unto "Caesar" (i.e. the government).
7. Would you consider Jesus an anarchist? Why or why not? (Luke 23:2)
8. Is witholding part of your taxes because of your convictions legitimate?
9. How is a servant greater than a king? (Matt. 20:25-28)
10. Name three figures of authority over you. Which are by your choice?
11. Do you believe in amnesty? How does that relate to forgiveness? (Matt. 18:21-35)
12. Could you as a Christian hold a political office? Why or why not?
13. Should you as a Christian take a stand against corruption and hypocrisy in high places? (Luke 13:32; Matt. 23:27-28)
14. Would you consider Jesus a civil disobedient? Why or why not? (John 9:13-16)
15. Is civil disobedience legitimate for a Christian?
16. To what extent is the public responsible for oppression, brutality, and expediency in government? How can the Christian respond?

(Contributed by K. C. Hanson, Placentia, California)

APPLES AND YOU

After kids are in the room, dump a pile of apples on the floor. The kids are to look over the apples and choose one that reminds them of themselves or "appeals" to them in some way. Then for the next five minutes, they are to analyze their apple. Really get to know it, every spot, bruise, color, etc. All apples then go back into one big pile and after some mixing up, the kids are told to find their apple. And they nearly always do. As they find their apple, they are to pair off and share with their partner by completing the following four sentences:

1. I picked this apple from all the others because . . .
2. The thing about this apple that reminds me of myself is . . .
3. The area in my life in which I naturally shine is . . .
4. The area in my life that needs a little polishing is . . .

After this sharing, each one closes his eyes and feeds his apple to his partner. After the apples are eaten, close with a short time of prayer for each other. (Contributed by Jim Hudson, North Platte, Nebraska)

APPRECIATION GAME

This is a small-group experience to be followed by a discussion. Form groups of from five to seven in each group. The groups sit in a circle with a chair in the center. One person in the group sits in the center chair with the rest of the group around him. As long as he sits in the center chair, he must remain completely silent. Each person in the circle then tells the person in the center three or four things he appreciates about him. This is done by each person one at a time. The kids are instructed to (1) Be Honest. Be as deep or as superficial as you like. Just don't be phony. (2) Speak directly to the person in the center. (3) Be specific and detailed. This continues until everyone has sat in the center chair, with everyone in the group telling what they appreciate about the person in the center. Following this experience, have the group discuss the following questions:
1. Was it easy to receive these compliments? To give them? Why?
2. Did you feel discomfort?
3. Did you want to avoid communicating directly with the other person?
4. Did you want to avoid, dismiss or reject these messages of liking?
5. Did some people in your group find it difficult to follow directions? About silence? About saying things of appreciation without cutting down the other person? About respecting the rights of others to speak?
(Contributed by Robert Fisk, Bellevue, Washington)

BACK DOOR DOCTRINAL STUDY

To better young people's knowledge of their faith, or the doctrinal position of their church, invite pastors or spokesmen from other churches in your community to speak and answer questions asked by the group. Don't be afraid to include the most far-out, un-Christian religious sects or cults in this series which could last many weeks. (Contributed by Chris Liebrum, Grand Prairie, Texas)

BACK RUBS AND THE GOSPEL

Here is a fun way to help people to experience touching and community in a safe and non-threatening atmosphere. (It feels good, too.) Each person is to give or to receive back rubs according to the following list which should be printed up so that everyone has a copy. Following the "back-rubbing" period (twenty minutes or so), follow up with a discussion. Some discussion questions are provided.

Rules:

1. You may receive a back rub only after you have given one.
2. The *giver* will be scored by the *receiver* on a scale of 1 to 10 with 10 being best.
3. On your sheet, the score is automatically 5 points for any back rub *received* by you.
4. You will receive a score from 1 to 10 only on back rubs which you give. The receiver will judge your back rub.
5. No score is valid without the initials of the other person (giver or receiver).
6. You may not refuse to give or receive a back rub if someone asks you.
7. The same person may be used only twice, once giving and once receiving.
8. The highest score at the end of the time limit wins.

The Back Rubs:	Score	Initial
1. Give to someone taller.		
2. Receive from someone shorter.		
3. Give to someone older.		
4. Receive from someone younger.		
5. Give to someone of the opposite sex.		
6. Receive from someone of the same sex.		
7. Give to someone with shoes on.		
8. Receive from someone without shoes on.		
9. Give to someone with blue eyes.		
10. Receive from someone with brown eyes.		
11. Give to someone wearing red.		
12. Receive from someone wearing green.		
13. Give to someone who lives less than one mile from you.		
14. Receive from someone who lives more than one mile from you.		
15. Give to someone who wears glasses or contacts.		
16. Receive from someone who doesn't wear glasses or contacts.		
17. Give to someone with an even numbered address.		
18. Receive from someone with an even address.		
19. Give to someone whose last initial is before yours in the alphabet.		
20. Receive from someone whose last initial is after yours in the alphabet.		

Questions for Discussion:

1. What are some feelings you had? Were you embarrassed? Those who could only give? Those who could only get?
2. Those who did both, did you like giving or receiving better?
3. Has this experience affected your feelings in any way with the rest of the group?
4. Are there any insights to be gained from this about Christian love?

(Contributed by Peter Tremain, Prairie Village, Kansas)

BALLOON WORSHIP

Pass out balloons and small slips of paper as the group assembles. As a *Call To Worship*, ask everyone to write on the slip the nicest thing they can say about someone else. "I love you," "I think you're great"—"You turn me on," etc. Then ask that they roll up the slips and place them inside the balloons and blow the balloons up and tie them. Hold them as the service progresses and as an *Offering*, have everyone bat the balloons forward over each other's head to the altar or worship leader. The "messages" become our offering to God. At the end of the service, ask the group to come to the front and grab a balloon, any balloon and POP IT. The message they receive from the balloon is the *Benediction* to the service, a message to us from God. Note: sometimes in the melee at the end, some balloons might be accidentally broken, so some people might not get one. It would be a good idea, then, to have some sponsors make two or three extra to have at the front. This could also be used in connection with some of the creative worship ideas in *Catch the New Wind*, published by Word, Inc. (Contributed by Prince Altom, San Francisco, California.

BIBLE STUDY METHOD

The following eight steps can help young people to have more effective personal Bible Studies or they can be used to give direction to group Bible Studies as well. In a group setting, have the kids break into small groups of three or four and work through an assigned passage of Scripture, using the steps below. Then have the small groups each share highlights of their Bible Study with the entire group at the close of the meeting period.

1. Before beginning your study, pray: "Father, reveal some new truth to me in this study. Speak to me as you have never spoken before..."
2. Read the assigned passage through at least 5 times, in as many different versions and translations that you have.
3. What do you consider the two most important lessons of the passage?

4. What did God say to you personally, that you needed most to hear? Write it down and share it with someone.
5. What *new* truth, if any, did you discover from this passage of Scripture?
6. What does this text teach about Jesus?
7. Were there any difficulties in understanding any portion of the text? If so, how did you resolve it?
8. What change, if any, do you intend to make in your life or your thinking as a result of this study?

(Contributed by Bob Gleason, Roseburg, Oregon)

BIBLE GOSSIP

A group of 15 to 30 people form a circle. Each person needs paper. The first person writes one not so well known verse and passes it with the pen to the next person. He reads the scripture; destroys the original; rewrites it by memory; passes his copy and the pen to the next person, etc., on down the line. The object is to discover how near the original the last copy will be. This could be an eye opener as to the necessity for memorizing Scriptures. Also, this shows in essence, the method of transmitting Scripture through the centuries. (Contributed by Roger Copeland, Hurst, Texas)

THE BIG FISHERMAN—ON LOCATION

Try a series of studies over a period of weeks or at a retreat on the life of Simon Peter. Each study is held at a location which relates to the incident being examined. Study his call to be a disciple by the side of a lake, or at the beach; his reaction to Jesus' Transfiguration at the top of a mountain; put him on trial on the charge of denying Jesus out of cowardice; and conclude with breakfast on the beach for a study of his restoration (John 21). All of these studies lend themselves to the production of an 8mm film or a set of slides which can be used to share the results with others in your church. (Contributed by David Scott, Riverside, California)

BODY LIFE GAME

This game is a good way to demonstrate the need for cooperation and unity within the Body of Christ as presented in New Testament Scripture. To set up the game, divide the entire group into five smaller groups, which will symbolize various members or parts of the body. Each group should be named accordingly, i.e., EYES, HANDS, EARS, FEET and MOUTH.

The object of the game is fairly simple. The five groups, all members of the same body, must work together to perform various tasks before LIFE dies. To symbolize LIFE, someone can be locked in a trunk or box and a road flare can be lit nearby. When the flare goes out, LIFE will be considered dead. The only way that LIFE can be saved is to complete the tasks which leads to the trunk key and lets LIFE out before the flare burns out (Flares are usually good for about 30 minutes.)

Each of the five groups (EARS, HANDS, EYES, FEET, MOUTH) should be equal in size and labeled in some way (Different color armbands or signs hanging around their necks, etc.). In order to complete the tasks, each group may function in only the way that it functions in a normal body. In other words, an EYE will not be able to hear and an EAR won't be able to see. EYES can only see and EARS can only hear. Therefore, everyone except the EYES must be blindfolded.

When the game begins, the blindfolds go on, the flare is lit and the group gets its first task. The instruction for that task is written and presented to the EYES, who whisper it to the EARS, who likewise whisper it to the MOUTHS, who then verbalize it to the rest of the body. Whenever the group must go anywhere, the FEET must carry the EYES (the only ones who can see) and the remaining members of the body must follow behind in a single file line, holding on to each other's waists. The EYES in that case are allowed to speak, giving directions to the rest of the body.

The tasks may be relatively simple ones. Three or four good ones are enough. A few examples are listed below:
    1. Crackers and juice should be fed to the MOUTHS by the HANDS while being guided by the EYES. The FEET will then carry the EARS to (place) followed by the rest of the body in a single file line.
    2. The EARS will be given a number (by the leader) between one and ten. The EARS must then hold up that many fingers for the EYES to see, who then tells the MOUTHS, who shout it to the HANDS and FEET. Everyone must then get in smaller groups of that number of people. The EYES may help everyone get together. (This can be repeated.)
    3. Splints and bandages can be provided which the HANDS should use to splint one arm and one leg of each of the FEET, guided by the EYES.

The above tasks are only samples. It is best to work out a few things that your group can do to fit each local situation. The last task should lead to the envelope which contains the key to the trunk. The HANDS must use the key to open the trunk, again guided by the EYES and carried there by the FEET.

The discussion which follows could include the following questions:
    1. Talk about the game and how each part of the body did or

did not function.

2. Did everyone do their part?

3. Why didn't some people get involved?

4. Relate this to Paul's analogy of the body (1 Corinthians 12: 14-26)

The game, although reasonably simple, must be thought through carefully by the leader before trying it out. One youth group used three different "bodies" and three different keys on the trunk, representing "Faith, Hope and Love." The possibilities are great with a little creativity. (Contributed by Bruce Otto, Minneapolis, Minnesota)

CARE COMPANY

This idea is designed to help bring about greater fellowship or *Koinonia* among members of the group. Begin with a 15 minute discussion of what "cliques" are and how they differ from "interest groups," etc. Then appropriate scripture can be read. (Romans 12:3-16, I Corinthians 1:11-13 and 12:12-27). Following the reading of scripture, groups of five are then formed (at random) and each person gives his name, age, school, etc., and shares two things he likes, and two things he dislikes. After all are through, a new group of five is formed and the same procedure is followed. At the conclusion of the meeting each person finds someone they don't normally associate with and after sharing the same information, close with a prayer for each other.

At the next meeting a "Care Package" is given to each person. It is simply a card or sheet of paper listing five persons (including themselves), chosen at random, who are members of their "care company." Also on the sheet or card is a "pledge," which each person is asked to accept and carry out as best they can:

> I PLEDGE TO:
> 1. Call or contact the members of my "care company" at least once a week just to see how things are going.
> 2. Make a personal effort to get to know them as well as possible.
> 3. Meet new people and expand my "care company" to at least ten by ___(date)___.
> 4. To pray for each member of my "care company" every day.

This can be an annual thing, and kids should be encouraged to keep it up all year long, and report how things are going with their "care company" on a regular basis. (Contributed by James Braddy, Sacramento, California)

CHRISTIAN BUDDY MACHINE

Have a guy dressed up like a robot with a sign on him that says, "Christian Buddy Machine — 10¢." A lonely man waiting for a subway tells the machine his problems, deposits 10¢, and the Buddy Machine gives him all the usual Christian "pat answers" to his problems. This can lead to a good discussion of the church or Christians who know "what to say," but who lack real personal love and concern. (Contributed by Sheldon White, Princeton, New Jersey)

CHRISTIAN RESPONSIBILITY

The following is a list of responsibilities that Christians have to each other, according to the Bible. Pass out the list to your group, read the passages, and then try to answer these questions:

1. How many of these responsibilities are being met in your group?
2. Is there one that surprises you or with which you disagree?
3. Is there one you are having difficulty doing?
4. Are these responsibilities optional or are they to be expected of all Christians?
5. Is there one you would like to work on as a group?

The meeting can be concluded by making a covenant with the other members of the group to work toward one or more of the responsibilities. Close with a worship service or prayer of dedication for your new goals. It is helpful to set an evaluation date to check on your growth.

Our Responsibility to Each Other as Christians:

To love one another
Eph. 5:1
Rom. 12:10
I Pet. 4:8
John 13:34-35
John 15:12-13
Heb. 13:1
I John 3:16-17 *(Lay down our lives for each other)*

To serve one another
Gal. 5:13
Eph. 5:21
I Pet. 4:9-10

Take material care of each other
Deut. 15:7
Rom. 12:13

Discipline each other
Gal. 6:1-2
Matt. 18:15
II Thess. 3:14-15

Pray for each other
Eph. 6:18-19
James 5:16

Forgive one another
Eph. 4:31-32
Matt. 18:21-22
Matt. 5:22 *(Don't hold grudges)*

Confess sins to one another
James 5:16

Carry each others' burdens
Rom. 15:1

Be patient with each other
Eph. 4:2

Worship together
Ps. 133:1

(Contributed by Linda Hudson, Oak Park, Illinois)

CHRISTMAS I. Q. TEST

Next Christmas, give the following "quiz" to your youth, to determine how much they *really* know about the Bible's most popular story. The results will undoubtedly be very embarrassing as well as lead to a better understanding of the events surrounding Christs' birth.

INSTRUCTIONS:

Read and answer each question in the order it appears. When choices are given, read them carefully and select the best one. Put a "T" or an "F" in the blank on all True or False questions. Guessing is permitted, cheating is not . . .

_____ 1. As long as Christmas has been celebrated, it has been on December 25th. *(True or False)*

_____ 2. Joseph was from:
    A. *Bethlehem*
    B. *Jerusalem*
    C. *Nazareth*
    D. *Egypt*
    E. *Minnesota*
    F. *None of the above.*

_____ 3. How did Mary and Joseph travel to Bethlehem?
    A. *Camel*
    B. *Donkey*
    C. *Walked*
    D. *Volkswagen*
    E. *Joseph walked, Mary rode a donkey*
    F. *Who knows?*

_____ 4. Mary and Joseph were married when Mary become pregnant. *(True or False)*

_____ 5. Mary and Joseph were married when Jesus was born. *(True or False)*

_____ 6. Mary was a virgin when she delivered Jesus. *(True or False)*

_____ 7. What did the innkeeper tell Mary and Joseph?
    A. *"There is no room in the inn."*
    B. *"I have a stable you can use."*
    C. *"Come back after the Christmas rush and I should have some vacancies."*
    D. *Both A and B*
    E. *None of the above*

_____ 8. Jesus was delivered in a:
   A. *Stable*
   B. *Manger*
   C. *Cave*
   D. *Barn*
   E. *Unknown*

_____ 9. A "manger" is a:
   A. *Stable for domestic animals.*
   B. *Wooden hay storage bin.*
   C. *Feeding trough.*
   D. *Barn.*

_____ 10. Which animals does the Bible say were present at Jesus' birth?
   A. *Cows, sheep, goats.*
   B. *Cows, donkeys, sheep.*
   C. *Sheep and goats only.*
   D. *Miscellaneous barnyard animals.*
   E. *Lions, tigers, elephants.*
   F. *None of the above.*

_____ 11. Who saw the "star in the east"?
   A. *Shepherds*
   B. *Mary and Joseph*
   C. *Three Kings*
   D. *Both A and C*
   E. *None of the above.*

_____ 12. How many angels spoke to the shepherds?
   A. One
   B. Three
   C. A "Multitude"
   D. None of the above.

_____ 13. What "sign" did the angels tell the shepherds to look for?
   A. *"This way to baby Jesus."*
   B. *A star over Bethlehem.*
   C. *A baby that doesn't cry.*
   D. *A house with a Christmas tree.*
   E. *A baby in a stable.*
   F. *None of the above.*

_____ 14. What did the angels sing?
   A. *"Joy to the World, the Lord is Come"*
   B. *"Alleluia"*
   C. *"Unto us a child is born, unto us a son is given"*
   D. *"Glory to God in the highest, etc."*
   E. *"Glory to the Newborn King"*
   F. *"My Sweet Lord"*

_____15. What is a "Heavenly Host"?
   A. *The angel at the gate of Heaven.*
   B. *The angel who invites people to Heaven.*
   C. *The angel who serves drinks in Heaven.*
   D. *An angel choir.*
   E. *An angel army.*
   F. *None of the above.*

_____16. There was snow that first Christmas:
   A. *Only in Bethlehem.*
   B. *All over Israel.*
   C. *Nowhere in Israel.*
   D. *Somewhere in Israel.*
   E. *Mary and Joseph only "dreamed" of a white Christmas.*

_____17. The baby Jesus cried:
   A. *When the doctor slapped him on his behind.*
   B. *When the little drummer boy started banging on his drum.*
   C. *Just like other babies cry.*
   D. *He never cried.*

_____18. What is "frankincense"?
   A. *A precious metal.*
   B. *A precious fabric.*
   C. *A precious perfume.*
   D. *An eastern monster story.*
   E. *None of the above.*

_____19. What is "myrrh"?
   A. *An easily shaped metal.*
   B. *A spice used for burying people.*
   C. *A drink.*
   D. *After-shave lotion.*
   E. *None of the above.*

_____20. How many wise men came to see Jesus?
   (Write in the correct number.)

_____21. What does "wise men" refer to?
   A. *Men of the educated class.*
   B. *They were eastern Kings.*
   C. *They were astrologers.*
   D. *They were smart enough to follow the star.*
   E. *They were "sages."*

_____22. The wise men found Jesus in a:
   A. *Manger*
   B. *Stable*
   C. *House*
   D. *Holiday Inn*
   E. *Good Mood*

_____23. The wise men stopped in Jerusalem:
   A. To inform Herod about Jesus.
   B. To find out where Jesus was.
   C. To ask about the star that they saw.
   D. For gas.
   E. To buy presents for Jesus.

_____24. Where do we find the Christmas story in order to check up on all these ridiculous questions?
   A. Matthew
   B. Mark
   C. Luke
   D. John
   E. All of the above.
   F. Only A and B
   G. Only A and C
   H. Only A, B and C
   I. Only X, Y and Z
   J. Aesops Fables

_____25. When Joseph and Mary found out that Mary was pregnant with Jesus, what happened?
   A. They got married.
   B. Joseph wanted to break the engagement.
   C. Mary left town for three months.
   D. An angel told them to go to Bethlehem.
   E. Both A and D
   F. Both B and C

_____26. Who told Mary and Joseph to go to Bethlehem?
   A. The angel.
   B. Mary's mother.
   C. Herod.
   D. Caesar Augustus.
   E. Alexander the Great.
   F. No one told them to.

_____27. Joseph took the baby Jesus to Egypt:
   A. To show him the pyramids.
   B. To teach him the wisdom of the pharoahs.
   C. To put him in a basket in the reeds by the river.
   D. Because he dreamed about it.
   E. To be taxed.
   F. Joseph did not take Jesus to Egypt.
   G. None of the above.

_____28. I think that this test was:
   A. Super   C. Fantastic
   B. Great   D. All of the above.

(Contributed by Gregg Selander, Whittier, California)

CLUE

Prearrange to have several games of Clue brought to your weekly meeting. The day before your meeting, contact several teenagers and tell them they are to cheat as much as possible in the game (have one teenage ''cheater'' for each game). After the game explain what has been done. Discuss the following: (1) What feelings did you have towards those who were dishonest? (2) Ask the ''Cheaters'' how they were treated by the others, (3) Discuss if the group considered it to be normal for there to be cheaters in the game and (4) Discuss the Biblical view of honesty. (Contributed by Paul Cox, Downey, California)

COMMUNITY

Using Acts 2:44-47 as a model, have the group define what the ideal community living situation would be for our culture today. Divide into small groups and attempt to cover these areas:

1. *Living quarters.* Should there be separate living quarters for each person? Family unit? Or one large facility shared by everyone?

2. *Meals.* Will everyone eat together? Separately? What about scheduling?

3. *Food.* Should it be bought? Grown? Include meat? Vegetables only?

4. *Income.* Should the group support themselves through a cooperative venture or each hold individual jobs and pool money? What about a budget? Allotments or allowances to each member?

5. *Location.* Should you locate in the city? Suburbs? Woods? Farm? Mountains? Another country?

6. *Decisions.* Will the group be governed by a leader, committee,

the whole group, or elected officials?

7. *Rules.* Will there by any?
8. *Maintenance.* Who will be responsible for upkeep, repairs, "dirty work?"
9. *Children.* How will they be cared for? How many allowed? What about eduation?
10. *Standard of Living.* Will you "just get by"? Live in poverty? Live comfortably? Try to do as well as you can?
11. *Entrance Requirements.* Who will you let into the group? Christians only? Certain age groups? Disabled? Elderly? Teens? Wealthy?
12. *Habits.* Will smoking, drinking or drugs be allowed? What about personal hygiene, cleanliness, etc? People who are sloppy or irresponsible?
13. *Religion.* Will you all attend the same church? Different churches? Start your own? Attend none?
14. *Law.* What about marriage? Taxes?
15. *Possessions.* Will members be able to keep their possessions? Pool them? What about personal items like cars? Stereos? Toothpaste? Clothing?

Have the group compare their models and try to agree on one ideal community living situation. If you can't agree, isolate the areas of disagreement and discuss why you were unable to compromise. Discuss your final model in light of the Scripture's model. Some questions for further discussion:

1. Has anyone had any personal experience with or in a commune?
2. What are the advantages (if any) and disadvantages (if any) of communal living?

THE CONFESSIONAL

This is an experiment for kids to do anytime they feel the need. With a recorder, go into a room where you can be completely alone and by yourself. Lock the door if necessary. Then turn on the recorder and make a confession of the one thing that most troubles you about yourself . . . the one thing that you could never tell another human being. Then rewind the tape and play it over. But listen to the confession as if you were God. And decide if you were God, what would you say to a person that made a confession like that. Remember God is more gracious and forgiving than you are. After this experience, erase the tape. If there were someone you could share this experience with, so much the better. But do not share it unless you feel absolutely free to. (Contributed by Jim Hudson, North Platte, Nebraska)

CUPCAKE

This is a simple object lesson best suited for younger kids. Have two volunteers come forward and give each a chocolate cupcake. They are to eat some of the cupcake and describe it—good, bad, delicious, so-so. Hopefully, they will consider the cupcakes to be very good. Explain that the cupcakes are going to represent life.

Next, place all the ingredients that went into the cupcakes in several small containers on a table. Have the volunteers taste each and describe how they taste to the group. Some will be bad, some good. Explain that these ingredients represent all the things that happen to us during our lifetime. Our lives are made up of both good things and bad things, and while we may be disappointed or discouraged by the bad things that happen to us, we can rely on the promise that "All things work together for good to them that love God" (Romans 8:28). Without the bad tasting ingredients, the cupcakes just wouldn't have turned out. Other scriptures that can be used in this lesson are Ephesians 5:20 and Proverbs 3:5. (Contributed by Marcella Stockin, West Valley, New Jersey)

DEATH DRUM

This idea works well in a worship service stressing hunger and starvation in the world. According to statistics (which you may need to update) someone dies of starvation every eight seconds. During the worship service, have someone beat a drum every eight seconds to symbolize another death taking place. The drum interrupting the normal course of the service very dramatically illustrates how we often try to ignore the problem of hunger in the world but it just won't go away unless we do something about it. (Contributed by Nancy Lee Head, Gulf Breeze, Florida.)

DISCOVERING LIFE

This idea could be used in an informal Sunday School Class, at a Bible Study, a Sunday night fellowship or a Youth Group meeting. First, instruct your group to look up Matthew 7:7-8 (or Luke 11:9-11). Let them dwell on this passage by reading it through two or three times and then meditating on how this wisdom applies to their life. Next, break into groups of four or five. Inform these groups that they are to find in the Gospels a factual incident where a person "sought and found." Use the whole Bible if you want. Then, have the groups discuss how they would act out this happening (be creative)! Stress that this can be anything from a comedy to a serious drama. After 10-20 minutes, have the groups come together and share what they discovered from the Scriptures by presenting their short play or skit and Scripture. When the skits are finished (after much thought, laughter, clapping, and excitement), bring them together in a serious mood by introducing and discussing three questions within their group or as a general group.

A. What personally could you do this week to ''seek and find'' for God?

B. Is there any certain answer you are seeking from God or doors that you would like opened?

C. Commit yourself now and during the next week to prayer and study of the Word for an answer. Come back to the next meeting ready to share what has happened.

(Contributed by Andy Hansen, Lansing, Michigan)

DON'T TALK WITH YOUR MOUTH FULL

In most of our affluent churches, a discussion on ''food and fasting'' can be very worthwhile with youth. Such a discussion can be wrapped around a study of biblical fasts to determine the relevance or need for fasting today. Below are a few quotes, references and discussion questions that might be helpful to stimulate interest in the topic.

Quotes:

1. ''Food is not the most basic essential in life. The greatest bodily need is Air. The second is not food, but Water. Third is not food, but Sleep! Food comes fourth but in thousands of Christians' lives, it seems to be put first. Too much food clogs the system. To over-eat is a sin of waste and a sin against the body, shortening the physical life and dulling the spiritual. If you are not its master, you are its slave!'' Winkie Pratney

2. ''The appetite for food is perhaps more frequently than any other the cause for backsliding and powerlessness in the church today. God's command is 'whether you eat or drink, or whatsoever you do, do all to the glory of God.' Christians forget this and eat and drink to please themselves. They consult their appetites instead of the laws of life and health. More persons are snared by their tables than the church is aware of. A great many people who avoid alcohol altogether will drink tea and coffee that in both quality and quantity violate every law of life and health. Show me a gluttonous professor and I will show you a backslider.'' Charles Finney.

3. ''It is important for us to distinguish between a desire or appetite for food and a hunger for food. It is doubtful whether the average individual, reared in our well-fed Western civilization, knows much of genuine hunger. The sensation of emptiness or weakness, gnawing in the pit of the stomach and other symptoms experienced at the outset of a fast are seldom real hunger. They are a craving for food

resulting from the long-continued habit of feeding ourselves three times a day without intermission for three hundred and sixty-five days a year.'' Arthur Wallis

Discussion Questions:

1. How do you react to Finney's statement? Why?
2. What do you think Finney meant when he used the phrase "the appetite for food"?
3. How could Finney link the idea of "powerlessness in the church" with the "appetite for food"? Do you think it is valid?
4. How is it possible to eat to the glory of God?
5. How much gluttony does it take to make one gluttonous?
6. What is your definition of fasting?
7. Is fasting a valid form of worship for people today? Why?

References:

1. The Bible, God
2. Buchinger, Otto H. F., *About Fasting—A Royal Road to Healing*; Thorsons Publishers Ltd.
3. Ehret, Arnold, *Rational Fasting*: Ehret Literature Publishing Co., Beaumont, Cal 92223
4. McMillen, S.I., *None of These Disease*: Spire Books, Fleming H. Revell Co., Old Tappan, N.J.
5. Shelton, Herbert M., *Fasting Can Save Your Life*: Natural Hygiene Press, Inc.
6. Wallis, Arthur, *God's Chosen Fast*: Christian Literature Crusade, Fort Washington, Pennsylvania.

(Contributed by Mark Senter, Arlington Heights, Illinois)

ENTERTAINING ANGELS UNAWARES

Begin your class as usual, but plan to have an interval where the kids will be free to move about and talk for about 5 or 6 minutes. While class is starting, have a really obnoxious looking person come in and take a seat in the back (he will be a friend of yours incognito, of course). While the move is going on, have this person try to approach some of the kids (he can be loud, drunk, very shy, paranoid, etc.). Just before the 5 to 6 minute period is over, he will leave. When everyone is situated again, read the scripture and explain the strange person. Have him come back in and the class can then discuss their reaction to him, how he felt, how Jesus would have reacted, and the mission of the church in reaching the socially outcast. (Contributed by Steven E. Robinson, Lubbock, Texas)

ENCOURAGE ONE ANOTHER

Give everyone a piece of paper and have someone help pin it on their back. Then ask the group to circulate and write one thing they like about each person on his piece of paper. This may take 5-15 minutes, depending upon the size of the group. Allow time for everyone to read his own piece of paper. Follow with a devotional on the need to encourage each other using such passages as 1 Thess 5:14: Hebrews 10:24. (Contributed by William Moore, Brainerd, Minnesota)

FAMILY COMMUNION

This can be a meaningful experience for families in a family retreat setting. Following a service emphasizing the family and the importance of family devotions, allow each family to have communion together as a family unit. Give the fathers the elements of communion and the mothers a candle. Each family then finds a place around the camp area to share scripture and communion together. After about fifteen minutes, all the families meet for a closing campfire service. The fathers can together light the campfire with their family's candle. (Contributed by Chester P. Jenkins, Allentown, Pennsylvania)

FAMILY CROSSWORD

The following "crossword puzzle" can be used to preface a discussion on the family. Divide the group into teams of less than five and

see which group can complete the puzzle correctly within the time limit. Afterwards, discuss the correct answers.

Across

2. What most family members think they are. Babies are especially this.

4. We think we have it
When we come of age.
But we learn how to use it
Before we leave the cage.

6. Mom and Dad
Are as different as can be
and from them we learn
How one plus one equals three.

7. Wear my school colors
To express this you see.
Take up for my sister
'Cause she's part of me.

8. Players don't do it;
Cheerleaders do.
When "hero's" home,
He may do it, too.

Down

1. When I feel happy and sad at the same time, my parents think that I'm a _____.

2. At school we have one
for chemistry.
The family is one also
So we learn how to be.

3. Parents have standards
Of good and bad.
Teens develop their system
In response to Dad.

5. When thinking of their family, some teens think they got a bad one.

(Contributed by Mark Senter, Arlington Heights, Illinois)

FELLOWSHIP GAME

Prepare ahead of time six 3 x 5 cards with the following instructions:

1. Go to the corner of the room and face it. Act as if you are reading your Bible and praying. Do not respond to anyone except your youth leader. (Make one of these).
2. Sit in the center of the circle and lock arms with the three others who will be there with you. *Do not* let anyone else into your circle. *Do not* respond to anyone except your youth leader and the three in your group. (Make 4 of these).
3. Try your hardest to become a part of the group in the center of the circle: try pursuasion, begging, crying, acting as if you don't care, force, and any other thing you can think of. If you fail to get in, go to the person in the corner and try to relate to him. (Make one of these).

To begin the game, have the entire group sit on the floor in a large circle. Give the 3 x 5 cards to individuals who will feel comfortable doing what the card instructs. Those who do not receive a card simply remain seated and watch. After the exercise, discuss the feeling and responses of each person in relationship to fellowship as presented in I John. Allow those who were watching to describe their reaction to what was going on. (Contributed by Gary Casady, Klamath Falls, Oregon)

THE FOOD STORE ROBBERY

This is an excellent "situational story" centered around the issue of stealing. There are many subtopics that can be discussed, such as the corporate structure, family stress, justice and law and order.

To use with your group, simply tell the story as it is presented below, and discuss the questions that are provided (or any other questions that may arise). You might find it useful to print up the story and distribute copies to each person. As you will discover, the circumstances of the story present some very difficult problems not unlike those that we have to deal with every day of our lives. The "answers" are not as clear as we would often like for them to be which is the beauty of an exercise such as this. It is through struggles with the hard questions that we grow and learn.

The story involves seven people:
1. The husband, Ed
2. The injured child
3. The teenage driver
4. The wife, Hilda
5. The plant manager
6. The banker
7. The food store owner

The Story

The automobile factory where Ed has worked for the past ten years is experiencing hard times because of a recession and is forced to lay off a number of employees. Management has left the responsibility to each of the plant managers. Ed's plant manager has been protecting his job for a long time and has always been worried that Ed might get his job. He lays Ed off to remove this threat.

Ed cannot find a job anywhere. After eighteen months of unsuccessful job hunting, his unemployment runs out and Ed is forced to sell his insurance so his family can have food and make the house payments. When that money runs out, Ed and Hilda discuss the possibility of applying for welfare. Hilda will not hear of it. She considers it degrading and a sign of failure. In fact, Hilda considers Ed a failure and constantly nags him to do something about their situation. She threatens to leave him.

One evening, one of Ed's children is playing in the street. (The child had been warned many times to stay out of the street). A stolen car driven by a nineteen year old runaway runs into Ed's child, seriously injuring him. The child requires hospitalization and the bills will be enormous. Of course, the runaway does not have any insurance or money.

In desperation, Ed goes to the bank to apply for a loan. Ed does have good credit, but the banker refuses the loan. (The banker has involved the bank's money in a number of questionable investments and has overextended the bank's loan limit.)

Ed explains the situation to Hilda. She explodes into a rage and hysterically threatens to leave and calls Ed a failure and a no-good who doesn't care about his child and his wife. She gives him an ultimatum to be gone when she returns and stomps out of the house. Distraught and confused, Ed robs the local food store. When his wife returns, he shows her the money and explains that a close friend loaned it to them. They use the money to purchase food and clothing for the children, but within a day Ed is arrested by the police. He explains, "All I wanted to do was feed my family."

After discussions with the city officials, the prosecutor decides to drop the case if Ed will pay back the money and seek counseling with the welfare department. But the store owner is a strong law and order advocate and refuses to drop the charges. He believes that Ed is a thief and ought to be punished. Ed is forced to go to trial where he pleads guilty and is sentenced by the judge.

Questions for Discussion:

1. Which person was most responsible for the robbery of the food store? Rank the characters from most responsible to least responsible. Give reasons for the order that you chose.
2. Was Ed wrong to rob the food store? Why or why not?
3. Hilda was certainly a nagging wife, but didn't she have something to nag about? Do you feel any compassion for Hilda?
4. Do you agree with Hilda's refusal to accept welfare?
5. What do you think Hilda did after Ed was arrested? What should she have done?
6. If you were the food store operator, would you press charges?
7. If you were the judge at the trial and Ed confessed to the crime, what sentence would you hand down?
8. Which person was the worst? Which was the best? Why?
9. What is your concept of "justice?"

(Contributed by Jody Kerr, Riverdale, Georgia)

FOOTBALL STADIUM

This can be a good "small group" experience designed to help members of the group not only learn more about each other, but to affirm each other's gifts and position in the Body of Christ. Picture the Christian life as a football game. Each person shares with the group where he feels that he fits into the picture and why. For example, one person might consider himself to be "sitting on the bench," and not very active. Someone else might consider himself to be a cheerleader, giving encouragement to the team, but not participating. Others may identify with the coach, the quarterback, or even an empty seat in the stands. Then allow everyone to share where they would *like* to be in the picture and why. This can be a great way to help kids visualize where they are today and where they want to be in the future. You might want to prepare a photograph or drawing of a football stadium with players, coaches, and spectators for each group to use or perhaps a list of possible participants in a football event to choose from. Close the experience with a round of affirming prayer for each other.

FOR BETTER OR FOR VERSE

Here is a possible way to form small groups for a retreat. Beforehand, choose some Bible verses and depending on the number of people per group, write a word or phrase from the verse on separate 3 x 5 cards. To identify the verse, place the ''book'' on one card and the ''chapter and verse'' on another. Finally, randomly distribute the cards and let the kids form the verses. Each group is created by the kids who hold cards from the same verse.

EXAMPLE: John 15:1

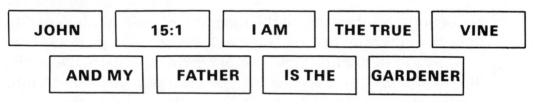

| JOHN | 15:1 | I AM | THE TRUE | VINE |
| AND MY | FATHER | IS THE | GARDENER |

(Contributed by Jim Shewmaker and Steve Kraftchick, Miami, Florida)

FREEDOM FOR ALL

Here's a fun way to open a discussion on the topic of "freedom." Divide the group into smaller groups and have each group come up with a short skit which would show what they would do if they were completely free to do their own thing, with no restrictions. Then have them present the skits to the group. Most will be very funny, showing such things as telling off their parents, teachers, etc., dropping out of school, living it up, traveling, and so on. Surprisingly enough, these skits actually help the kids to see the chaos and futility of "complete freedom." The following questions can then be used for an in-depth discussion of the topic:

1. What does the word "freedom" mean to you?
2. If you were "completely free," what would you do?
3. If *everyone* were "completely free," and did their own thing, what would be the result?
4. Discuss Romans 6:16-23 and Paul's concept of man as a slave.
5. Discuss Romans 7:21-25. What was Paul's problem and where did he find "freedom" from it?
6. How does Christ define freedom? (See John 8:31-34.)
7. Discuss freedom vs responsibility. (See Galatians 5:13.)

(Contributed by Wayne Renning, Williamsburg, Iowa)

FRUIT PICKING

This small group experience is based on Galatians 5:22-23, where the ''fruits of the spirit'' are listed. Print up that list and pass it out to everyone in the group. The list can look like this:

1. Love _____
2. Joy _____
3. Peace _____
4. Patience_____
5. Kindness _____
6. Goodness_____
7. Fidelity_____
8. Gentleness _____
9. Self-Control _____

Following a brief lesson on the meaning of each of the nine "fruits," have the kids refer to their lists. Ask everyone to jot down the name of a person in the group who most exhibits a particular fruit in his life, next to the fruit on his list. For example, you might put some-one's name next to "Peace" because they rarely cause division in the group, or next to "Joy" because they are so happy.

When everyone has completed writing in names on their list, then ask one person to sit silently while the others share where they jotted down his name and why. When everyone is through, ask this person to share which of the fruits he feels the least of in his life and why. Go around the group until everyone has had a chance to do this.

This experience is best when conducted in smaller groups that have had plenty of time to get to know each other. There should be less than eight in each group for best results. That assures that no one will be left out. Instruct kids that they may put more than one name next to a fruit on their list.

GOOD SAMARITAN

The following material can be used to plan a meeting around the parable of the Good Samaritan (Luke 10:25-37). You should familiarize yourself with the parable and get as much background material on Samaritans as possible. Since this is one of the most familiar of the parables, one of the chief objectives of this meeting will be to provide new insights and understanding to details that enrich the story, but which are often lost in the telling. The meeting may include the following exercises:

1. As the group enters, seat all the left handed members (or any other obvious distinguishing characteristics that might make up a minority group) separate from the rest. This should be preferably in the worst chairs, on the floor, behind some obstacle, facing the wrong way, or any other undesirable place. No explanation is needed at this time.

2. Begin with a discussion on "Samaritanism." Use a "con-

cordance'' to find four or five references to Samaritans. Have the group read them, and ask what general attitude toward Samaritans prevailed in New Testament times. Why? Have the group list five or six parallels (contemporary) to this situation. (e.g. Catholics in Northern Ireland, Turkish people on Cyprus, Palestinians in Israel, etc.)

3. Give each person a slip of paper and pencil. Ask the group to write their answers (without signing their names) to this question: In the last six months, have you ever acted like the ''priest'' or ''Levite'' in the parable? Then have them pass their papers around. Each person should then silently read the answer he ends up with. Have the kids share with each other their reactions to this exercise—how they identify with the writer of the one they received.

4. Ask the group how they feel about the ''left-handers,'' (the ''Samaritans'') in the room. Did they do anything for them? How do the ''Samaritans'' feel?

5. Have the class break into groups of four and discuss the two questions, ''Who is my neighbor?'' and ''What does it mean to be a neighbor?'' If necessary re-read the passage and point out the Christ's response to the first question might help answer the second.

(Contributed by Keith Geckeler, Escondido, California)

GOSPEL NEWS

As a discussion starter, pass out parts of the daily newspaper to the kids as they arrive. Then ask them to find in the newspapers examples of where the "Gospel of Jesus Christ" is at work in the world, or where they think the Gospel is needed in a particular situation. (Contributed by Charles W. Stokes, Amory, Mississippi)

GRATITUDE GAME

Distribute to each person several slips of paper (one less than the number of people present). Ask each person to write one thing about every person present for which the writer would be thankful if he had that particular blessing. Collect the slips and read them out loud. The game may reveal that we take for granted something wonderful which others recognize as a special gift from God. We may have more to be thankful for than we think. This game is best with smaller groups (under 30) and is appropriate at Thanksgiving time. (Contributed by Jim Olia, Madelia, Minnesota)

GRAVEN IMAGES

Read the second commandment given to Moses to your group or study together the story of the golden calf which followed the receiving of the ten commandments. Then give each youth the necessary materials to sculpture a modern day ''image'' out of balsa wood or clay. The sculptured images can be realistic or symbolic, but should represent things that young people often put before God. A discussion can follow, with each person sharing his image and the images can further be dedicated to God by their destruction. For example, the wooden ones could be burned or the clay ones could be heaped together and re-molded into a symbol of the Faith. (Contributed by Rose Tozer, Ellensburg, Washington)

THE GREAT FISH CONTROVERSY

The following "parable" is excellent for stimulating discussion on evangelism and the ministry of the church:

For months, the Fishers' Society had been wracked with dissension. They had built a new meeting hall which they called their Aquarium and had even called a world renowned Fisherman's Manual scholar to lecture them on the art of fishing. But still no fish were caught. Several times each week they would gather in their ornate Aquarium Hall, recite portions of the Fisherman's Manual and then listen to their scholar exposite the intricacies and mysteries of the Manual. The meeting would usually end with the scholar dramatically casting his net into the large tank in the center of the hall and the members rushing excitedly to its edges to see if any fish would bite. None ever did, of course, since there were no fish in the tank. Which brings up the reason for the controversy. Why? The temperature of the tank was carefully regulated to be just right for ocean perch. Indeed, oceanography experts had been consulted to make the environment of the tank nearly indistinguishable from the ocean. But still no fish. Some blamed it on poor attendance to the Society's meetings. Others were convinced that specialization was the answer: perhaps several smaller tanks geared especially for different fish age groups. There was even division over which was more important: casting or providing optimum tank conditions. Eventually a solution was reached. A few members of the Society were commissioned to become professional fishermen and were sent to live a few blocks away on the edge of the sea and do nothing but catch fish. It was a lonely existence because most other members of the Society were terrified of the ocean. So the professionals would send back pictures of themselves holding some of their catches and letters describing the joys and tribulations of real live fishing. And periodically they would return to Aquarium Hall to show slides. After such meetings, people of the Society would return to their homes thankful that their Hall had not been built in vain.

(Written by Ben Patterson. Reprinted from *The Wittenburg Door* by permission.)

GYPSY LIBRARY

This works well on a college campus and might be worth trying on your high school campuses. Gather together Christian paperbacks from your teens, which they have read and been influenced by. Have them make a sign with "Gypsy Library" on it and a catchy title such as "Beg, Borrow, or Steal." Then at school, before classes, at noon, or after school, they spread the books and sign out on a blanket or table in a crowded place. When persons stop to glance at the books, the teens manning the library that day, tell the onlookers to help themselves, the books are free. It's a good witnessing opportunity and a way of using books instead of leaving them to gather dust on book shelves. It's best to have some small booklets too, as many people feel inhibited from taking large books, but will be glad to take a smaller one. Suggest to the takers that they pass them along to others after they read them or bring them back to the library and switch for another. (Contributed by Dan Wilcox, Westminster, California)

HEAVENLY TRIP

The imagination is one of God's greatest gifts. This exercise gives young people a chance to really let their imaginations run wild and learn something from the experience at the same time. Have everyone in the group lie down on the floor and get in as comfortable a position as possible. The room should be darkened, although total darkness is not required, since the kids will be instructed to close their eyes. Move through the instructions below slowly. Take your time, speak softly, and allow the kids to develop each idea in their heads before moving on to the next. When you finish, discuss with the kids how they felt and what their experience was like. You can then relate the discussion to a Scriptural view of Heaven and eternal life.

Instructions:

1. *Close your eyes* (after you find a comfortable place, not too close to anyone else). Forget about the others in the room. Say nothing so you don't distract others who are doing their own thing. Let your imagination run wild . . .

2. *Get in touch with your senses.* Slip off your shoes and silently stamp your feet . . . Drum with your fingers on the floor or table . . . Sit or lay perfectly still and try to tune into the signals your nerves all over your body are sending:
   a. Start with your feet . . . your toes . . . the arch of your feet . . . your ankles.
   b. Your legs . . . your calves . . . knees . . . thighs

c. Your torso . . . stomach muscles . . . back . . . chest
d. Your hands . . . finger tips . . . fingers, palms, wrists
e. Your arms . . . forearms . . . elbows . . . biceps
f. Your neck . . . your head . . . jaw muscles . . . eye muscles

3. *Keep your eyes closed* while I suggest some ideas that you may associate with. Put yourself into it and let your imagination go where it will.
   a. You are riding on a roller coaster (the climbs, over the top, curves, dips . . .)
   b. You are standing inside the observation window of a tall building (you see all the smaller buildings and tiny cars, people, below you . . .)
   c. You are overlooking the Grand Canyon.
   d. You are standing up on top of one of the two uprights of the Golden Gate Bridge on a foggy, windy day (you can feel the bridge sway beneath you).

4. *Go back in your memory.* It is one of those summers when you had enough time to do the thing you enjoy most of all . . .
   a. Experience doing it again.
   b. See yourself doing it.
   c. Feel it.
   d. Smell the smells that go along with it.
   e. Taste it, if there were associated tastes.

5. *You find yourself in a strange place* . . . You didn't come here on purpose . . . You don't know what to expect . . .
   a. You are alone.
   b. The room is warm, but not too warm.
   c. The colors of the walls and carpets are soft.
   d. You see a face—it's your best friend coming into the room, too. You greet each other, share your confusion, talk about other experiences you've been through together . . .
   e. Other friends and people you like join you one-by-one, some you haven't seen for years . . .
   f. Jesus enters the room. He greets everyone personally. You meet Him. Then He announces, "Inasmuch as you accepted my gift for life . . . made me first in your life . . . and spent your life seeking first to provide for the well being of others . . . you may spend eternity with those who are your best friends, or are willingly indebted to you. Every personal need will become a source of maximum enjoyment with your friends. Every point of conflict will be happily resolved to everyone's satisfaction. You will experience dimensions of peace never before imagined . . ."

6. *Welcome back to Earth!* It was only a dream.
(Contributed by Jerry Boutelle, South Holland, Illinois)

HOSPITAL BLITZ

Most hospitals have a clergy file and the saddest category is labeled "no church affiliation." Get an o.k. through the hospital administration for a night to bring your kids quietly to perform some real ministry.

In twos, take halls or sections and visit with those that seem to want it. *No* little gifts or hand decorated greeting cards — just stop in, identify yourself, talk — mostly listen, and leave.

Brief the kids on hospital etiquette such as never sit on or lean on the bed; always talk softly, if the patient is hard of hearing move closer, don't get louder; be cheerful, it's not a funeral, and never begin by asking, "How do you feel?" A better opener is, "How are things going?" (Contributed by Jim Bourne, Warner Robins, Georgia)

ICE CREAM SHARING

This simple idea is an excellent way to get discussion going on the subjects of trust, distribution of worldly goods, roots of revolution, discrimination, and other aspects of human relationships. At a meeting, camp, or outing with the young people in your group, provide some ice cream for part of the group only, such as the staff and maybe one or two of the kids. Say nothing to the rest of the group. Just serve the ice cream to the selected few while the others look on. It doesn't take long for real hostility to begin building up. Those who have been deprived of the ice cream become so resentful that even when they are later offered ice cream as a peace offering, they often refuse. If they don't get ice cream to begin with, then they usually don't want any at all. After playing this little game, reveal your true intentions and ask the deprived group to really share their feelings during the experience. You can get a lot of mileage out of a gallon of ice cream. (Contributed by Al J. Opdyke, Turlock, California)

IDEAL CHURCH

Issue five cards (index size) to each person. Ask each to write one idea on each card with the theme, "The Ideal Church would be one that...." Give a few minutes to complete. Then, ask each to rank and order in importance, from 1 (most important) to 5 (least important). Mark the rank on the BACK of the card. Then, in a sharing time, trade cards (one for one) with others, that each might accumulate the five best cards they can for their "ideal church." Instruct the group to discard three, keeping the best two. With these two cards, find others with whom you can form a "church" consisting of several members of the group. (Perhaps four to five people.)

Each church group should name their church as they see fit after discussion. Then, each group, if time permits, should design a symbol for their church. The wrap-up would be for each group to present their church to the group, explaining their goals as a church community, in addition to explaining their symbol and meaning. This is great for Senior Highs or adult groups and it really gets some discussion going about what is important in the "Ideal Church." (Contributed by Arthur Homer, Tioga Center, New York)

JESUS ON TRIAL

The following "trial" is ideal with a study of the book of Mark but can be used anytime. Before the trial, read the following scripture:

1. Mark 14:43-52 (Arrest of Jesus)
2. Mark 14:53-62 (Jesus before the Council)
3. Mark 15:1-15, John 18:28-38, Luke 23:1-5 (Jesus before Pilate)

Then divide the group in half. Group one is the prosecution and group two is the defense. The prosecution must build as tight a case against Jesus as possible. The accusations are as follows:

1. Christ was going to tear down the temple (Mark 14:58)
2. Blasphemy, claiming to be God (Mark 14:61-64)
3. Claimed to be King (Luke 23:2)
4. Misled the people, telling them not to pay taxes (Luke 23:2)
5. Instigating riots (Luke 23:5)

They may also present additional charges if they can present evidence from scripture, such as disregarding the Sabbath, disturbing the peace, etc.

Instruct the second group to work up a defense by first examining the charges and then refuting them with Scriptural evidence. Have each group work in separate rooms and let them prepare their cases by listing their charges or defenses with the appropriate scripture. This should take about 20 minutes.

Have the groups return and explain that they will also have to act as judge and jury. They must be honest and objective and judge only according to evidence presented. This could mean that Jesus would be found guilty if the defense didn't do its "homework." Have the prosecution first present its case with a sponsor listing the charges with scripture references on a blackboard or overhead projector. The defense then answers the charges with evidence and references listed opposite the charges. Following this presentation, a short "recess" is taken so that each group may bring their thoughts together and the defense has an opportunity to check out any charges unanswered. Take about five minutes for this. The groups then return and wrap up their cases. A spokesman for each group gives its "summation." The jury (everyone) then deliberates (discussion) and votes whether or not Jesus was guilty of the charges made against Him and whether or not He deserved death on the cross. (Contributed by Baxter Swenson, Denver, Colorado)

JIGSAW PUZZLE

Take a picture of the youth group. Cut it up into as many pieces as there are people. Send each youth a piece of the puzzle with instructions to bring it to the next meeting. The number of pieces missing dramatizes the completeness or incompleteness of the Body of Christ. (Contributed by Jim Hudson, North Platte, Nebraska)

KINGDOMS

This is a "table-top" discussion game which requires the construction of the game board (about 24 x 36 inches) on cardboard and the discussion cards shown below.

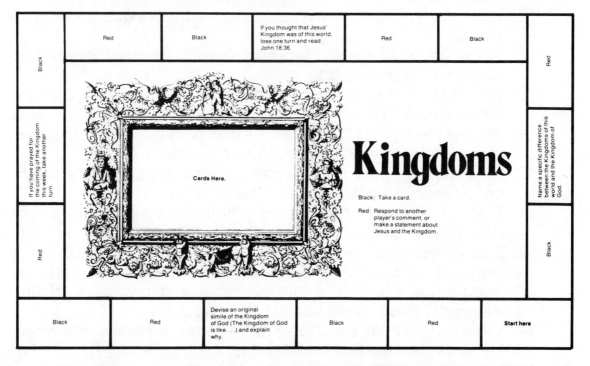

The object of "Kingdoms" is to facilitate the examination of Christ's teachings concerning the "Kingdom of God" and its implications. The intent of the game is to get players to think creatively concerning the Kingdom of God and its relationship to other Kingdoms.

Each player rolls dice to determine the amount of spaces he moves his marker (any small object) around the board. He then responds according to the type of square he lands on:

a) On a black square he takes a card and answers the question.

(Note: the scripture references usually denote the source of the question rather than the answer.)

b) On a red square the player may comment on another player's answer or make a statement about the Kingdom of God.

c) On a written square the player responds as it requests.

Players may go around the game board as many times as they wish, according to interest. Questions to be written on the game cards are listed below:

1. Since the masses did not hear Jesus' interpretation of the parable of the sower, how would you interpret it? (Matt. 13:3ff)

2. Is the Kingdom of God without order or rules? Do the Ten Commandments still govern us?

3. In what way have you made preparations for entering the Kingdom like the five wise virgins? (Matt. 25:1-13)

4. At what degree does money inhibit a man's entering the Kingdom? (Mark 10:23-26)

5. How was (or will) Jesus' phophecy that some of his disciples would not die before He came into His Kingdom fulfilled? (Matt. 16:28)

6. In what ways, and in what areas, does the Kingdom demand our all?

7. Name some of the attributes of people who will inherit the Kingdom. (Matt. 5:3, 10)

8. How does "Seek ye first the Kingdom . . ." relate to capitalism? (Matt. 6:33)

9. What is the "will" of the Father? Is that synonymous, or in some other relationship with the "Kingdom"? (Matt. 6:10)

10. How and why is John the Baptist referred to as having a different position in the Kingdom? (Matt. 11:11)

11. Was the Kingdom inaugurated with the coming of Jesus and His signs? (Matt. 12:28)

12. Do you feel more like a sheep or goat and why? (Matt. 25:33)

13. Why did Jesus differentiate between His disciples and the masses for interpreting the parables and mysteries of the Kingdom? (Matt. 13:10, Mark 4:11, Luke 8:10)

14. What do you think the substance of Jesus' message was when He "preached the Kingdom"? (Matt. 4:23, Luke 19:11)

15. How could Jesus speak of the Kingdom in varied time sequence (i.e. in you, at hand, near, to come)? (Luke 17:21, 21:31, Mark 1:15, Matt. 6:10)

16. How will the Kingdom of God bring the fullfillment of the Passover? (Luke 22:14-16)

17. Have you ever been guilty of "castling" (i.e. making the Kingdom of God so other worldly that it has no present significance?)

(Contributed by K.C. Hansen, Placentia, California)

LABOR GAME

This game is based on the "Parable of the Labourers in the Vineyard" (Matthew 20:1-16). This sometimes perplexing parable can become real by allowing your youth to experience the frustration of the workers that complained about equal distribution of pay at the end of the day, even though all did not work as long or as hard. The owner (God) was just and kept his promise — paying exactly what He said He would. This would have satisfied the workers until greed crept in. The following simulation game will help kids to understand this parable more fully.

As the kids enter the room, have several tables prepared with a puzzle, "brainteaser," or skill to do on each one. Some should be very easy, others impossible. Have points for each puzzle — depending on the difficulty, and each person is to keep track of his own score. After 20 and 30 minutes call a stop. Go to each young person, ask how many points he has, and then reach into a bag and give him a prize. The prize can be very small, just be sure every prize is exactly the same for everyone in the group.

As you slowly do this, it will soon be obvious to everyone in the group what is happening. No matter how high or low the score they tell you, they are all receiving equal payment. Allow free talk as you distribute the reward. Follow by discussion, prodding with questions such as "How do you honestly feel?"; "What is your attitude toward the "prize-giver?"; "How do you feel toward the other young people?" Ask the one that scored the highest and the one that scored the lowest how they feel. Follow by reading the scripture account of the parable and discuss greed, envy, lust, and competition, and how these things can foul up ones relationship with God. (Contributed by Jim Bourne, Warner Robins, Georgia)

LAMED VOVNIK CONVENTION

There is a charming Jewish legend which states that the world exists due to the presence of only thirty-six righteous people. The Jewish name for these people is *lamed vov* (pronounced "lah-med vov"), which indicates thirty-six. These people may be of any station in life, poor or mighty, men or women, hermits or public figures. The only thing we know about them is that they are alive and that they do not know that they are *lamed vovniks*. If they claim to be, then they cannot be.

To conduct a "lamed vovnik convention," divide your group into as many small groups as you wish, and have each group nominate several individuals whom they think might qualify as a "lamed vovnik." They should be righteous, selfless, and the kind of persons on whom the welfare of the world might rest. Each group should take 10-15 minutes for this. Set a maximum number of people that each group may nominate.

When the groups have finished, have a "nominating convention." Each group announces its choices and explains why they nominated who they did. A list can be kept on a blackboard, and a final vote can be taken to arrive at the entire group's guesses at who the thirty-six *lamed vovniks* are.

Many famous people will undoubtedly be nominated, but the beauty of the exercise is that many ordinary people, not well-known, will undoubtedly be favorites. At one "lamed vovnik convention" a man named David Rapaport was elected, when a persuasive young man nominated him with the words, "Most of you wouldn't know him, but when I need help or advice, he's always there to help me or steer me through times of trouble." Another notable nominee was an anonymous man on an immigrant ship who helped the father of one of the young people who said, "He gave dad some food and a little money, and did the same for many others on the boat. But no one remembers his name . . ." Perhaps the best thing about the activity is the shift of emphasis from fame to humility. True models begin to emerge and kids begin to put some handles on what righteousness is all about. (Contributed by Stephen E. Breuer, Los Angeles, California)

LETTER OF COMPLAINT

Have the kids write a letter to any larger manufacturer, business, or organization and complain about one or more of their products and/or services. The complaints must be completely legitimate, such as false advertising, pollution of our natural resources, high prices, or any one of hundreds of possibilities. Each kid must select his own company to write to, and request a reply. When the replies come in, have the kids then post a copy of their letter and the reply to it which they received. The discussion possibilities are great.

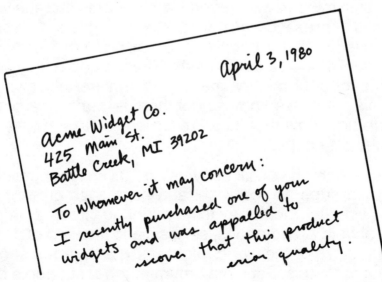

LETTER TO AMOS

The following is good after a study of the Old Testament book of Amos. Pass out copies of this "open letter" to Amos and discuss the arguments presented. Some suggested questions for discussion follow:

Dear Mr. Amos,

Your intemperate criticisms of the merchants of Bethel show that you have little understanding of the operations of a modern business economy. You appear not to understand that a businessman is entitled to a profit. A cobbler sells shoes to make money, as much as he can. A Banker lends money to get a return on his loan. These are not charitable enterprises. Without profits, a tradesman cannot stay in business.

Your slanders reveal also a lack of appreciation for the many contributions made to our land by the business community. Visitors to Israel are greatly impressed by the progress made in the past few decades. The beautiful public buildings and private homes are a proud monument. Increasing contacts with foreign lands add to the cultural opportunities open to our citizens. Our military strength makes us the envy of peoples already swallowed up by their enemies.

Despite the great gains during Jereboam II's reign, there is some poverty. That we admit. But is it just to blame us for the inability of some people to compete? You say that the peasants were cheated out of their lands. Not so! They sold their property. Or in some cases, it was sold for back taxes. Some peasants put up the land as collateral on a loan, then failed to meet the payments. No one was cheated. The transactions to which you refer were entirely legal. Had you taken the trouble to investigate the facts, your conclusions would have been more accurate.

The real reason for poverty is lack of initiative. People who get ahead in this world work hard, take risks, overcome obstacles. Dedication and determination are the keys to success. Opportunities don't knock; they are created by imagination and industry.

Our success can be an inspiration to the poor. If we can make it, they can too. With the growth of business, Israel grows. More jobs, better pay and increased opportunity for everyone. The old saying contains more than a germ of truth; What's good for General Chariots is good for the country.

Yours for Israel,

Discussion Questions:

1. Evaluate the merchant's arguments in light of justice. At what points do the businessmen convince or fail to convince you?
2. Suppose this letter were written today—how would you react? Where do the rights of the individual stop? Can justice be administered without striking a balance between individual rights and rights of the community?
3. What about Justice, Just Us or Just U. S.??????

(Contributed by Homer Erekson, Fort Worth, Texas

LETTER TO THE EDITOR

As a way to get kids more involved in the world, have them all write a letter to the editor of a newspaper of their choosing, about any current issue which they feel strongly about. They may write as many letters as they wish, but the idea is to get one published. As they become published, they can be posted in the group meeting room for all to see.

LIFE LETTERS

Following a discussion of "suicide," have kids write a "life letter" to a potential suicide victim, which expresses their reasons for their belief that life is worth living. After about twenty minutes of writing, have the kids share their letters with the rest of the group (if they want to). This gives some people a chance to share their faith and provide a unique learning experience as well. (Contributed by Dave Wilkinson, Los Angeles, California)

LIFE SKILLS

Print up a number of cards with the words, "I am a _____" on them. Give each person ten of these cards.

On each card, the person fills in a word or two that describes who or what he or she is. (Example: "I am a student," or "I am an American," etc.) After each of the cards have been filled out (allow five minutes for this) each person stacks the cards in the order of the characteristics he would most easily give up in his life, to those he would least be willing to give up. In other words, the card on the bottom would be something about him that he would find most difficult to give up. (Such as "I am a Christian").

Next, divide up into small groups no larger than eight per group. Each person then shares their top card with the others in the group. This is done by going around the circle, with each person laying their first card on a table in the center and commenting on it if they want to. Then they go around the circle again, this time laying down their second card, and so on until all ten cards have been revealed.

The value of this game is dependent on the attitudes of the individual players. Some people find it difficult to even write down the things that describe them. But this can be a very effective means to helping people "open up" to each other in a new way, thus deepening relationships on a human level. A game such as this can be followed up by a discussion on "The Whole Person"—the idea that all of us are made up of many characteristics, all of which are important to God. There is often agony in having to give up even one tenth of your personal identity. Some people may have written down things that they would *like very much* to give up in their lives. Allow them to share their thoughts with others and perhaps discuss ways to accomplish this. (Contributed by Paul Loewen, Steinbach, Manitoba, Canada)

LIGHT TRIP

This is a "mind trip" which allows kids to use their imaginations in a controlled situation. Everyone lies flat on his back on the floor. No one should be touching and all lights are out. The leader asks everyone to close their eyes and then he gives the following story/instructions:

> "Place your hands on the center of your being. It's warm in the center of your being. So warm there begins now a glow coming from the warmth. A glow that's increasing — into a radiant white light. Now the light is great and it is beginning to move throughout your body. It moves into your face, out your arms through your fingers, down your legs and feet. Your entire body is a beautiful radiant light. The whole room now is filled with this light that is coming from everyone in the room, and it feels so warm.
>
> Now the light begins to move, down the halls, into the rooms, filling the building. And now it moves into the alley and parking lot, and into the streets. It's beautiful!
>
> The light continues to go through the streets til it fills *(the place where you live)* Lincoln, Nebraska. And it's still going. It's moving out across the state — into the next state, filling the entire country with light. But it doesn't stop. It keeps on moving slowly across the oceans into Europe — and on until the entire world is filled with this beautiful light that is emanating from within you.
>
> The light is beginning to fade now. It seems to be moving back into our country. Moving back to Lincoln. That light is coming back to the church (where we are laying on the floor) — back into this room. The room is all aglow with the radiant light.
>
> The light now travels back through your toes and finger tips, and into the center of your being. The light is there in the center of your being. It's warm, bright, and it's still there."

Now ask everyone to curl up in a fetal position and remain quiet until the lights are on. Then they can open their eyes and discuss the experience. It's a good way to get kids to think of themselves as "light" in the world. (Contributed by Mary McKemy, Lincoln, Nebraska)

LINES OF COMMUNICATION

The following exercise is designed to help young people to visualize and evaluate lines of communication and relationships between themselves and others in the youth group or the church community. In so doing, the "Body of Christ" is strengthened as decisions are made regarding weak areas that need correction.

Divide the group into smaller groups of from 4 to 8 persons. Each group should have a leader who has been prepared for this exercise. Each person is given an envelope containing pieces of construction paper cut into various shapes, a large (14 by 22) piece of construction paper and a pencil. Glue should be provided also.

The leader explains that the pieces of construction paper in their envelopes are to represent the people in the youth group (or the whole church, or whatever). Each person first chooses the shape or combination of shapes that he or she feels best represents himself or herself. (Be creative and honest.) Each person should write their own name on this shape.

The large piece of paper represents the group (or church) as a whole. Each person should place the piece(s) of paper chosen to represent himself where he sees himself in relation to the rest of the group. (e.g. in the center of things, on the sidelines, etc.) Next, each person should choose shapes of paper that they consider best represent the other people in the group or church and designate these by writing names on them. Then they should be placed on the blank sheet in such a way that their position represents their relationship to you. Glue them all down.

Finally, draw the "lines of communication" that exist between you and the others using the following types of lines:

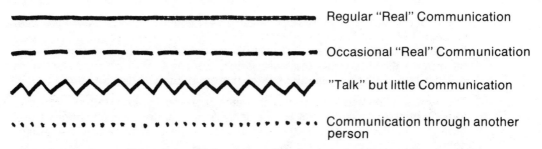

Regular "Real" Communication

Occasional "Real" Communication

"Talk" but little Communication

Communication through another person

(show by the route of the dots which person the communication passes through)

Other types of lines can be added for other "types" of communication (or non-communication).

Wrap up the exercise by allowing the participants to voluntarily share and explain their sheet to the rest of their small group. Each person should be encouraged to also share which relationships they feel should be changed or communications improved, and how they propose to do this. (Contributed by Philip Beaudoin, Independence, Missouri)

LORD OF THE FLIES REVISITED

This is a rough, active simulation game which shouldn't be tried unless the leadership is really in control of the kids.

Everyone in the group is to imagine that he is part of a huge family that has been shipwrecked on a desert island. The head of the family, much beloved and respected, has taken the only remaining boat, a motor launch, and has headed for the mainland for help. He has left instructions behind (see letter), a project (cleaning up the fellowship room or something similar), and promises to be in radio contact with the family from time to time. He has also promised that he definitely will return.

There are already people on the island. The "Wuggawuggas" are savages who will attack any foreigners who land. There are also some "hippies" who have fled San Francisco looking for a beautiful place where they can do their thing in peace.

The family should first have their situation explained to them. Then the letter from the family head should be read. A temporary family head should be elected (try to elect someone who can really lead), and a small project assigned. Then the head "hippie" is introduced. He explains that it's great to be a hippie on the island because there's absolute freedom, no responsibility, and you can get high on the candy the hippies have brought with them (have a bag of candy with enough for everyone in the group to have *one* piece). The hippies have a truce with the Wuggawuggas because they give them candy which gets the Wuggawuggas high and temporarily un-savage. So, to get the best possible life out of the island, the best thing to do is to convert from the family and join the hippie commune. Family members may become hippies at this point. Then the chief of the Wuggawuggas is introduced (with war-paint, costume, big, hairy tummy, if possible). He threatens the family with beatings and constant warfare unless they convert and become Wuggawuggas. Family members may become Wugga-wuggas at this point.

Now comes the rough and tumble: the Wuggawuggas retire to their turf and organize a raid. Each Wuggawgga is given a newspaper which he rolls up and uses as a club. He gets war paint (washable magic marker) and takes off his shirt (if he's a boy). When the tribe is organized, they whoop in and raid the family and the hippies. Tribute is demanded from the hippies until all the candy is gone, and then hippies may be bopped on the head. Caution your kids to take it easy and avoid clobbering people. The important thing is to mess up the family project.

The family meanwhile, gets organized to do their project. Prime some of your leadership in advance and get their commitment to stay with the family in case there is wholesale defection. The problem of the family is to figure out some creative way to get their project completed before the Wuggawuggas can mess it up.

The key to a successful game is having your leaders prepared and in control of the situation. If things get hairy, blow a whistle and call a halt. Re-organize and start over again. After a couple of Wugga-wugga raids, call a halt and discuss. Total time: about an hour.

The following "radio briefings" should be read periodically during the game to the family:

"Nothing's happening to you that isn't happening to everyone else who stayed with the family. There's always a way out of your predicament — use your imagination and look for ways."

I. Cor. 10:13 (paraphrased)   Josh Davidson
                                      Head of the Family

"Don't be taken in by the hippies or fall in love with their way of life. Everything they do is made of froth and will be blown away the first time there's a good wind. One of these times they'll run out of candy, and then they'll be worse off than you. But you hang on and follow my instructions, and you'll be O.K."

I John 2:15ff (paraphrased)   Josh Davidson
                                        Head of the Family

"You may think you're fighting Wuggawuggas: but it's much more serious than that. You're up against a whole evil system — so keep in shape. Use your equipment the way it was intended and hold your ground."

Eph. 6:12ff (paraphrased)   Josh Davidson
                                      Head of the Family

The *letter* to the family is a paraphrased condensation of John 13:

Dear Family,
    I just want to remind you about our last night together in the hope that it will help you endure living on the island. I'll be back soon, don't forget, but in the meantime, I want you to live together in such a way that I can be proud of you, and in such a way that life will be good for all of you.
    Remember that last night when I was eating with you — how I took off my jacket, rolled up my sleeves, and went around to each of you to shine your shoes? And remember how one of you said, "You'll never shine my shoes!" And I replied, "If I don't shine your shoes, you have no part of me." And he said, "Shine them, then, and I've got another pair in my duffel bag."
    I don't want you to forget that. I did it for a good reason. I'm the head of the family, and yet I shined shoes for each of you. If I did it, you ought to do it for each other. If outsiders see you shining shoes for each other, they'll know there's something great going on in our family.
    So, love each other — the same way I love you all. If you love each other that way, everybody will know that you're members of my family.
    I'll be sending briefings to you from time to time by radio.
    Don't forget what I said. And don't forget, I'll be back soon.
                      Love,
                      Josh

You can adapt this game any way you want, changing the names of the groups, adding more groups, or whatever your own creativity comes up with. Close with a discussion using questions such as these:

1. To the family head and members who stayed to do the project: how does it feel trying to get all this together? Do you see any similarities between your experience and Christian life?
2. Hippies: did you enjoy being hippies? Why or why not? What problems?
3. Wuggawuggas: how did you like being savages? Can you see it as a way of life?
4. How is this stiuation like our human predicament?
5. What should the family's attitude be toward hippies? Wugga-

wuggas? Did it occur to you during the game that you might win some of them back to the family?

6. Why did members of the family convert so quickly to being either hippies or Wuggawuggas?
7. How can we form a stable Christian family?
8. Do you see the story of Christ and His disciples in this game?

(Contributed by Dave Phillips, Pittsburgh, Pennsylvania)

LOVE GROUPS

This exercise is a five session project which is designed for more informal times with your youth group, although it could be used for Sunday School under certain conditions. The basic purpose is to let the youth be creative and imaginative about the subject of Christian love through many different activities. The teacher or youth leader acts as a traffic director and organizer and supplies very little direct lecture-type teaching.

The basic format of the five sessions has each youth working in an activity group for the first four sessions. Each of these activity groups is working on something directly related to the subject of Christian love. During the class period (while the activity groups are working), the leader stops all the groups for one of a variety of give and take sessions which include mini-lectures (3 minutes), discussion, a short film, or whatever, all dealing with the subject of love. The fifth session is devoted to presentation and action of each of the activity groups' finished products. (For example, the drama group would present their drama, and the "love banners" group would auction off their banners, etc.) Adults or other youth groups can be invited to the fifth session to see and hear the presentations.

Following are ten sample "love groups:"

1. *The Signs of Love Slide Show:* This group will shoot pictures of "signs of love" all around them, have them developed, and create a slide show with narration or music.
2. *Drama:* This group will prepare a play on some facet of Christian love. It can be original, or it can be a well-known Bible story.
3. *The Multiple Listing Group:* This group will come up with lists centered around Christian love. For example, a list of "What love is," or "What it is not," or "Ways to demonstrate love," etc.
4. *The Crossword Puzzle Group:* This group will design one or more crossword puzzles based on the subject of Christian love.
5. *The Poetry Group:* This group will write original poetry about Christian love.

6. *The Cartoons Group:* This group will publish a booklet of Christian love cartoons. They can be original or from other publications.
7. *The Bible Scholar Group:* This group will research the concept of Christian love in the scriptures using commentaries, other books, etc., and write a report on the findings.
8. *The Love Banner Group:* This group must have some artistic and sewing ability, because they will produce banners on the subject of Christian love.
9. *The Songwriting Group:* This group will compose Christian love songs and perform them. They can be completely original or new words to familar tunes.
10. *The Love Object Group:* This group will produce love-related art objects to auction off or give away, such as love necklaces, plaques, calligraphy, paintings, or whatever.

Each group should be supplied with the necessary items to complete their work and the kids should be encouraged to work at home on their project as well. A textbook (such as Francis Schaeffer's *The Mark of the Christian,* published by Intervarsity Press) can be used during the class sessions as a common study guide. (Contributed by Tim Doty, Tigard, Oregon)

A MAD LATE DATE

The following is a short play which is useful for getting discussion going on the obvious areas of friction developed in the play as well as general family and parent-teen relationships.

Characters needed:
1. Father
2. Mother
3. Daughter (Christy)
4. Son (Donald)

The setting is the breakfast table. Everyone except Christy is seated. Father is reading the paper, Mother is pouring coffee, and Donald is toying with his cereal. Christy hasn't come in yet.

Mother: Quit playing with your food, Donald. You'll be late for school.
Father: I'll have some more coffee, dear.
Donald: Speaking of being late, what about Christy last night? Man, if I came in that late, I'd be flogged till daylight.
Father: You let us worry about your sister. Anyway, you have to be able to get a date first.
Donald: Funny, funny!
Mother: You know, I am worried about Christy. This is the third time this has happened and . . . (Christy enters and interrupts.)

Christy:	. . . And every time there was a perfectly good excuse. Just like last night.
Donald:	Some reasons! Out of gas, flat tires . . . What's it going to be this time?
Christy:	It's none of your business, smart aleck.
Father:	Well it is *my* business, Christy. You know how worried your mother and I become when you are late.
Mother:	Yes, you could have at least called and let us know you had problems.
Donald:	Kind of hard to find a phone booth out at Folsom Lake.
Christy:	Knock it off, bird brain. I couldn't call. Coming home from the game we stopped at Eppie's and the service was just terrible . . .
Mother:	Couldn't you have called from there?
Christy:	No, Mom. We left in plenty of time — 11:00. But we hit some traffic downtown because of the big fire. Just no way we knew that was going to happen.
Donald:	Ha! That greaser you were with probably planned the whole thing.
Father:	That's enough, Don. Christy, you know the rules around here. We've asked you to be in by 12:00 and this is the third time you've been late. I'm just going to have to put you on a one week restriction.
Christy:	But Dad you don't understand. We couldn't help it!
Father:	I know you have a good reason, but rules are rules. And this isn't the first time.
Christy:	So what if it is the fifteenth time? I couldn't help it and I don't think it's fair that I get restricted.
Donald:	Fair? If it had been me, I would have been chained and muzzled to the bed post for a month!
Christy:	Yeah, you *should* be chained and muzzled with that mouth of yours.
Mother:	Regardless, Christy, we must have some rules and both of you have to obey them. I think your father is right. Anyway, I don't know if I like you dating that . . . that . . . oh, what is his name?
Donald:	You mean Greasy Gary?
Christy:	Shut up dummy! Now I know why I'm on restriction, you never have liked anybody I've dated. If it wasn't him, you'd find something else . . .
Father:	(Interrupts.) Now just a minute. The matter of liking who you're dating has nothing to do with it. I might say, however, you could be a little more choosey.
Christy:	Choosey! Who would you want me to date? One of those creeps at the church?
Mother:	Creeps? Where did you pick up that language?
Donald:	From Greasy Gary. I think that's his middle name.

Christy:	Okay, smart mouth . . .
Father:	Both of you calm down. If this is going to be your attitude, Christy, you can forget about going anywhere for the following week as well. Your mother and I could use a little help around here.
Christy:	WHAT, YOU CAN'T BE SERIOUS! What about Donald? All he does is sit around and flap his mouth making corny jokes.
Mother:	Now, Christy, that's enough. There's no need to bring your brother into this. I think it is time we be just a little more considerate of each other.
Christy:	Why don't you start with me? I come in a lousy 45 minutes late and you act like it was three hours. Then you start harping on who I date. All you're concerned about is your silly rules and regulations.
Father:	You don't need to raise your voice to your mother. And rules and regulations are something to be concerned about. But more important is your behavior to those rules. Either you shape up or else.
Donald:	Or shape out . . . that shouldn't be hard for you.
Christy:	(in tears) I've had enough! I'm leaving! Nobody understands me. You just don't care.
Mother:	We do care Christy. You are the one who doesn't understand. Why, when I was your age . . .
Christy:	Now comes the second lecture! Well, times are different and you are *not my age!*
Father:	I think I've heard enough. Both of you get off to school, and Christy . . . I want you home at 4:00 sharp.

(Contributed by Jim Braddy, Sacramento, California)

MAP OF ME

Give each person a large sheet of paper and a marking pen or crayons. Have each person then think of himself as a *place* and draw a map which would describe that place. For example, what would you look like if you were a city, or an island in the middle of the ocean? What kinds of buildings, hills, valleys, roads (some under construction), areas of interest, etc? Allow each person to describe what he or she has drawn to the entire group. This is great as a way of getting kids to open up about their lives and their individuality. (Contributed by Andrea Sutton, Ipswich, Massachusetts)

MAUNDY THURSDAY EXPERIENCE

This is an excellent way to help make Easter Week more meaningful for your young people. Have the kids meet on "Maundy Thursday," the Thursday prior to Easter and participate in the following events:

1. Begin with supper in small groups in homes. Prepare a discussion guide about "what happened" at the Last Supper. Have one of the kids lead the discussion after the meal, around the table with all the left-over food and dirty dishes on the table.
2. Meet at the church (or elsewhere) with the entire group and have a Communion Service, with all the members of the church, if possible.
3. Take a short trip to "Gethsemane." This can be a nice park, isolated, with trees, brushes, hills, etc. Attempt to experience in some way the feelings and thoughts that Jesus must have had at Gethsemane. Sit together in a close group, and have someone relate the story of Gethsemane from the Bible. Someone can sing the Gethsemane song from the play "Jesus Christ, Superstar," and perhaps another can do an interpretive dance to it.
4. Point out that, just as Jesus, we have our "Gethsemanes" too. Have a few in the group share a time in their life when they felt something of what Christ must have felt. This can be very impressive.
5. Close by joining hands in a large circle and singing Easter songs together.

(Contributed by Kenneth Dunivant, Cullman, Alabama)

MELODY IN "S"

Here is a fun version of an old story. Use it however you wish.

Sure enough, the scholarly scribe stood up and slyly said to the Savior, "Sir, surely you surmise that I seek a sustained subscription to a solid life beyond the solid shale sepulcher. So what steps shall I secure for such a sub-sistence?

The Savior said, "What saith the statutes?" The stupid scribe responded, "It says, 'Serve, Sigh for and Sway with your Savior with all your substance, soul, spirit, and strength. And sway with the sire who settles by your side as you sway with yourself.'"

"Sure," said the Savior, "Stay so and you shall survive." So, the silly scribe, seeking to save his skin, said, "Sir, I solicit you to set before me my sidekick." The Savior sent home his statement by citing a sample:

A sorry sap was sauntering slowly side to side when suddenly six serious assassins set themselves to smash that silly sap. Stripped, stunned and shaken, he stumbled and sank to the solid slate of the sidewalk. After seemingly several seconds slipped by, a slothful sort of celibate saw the simple soul seething on the sidewalk; so he stopped and then simply strolled by. Soon a selfish shepherd who subsisted on a small salary stalled a second and left the sorry simpleton stranded. Suddenly, a stalwart Samaritan slid straightaway to the subdued subject who was stunned. Seeing the seriousness of the situation, he restored the strength of that sorry soul and sitting him in the saddle of his staunch stallion, surveyed him safely to some septic sanatarium where he secured some serious substantial sleep for that stranded sojourner.

"So," said the Savior, "Seeing such circumstances, who seems to be the sympathetic saint in such a situation?"

"Surely, the Samaritan," stammered the scribe.

"Superb," said the Savior, "So must you shape yourself."

(Contributed by George E. Gaffga, Liberty, New Jersey)

MIND TRIPS

These "mind trips" are really nothing more than imaginative daydreaming. They are used to promote greater self-awareness and to generate discussion. Yet, it is possible that they may release feelings causing temporary pain and anxiety. That is, a person may not like what his mind tells him . . . there would be considerable anxiety if, for example, one saw his inmost self (Who Am I exercise) as a dark, empty room. Therefore, one needs to use some caution as he proceeds.

1. Move through the exercises slowly. Some time must be allowed for the imaginative process to work . . . Be deliberate in giving the suggestions.
2. Avoid pressuring anyone into doing these exercises. If they don't wish to participate, ask them to sit quietly or to leave the room.
3. Anyone can stop himself at any point in the exercise. If one is reaching some level of anxiety and wishes to discontinue, he may "imagine" himself awake, open his eyes, get his bearings and not participate further. There is no trance or hypnosis or anything like that involved in these exercises. It is like daydreaming. You are always in control of yourself.
4. It is rare that anyone would reach such an anxiety level as described above. It is even more rare that someone would become upset or frightened in the course of these exercises. But it could happen. In that infrequent emergency: Hold the person in your arms, reassure him, speak soothingly to him. Calmly help him return his attention to the immediate reality. As I said, it would be extremely rare for this kind of thing to happen. But it is possible.
5. Always discuss the exercise and what went on in the mind. It is good for everyone to have the chance to share what they dreamed. Some analysis of symbols can be made but it is best to let each person analyze his own dream for its meaning. There

will always be an interesting and amazing variety of happenings in these mind trips. Nearly everyone enjoys these experiences and comes to feel a new degree of insight into themselves.

6. The leader could also stress the fact that what one sees in his mind is only a temporary picture. That is, if one were to repeat the exercise tomorrow some changes would take place. One might even imagine something entirely different. No long lasting significance need be given these mind trips. But again, they can help promote greater self-awareness. And they are fun.

JESUS TRIP

Close eyes, relax, breathe deeply, concentrate for just a few moments on relaxing. This is important to begin.

When you are relaxed, listen to leader's suggestions, don't try to force something to happen in your mind, just let it happen.

Begin by imagining yourself walking down a road. Any road. As you walk, notice the things around you. What kind of a road? What scenery? Are you enjoying your walk? What's happening around you?

Continue walking and observing. But notice a figure behind you on the same road going in the same direction. As the figure gets closer to you, you realize who it is . . . it's Jesus. Notice what he looks like, how he's dressed.

As he catches up with you, he says hello and the two of you begin to talk. Take two or three minutes and just let your conversation go where it will. For a few minutes share with Jesus and let him share with you.

As you continue walking down the road, you come to a "Y" in the road; you realize that Jesus must go one way and you must go the other. You have time to ask Jesus one last question . . . make it an important one . . . and he will answer. Ask your question and listen to his answer.

Then say goodbye . . . Jesus goes one way and you go the other.

When you are ready to, open your eyes, look around, remember where you are.

Share your experiences with the group. Break up into smaller groups to discuss what happened if you would like to. Write some things down if you would like to remember to.

WHO AM I?

Close eyes, relax, breathe deeply, concentrate on relaxing for just a few moments. This is important to begin.

When you are relaxed, listen to the leader's suggestions, don't try to force something to happen in your mind, just let it happen.

Begin by imagining yourself walking down a long corridor. This corridor or hallway leads deeper and deeper inside yourself. As you walk it takes you deeper and deeper into your mind.

You can begin to see an end to the hallway. It leads to a room deep inside yourself. This room is your inmost being. You are now approaching the doorway to your room . . . your inmost self.

As you come to the doorway, open it and look inside. What do you see in your room? Remember this room represents yourself, what you're really like, what's important to you.

Before you step into the room, notice a few things. What size and shape is your room? What color? Is it light or is it dark? Are there windows? Where does the light come from? What kinds of furnishings are in the room?

After you have noticed these things, step into your room and walk around it. Look closely at what is there. Don't be surprised by your room; remember it's you. Are there any blurred or vague areas in your room that you can't make out? Do you enjoy being in your room? Just wander around and look for a few minutes.

After you have toured your room, come back to the doorway. Turn and take one last look at your room. Then step back out, through the doorway into the corridor or hallway, and come back up the long hallway until you return to the present.

Then open your eyes, look around you and get your bearings.

Share your room with the group or break up into smaller groups to discuss what your room was like. Why do you think you visualized your room as you did? What did the things you saw mean to you? What do you think this says about you?

Remember that your room would change every time you would do this because you change. Thus, your room might be dark and foreboding one time and light and gay another time, depending on what's happening to you at the time.

PARADISE

Close your eyes, relax, breathe deeply, concentrate for just a few moments on relaxing. This is important to begin.

When you are relaxed, listen to the leader's suggestions; don't try to force something to happen in your mind. Just let it happen.

Begin by imagining that you are floating on your back down a river. You cannot sink. You are relaxed and just floating along. Breathe deeply and let your body float.

It's a gentle little river that is winding its way through a beautiful forest. It's a sunny day, and the sun is warming your skin. You float past trees and great fields of beautiful flowers. There's a meadow. Smell the grass and flowers. Hear the birds. Gaze up at the sky.

Swim over to the edge of the meadow and climb out of the river. Walk across the meadow. Enjoy the grass on your ankles, the lightness in your step.

On the other side of the meadow is a large tree. It has a door in it. Behind that door is your personal paradise. Open the door and look inside. What do you see in your personal paradise? Look around first, then step through the door. What do you see? What is happening?

For a few minutes just enjoy being in your paradise . . .

You realize now, that you cannot stay here. You must return. You hate to leave but you know you have to. Step back to the door. Step outside, through the door, turn . . . take one last look, then close the door. Walk back across the meadow, thinking about and enjoying what you have just seen. Enter back into the river and swim slowly and lazily, with no effort, back up the stream. Swim past the meadow and through the forest.

When you have returned, open your eyes, look around and remember where you are.

Share your personal paradise with the group or break up into smaller groups and discuss what it was like.

(Contributed by Jim Hudson, Fresno, California)

MOLD ME

Give each person a lump of clay or "Playdough" and have each one mold it into "an image of their life." This can be abstract or an actual likeness. Allow each person to share and explain his sculpture with the rest of the group.

Next, study II Timothy 2:20-21 and have each person shape their clay into a type of "vessel" that they wanted to be. Again, these can be shared and explained by each person. Following an act of "dedication" in which each person asks to be "filled" and "used" by God, the vessels can be allowed to harden and put on display. The song "Spirit of the Living God" is an appropriate song of dedication. (Contributed by Jack Keyte, Kansas City, Missouri)

MOMENT OF DISILLUSIONMENT

This is a Bible study and role play on John 13:1-14:11. Read the passage aloud in groups of twelve. Assign the following parts to be read by members of your group:
1. Jesus
2. Judas Iscariot
3. Peter
4. Disciple whom Jesus loved
5. Thomas
6. Philip

A narrator should read all of the parts which are not directly attributed to a person. After reading the passage once, reread the passage playing the same roles. Perhaps you will want to arrange yourselves in a manner similar to the way in which the disciples must have been seated.

After the second reading, discuss the following questions:
1. If you had been Peter, how would you have acted when Jesus tried to wash your feet? Why? How did Peter act? How should he have acted?
2. Why did Jesus wash the disciples feet? How can leaders in our group "wash" others feet?
3. Why did the disciples not understand what Jesus meant when he spoke to Judas Iscariot? (12:26-28)
4. Why did Jesus tell his disciples not to be troubled? (14:1)
5.   If two of the spiritual leaders of this youth group suddenly "wiped out" in their Christian lives, how would you react?

(Contributed by Mark Senter, Wheaton, Illinois)

MONITORING YOUR MORALS

The following are true-false questions to be answered individually by the members of the group, then discussed collectively by the entire group. Explain that the answers given should be honest opinion, not answers which might be considered "correct" by the church or youth director. Be prepared to work through each question thoroughly in the discussion period.

1. Over eating is as wrong as smoking or drinking. _____
2. While your father was walking home from work one night, a robber came from the shadows and demanded all his money. Your father gave his wallet to the robber. He looked in the wallet and asked "Is this all the money you have?" Your father said, "Yes." The thief crept away satisfied, but your father had lied to the thief: he had a twenty tucked away in his shirt pocket. This was wrong. _____
3. To goof off on your job is as wrong as if you stole money from your boss. _____
4. There are degrees of sin with God and He won't punish us for the little ones. _____
5. Killing a man is justified when a person is called by his government to defend his country. _____
6. As Christians, we are to obey all people who are in a position of authority over us. This means police officers, parents, teachers, youth directors, etc. _____
7. You are late for church so instead of driving at the 45 mile per hour speed limit, you drive at 50. Because you are going to church this is not wrong. _____
8. Going into your history final, you are just squeezing by with a C. Passing or failing this test could mean the difference between passing or failing this course. There are several questions you don't know, so you look on your neighbor's paper, an A student, and copy from him. When you get your paper back you found that you would have flunked without the correct answers from your neighbor's paper. Cheating was justified in this case. _____
9. You are very much in love with your girl friend and plan to get married. On a date, you get carried away and she gets pregnant. Because you love her as your wife, the act was not wrong. _____
10. There is a guy at school that really gets on your nerves. If there was ever a person that you hated, it would be this guy. The feeling you have for this guy is as wrong as if you killed him.

_____

(Contributed by Bob Gleason, Roseburg, Oregon)

THE MORAL OF THE STORY . . .

Read a story (proverb, fable, Biblical, or make-believe) and leave out the "moral" at the end, if there is one. Challenge each person to write down what they think the moral of the story could be. They can then share them and discuss. It's amazing how many different things you can learn from one simple story. (Contributed by Nido Qubein, High Point, North Carolina)

M.U.S.T.

The following is an idea to make the summer months more of a challenge for your youth. At the beginning of the summer, give the youth group the name *Metamorphosis Union in the Summer Time* (M.U.S.T.). Metamorphosis means "change," and as a key verse, you can use St. Paul's admonition about being "changed from within by the power of God" rather than being changed by how the world squeezes us into its mold (Romans 12:2)

To begin with, have the kids write letters *to themselves* about how they would like to change as a person during the summer (and beyond if they care to). These are sealed in self-addressed envelopes. During the summer, the kids attempt to expose themselves to as much as possible in the way of activities, projects, study, and each other to help bring about personal metamorphosis. The emphasis is focused on personal development and maturity, with special individual projects and activities designed by the youth minister. At the end of the summer, mail the letters which they wrote to themselves back to the kids and have them discuss any metamorphosis that took place during the summer. (Contributed by Glenn Jolley, Santa Barbara, California)

MYSTERY GIFTS

Wrap several mystery gifts, using seasonal paper for wrapping. Vary the size of the boxes. Have several kids come up and select a "gift" from a box or pile of gifts. They open (before the audience) then give an impromptu "parable", thought, lesson, or something with the "gift" as a theme. If the treasury is able, the participants may keep the gifts. This is a great way to enhance creativity at Thanksgiving or just anytime. (Contributed by W. C. Arnold, Madison, Tennessee)

MYSTERY GUEST

Divide the youth into small groups of three or four per group. Then have each group choose a Bible character and research and collect information about him or her for ten minutes. Each group then takes the stand, and the rest of the youth ask questions of the group to try and discover who the character is. Each question must be answered "yes," "don't know," or "no." If ten "no" answers are given before the identity of the Bible character is guessed, the group "wins." The game can be played with "flip cards" similar to the TV show "What's My Line." (Contributed by James Brown, Rochester, Pennsylvania)

NAILING OUR SINS TO THE CROSS

As a symbolic representation of how Christ took our sins with Him to the cross, have students write their sins down on pieces of paper and one at a time nail them to a wooden cross. After a time of individual silent prayer, the sins can be removed from the cross and destroyed, symbolizing how our sins have been erased from God's memory forever. (Contributed by Lanny Bruner, Longview, Washington)

NEWSPAPER PRAYER

Here's a great creative worship idea. Pass out several morning newspapers to the participants in the service. Include the funnies, sports, and the weekly magazine. Invite people to share things that they find in the paper which need God's guidance (prayer requests) or for which they want to praise or thank God for. After a sufficient number of people have shared, close with a summary prayer, group prayer, or a song. This can be used as an illustration for an approach to family devotions or as a meaningful way to get people to participate in the service.

NEWSSTAND

Listed below are thirty popular magazines found on most newsstands that reflect a wide range of interests. There are many others, of course, and you may want to add or subtract titles from the list before using it.

1. Rolling Stone
2. T.V. Guide
3. Ladies Home Journal
4. Holiday
5. Psychology Today
6. Surfer
7. Time
8. Playboy
9. Sixteen
10. Sports Illustrated
11. Readers' Digest
12. Mad
13. Hot Rod
14. Intellectual Digest
15. U.S. News & World Report
16. Better Homes and Gardens
17. Parents
18. Playgirl
19. Esquire
20. Police Gazette
21. Consumer Reports
22. Ms.

23. Wall Street Journal
24. Glamour
25. National Geographic
26. Hollywood Reporter
27. Decision
28. Ramparts
29. National Enquirer
30. People

Divide into small discussion groups of not more than eight each (four to six in a group is usually best). Try to avoid "cliques" getting together into the same group. Perhaps a random method of selecting groups might help. Print copies of the above list and distribute to each person. The three questions below are asked one at a time and each person is allowed to share his or her response with the others in the discussion group. Anyone may pass if they wish.

1. Which magazine(s) best describes you right now? Explain why. Which magazine(s) best describes the way you would *like* to be?
2. Due to a sudden paper shortage, the government will only permit three magazines to continue being published. Those three magazines are to be determined by a vote of the people. Which ones will you vote for?
3. If you had one full page in any magazine to do with as you wish, how would you use it? What would be printed on the page, and in what magazine would it appear?

Allow ample time after each question for everyone to respond. Remember that in a discussion such as this, there are no "correct" answers. The important thing is that everyone has the opportunity to express himself openly and honestly, which invariably leads to more openness, better understanding and communication among the members of the group. You may want to "wrap up" the experience, however, with a challenge or lesson that gives added content. Ques-

tion one is an introductory or self-analysis type of question. Question two deals with values and priorities, and question three with communication. Any of these topics can be discussed. Further application is left up to you and your objectives.

OBSERVATION GAME

Send a person out of the room. While he is gone, ask the others to tell things about the person's appearance. For example, what color is his shirt, does he wear glasses, what kind of shoes, pants, etc. Write it down on a blackboard and have the person re-enter. Compare with the descriptions. Follow up with a discussion on how much we notice about each other. It might be a good idea to "fix" the person up ahead of time, that is give him some distinct things for him to wear, like a leather watch band, a pencil in his ear, monogrammed shirt, etc. (Contributed by Jim Olia, Madelia, Minnesota)

PARABLE

This is an excellent way to get young people involved in the parables of Jesus. Divide into small discussion groups and give each group a parable from the Scriptures. Then have the groups work on the following questions concerning their parable:

1. What do you feel was the meaning of the parable in Jesus' time"?
2. How does it speak to us now?
3. What do you find most profound in its message?
4. Prepare a short modern skit of how you think this parable would have happened in 20th Century America?

The groups should be allowed enough time to work through each question and prepare their skit. Then the entire group meets together and each small group presents their skit and shares their thoughts on the parable that they worked on. The discussion / preparation period and the presentation of the skits can be done in two different meetings, over a period of two days, or two weeks if desired. Either way, the experience can be very rewarding. (Contributed by Randall Foos, San Diego, California)

PARABLE PLAYS

Give groups of five to eight kids each a parable of Jesus. Have them re-create the parable in play form and present it to the whole group. After the plays have the whole group discuss the meaning of the parables. Encourage the kids to up-date or add their own creativity to the parable plays to make them more understandable. (Contributed by James Brown, Rochester, Pennsylvania)

PARENT BLUNDERS AND TEEN GOOFS

Give each kid a mimeographed sheet which contains two columns of "Yes" and "No" answers, ten to each column. Then give the following questions to them orally and have them circle their response after each question. The kids should be as honest as they possibly can, and they need not put their names on their answer sheets.

In column one, they answer questions relating to their parents' attitudes toward them, and in column two, questions about their attitudes towards their parents. The total number of "yes" and "no" answers in each column can be totaled after the quiz and may then be used as a basis for discussion. Normally, whenever the parents score a high number of "no" answers, so does the kid. (And viceversa). For example, if a kid says his parents do not act like they trust him, he will undoubtedly answer "no" to the questions about trying to earn and keep his parents' trust. The answers should show that both parents and teens have a 50-50 share of the responsibility for their problems.

Parent Blunders:
1. Do your parents listen to you when you have a family discussion?
2. Do your parents act like they trust you?
3. Do your parents treat your friends nicely and make them feel welcome?
4. Do your parents admit their mistakes when they have been wrong?
5. Do your parents openly express and show their affection for you?
6. Do your parents avoid comparing you to brothers or sisters, or other youth?
7. Do your parents keep the promises that they make to you?
8. Do your parents show their appreciation and give you credit when you do something good?
9. Do your parents set a good example for you in their personal honesty?
10. Do your parents use the kind of language in front of you that they told you to use?

Teen Goofs:
1. Do you listen to your parents when they want to share an idea or advice with you?
2. When your parents say "NO" to your plans, do you accept that answer without complaining?
3. Do you try to understand the pressures and problems that sometimes make parents grumpy and hard to live with?
4. Do you say "Thank you" for everything that your parents do for

you?

5. Do you try to plan something nice that you can do for your parents occasionally?
6. Do you say "I'm sorry" when you know you have been out of line or have said or done something you shouldn't?
7. Do you try to earn and keep your parents trust by doing what they expect of you?
8. Do you play fair with them and discuss things honestly, without covering up for yourself?
9. Do you ask your parents' advice about decisions that you have to make?
10. Do you try to avoid problems and arguments by doing what you're supposed to before you have to be told?

(Contributed by Bill O'Connor, San Dimas, California)

PARKING LOT PALESTINE

Here's a creative way to add a new dimension to the events of the Bible. Have the youth group research and map out a large map of the Holy Land (to scale) that can be "painted" onto the parking lot of the church. Major cities and locations can be marked and one kid can be assigned that place to research and learn about the events that took place there. Displays, photos, and other "sets" can be put at each location (such as three crosses at Mt. Calvary, an "ark" at Mt. Ararat, etc.) Then the youth group can give guided tours to adults and children of the church with each "guide" telling about the events that took place in his or her area. With some creativity and a lot of work, this can be a very meaningful and worthwhile project. (Contributed by Winifred Bartunek, Hiram, Ohio)

PAUL'S DILEMMA

The following is a contrived situation involving a teenage boy named Paul. He faces a problem for which he receives "advice" from friends and relatives holding various points of view. This situation can be either read to the group by the leader or acted out in a sort of role play. After presenting the situation to the group including all the advice which Paul receives, discuss the questions provided at the end with the entire group.

The Situation:

Paul is a junior in high school. He is relatively well accepted by his friends. He makes average grades and is a member of several school organizations: choir, the basketball team and student council. He has been friends with one group of five guys through most of his junior high and high school years. His parents are respectable members of the community. His father is a lawyer and his mother the secretary of a popular civic organization. The whole family is active in a local church where his father and mother hold leadership positions.

Paul's problem is this: he has been close with this group of five guys for a long time and their values have always been quite similar. But lately, the guys have been experimenting with drugs and alcohol. Although Paul has participated until now, he is beginning to feel more and more uncomfortable. He has discussed the problem with his buddies and they do not feel uncomfortable. If Paul decides to stop going along with the group, it may cost him his relationship with the guys. He approaches a number of acquaintances seeking advice:

Youth Group Sponsor: He is concerned that Paul may get sucked into the habits of his buddies. His advice is to break the relationship pointing out that Jesus never allowed relationships to get in the way of his convictions. He refers to others such as Martin Luther who did what they knew was right regardless of the circumstances.

Paul's Uncle: His favorite uncle who is also a lawyer, listens nervously as Paul confides that he really doesn't see what is so wrong with all of these things. It's just that he doesn't feel right. Paul's uncle immediately attempts to point out through statistics the dangers of Marijuana and alcohol. He attempts to rationally investigate all of the "phony" justifications for using grass and alcohol and makes a case for abstinance, the only really logical and safe conclusion.

Sunday School Teacher: He points out that you are either "with" Christ or "against" him. You either are committed or not committed. What is at stake is behaving like a Christian should and renouncing every "appearance of evil" or capitulating and being "worldly" and "sold out" to sin.

Youth Director: He relates to Paul a true story of a close friend who was bothered by the direction his friends were going, but didn't have enough courage to stand for his conviction. The result was that he became heavily involved in drugs, disgraced his family and friends and eventually committed suicide. He suggests that Paul has great potential to influence hundreds of young people and he could blow his chances of potential greatness. In fact, the youth director confides, he was just going to ask Paul to take a leadership position in the group.

A Neighbor (who is also a policeman): He confronts Paul with the fact that he saw a report on some of Paul's friends who were on the brink of getting into trouble with drugs, etc. The neighbor is concerned that Paul understand the legal implications of his friends' behavior and counsels him to stay away lest he and his friends get busted. He then goes on to explain that he personally does not see what's wrong with a kid experimenting with Marijuana, but that we must all obey the laws otherwise there would be total chaos. Laws are there for our protection and we must follow them.

The Pastor: He points out that the church has always spoken out against "non-Christian behavior" and that ever since the church was founded such things were not acceptable for church members. The purity of the church, whether it's local body of believers or "the church universal," has always been a focal point for "our doctrine."

His Girlfriend: She points out that she does not care what anyone else says, he must do what's right. If he made the wrong choice, he would never be able to live with himself. She reminds him that if his parents knew he was experimenting with Marijuana and alcohol, "his mother would be crushed" and "his father would be humiliated." "Besides," she says, "What about me and our relationship? You know what I think of your group of friends and what they are doing, and if I meant very much to you, you would think carefully about what you're doing."

Paul's Older Brother: He thinks Paul is too narrow and making an issue out of nothing. He feels Paul is experiencing false guilt produced by the unenlightened views of their parents. He points out that he regularly smokes pot and drinks and still maintains a high grade point average and also holds down a good job. He counsels Paul not to get involved in heavy drugs or excessive drinking, but warns him not to sacrifice his good friendships for a "non-issue."

Questions for Discussion:

1. Evaluate each of the arguments given to Paul. What are the strengths, if any, and what are the weaknesses, if any?
2. Which person do you most agree with? Why? Least agree with? Why?
3. What answer would you have given Paul? What would you do in Paul's situation?
4. Is there a "right answer" to Paul's Dilemma?
5. What were Paul's alternatives?
6. If Paul had weighed all the alternatives and made what you considered to be a wrong choice, what would you say to Paul if you were:

      a. a close friend   e. a youth director
      b. a girlfriend   f. a minister
      c. a parent   g. a school counselor
      d. a brother/sister

(Adapted from an idea contributed by Al Simons, Wichita Falls, Texas)

PEACE, LOVE AND JOY WORSHIP

This is an excellent "creative worship" idea, which is simple, yet effective. As each person enters the room, give him (or her) a "peace" flower, a "love" flower or a "joy" flower. Balloons may be substituted for flowers if you choose, with peace, love or joy written on them. Regardless, the purpose is to divide the group into three groups so the reading below can be read by the appropriate groups, as a responsive reading. The "verse" in each section may be read by the leader and the response (the bold type portion) by the group, or the group can read the entire segment, or the boys in the group can read the verse with the girls answering with the response, or any other way you want. However you feel the most meaning can be read into it is the best way.

"Peace, Love, Joy"

LOVE: Love is very patient and kind, never jealous or envious, never boastful or proud. (Cor. 13:4)
I asked God for love
Instead He showed me
How He could love through me.

JOY: He is my strength, my shield from every danger. I trusted in Him and He helped me. Joy rises in my heart. (Psalms 28:7)
I asked God for joy
Instead He let me fully trust
From whence my joy came.

PEACE: Since we have been made right in God's sight by faith in His promises, we can have real peace with Him. (Romans 5:1)
I asked God for peace
Instead I was confessing everything.
Then my peace came.

LOVE: Love does not demand its own way; it is not irritable or touchy, nor does it hold grudges. (1 Cor. 13:5)
I asked God to give me my own way.
Instead He let me give to my family
Yes, mother, father, brother and sister.

JOY: We confidently and joyfully look forward to becoming all that God has had in mind for us to be. (Romans 5:2)
I asked God to make me successful
Instead He gave me humility
Joyfully, I followed His will for my life.

PEACE: "His peace will keep your thoughts and hearts quiet and at rest as you trust in Christ Jesus." (Phil. 4:7)
I asked God that I might worry less,
Instead He took all the worry from me
And peace was mine.

LOVE: If you love someone you will always believe in him, always expect the best of him and always stand your ground defending him. (1 Cor. 13:7)
I asked and expected too much, God
Instead I learned to love my family,
And all around me in a positive way.

JOY: O God, in mercy bless us. Let Your face beam with joy as You look down at us.
(Psalms 67:1)
**I asked God for discipline in
Church Attendance
Instead He showed me what worship
Is All About.
O joy in His worship!**

PEACE: He will give His people strength, He will bless them with peace (Psalm 29:11)
**I asked God for peace in all the world.
Instead He showed me His timing
In my life and for mankind.**

Close with a round of prayer, passing the peace, batting the balloons or however you wish. (Contributed by Cindy Baw, Orlando, Florida)

PENTAGON

This game is not only fun to play, but is also excellent as a simulation game to teach the inter-dependence of members of the Body of Christ.

Divide into any number of teams, with six people on each team. Each team will have five "players" and one "runner." The five players are seated in a pentagon-shaped arrangement with approximately 10 feet separating each player. The runner is in the center.

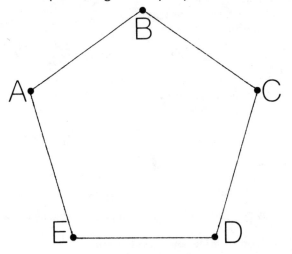

A deck of ordinary playing cards is shuffled and the five players each receive a card. They are to keep the cards concealed and not reveal to anyone which card they have. The object of the game is for each player to learn what cards the other players on his team have, through a process of note-passing. No one may tell another player what card he has. He must write notes. No talking is allowed or the team is disqualified or penalized.

Each player has a scratch pad with plenty of note-paper and a pencil. He may only communicate directly with the players to either side of him. For example, A may communicate with B and E, B may communicate with A and C, etc. He must remain seated at all times and give his note to the runner, who delivers everyone's notes back and forth. Each note should state who is sending it and from whom:

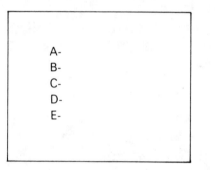

When a player writes a note, he raises his hand until the runner picks the note up and delivers it to whoever it is to. He may only send one note at a time and each note may only give or ask information concerning one player at a time. In other words, a note *cannot* say "B has the Jack of Hearts, C has the two of Clubs, and E has the six of Diamonds." That message would require three notes. Once a note has been read and / or answered, it is discarded (wadded up and thrown on the floor.)

Each player should be keeping a record of information that he receives. He should have a piece of paper with the following list:

A-
B-
C-
D-
E-

As soon as the list is complete and he knows which cards all of the other four players have, he stands up. While standing, he may still give and receive notes to assist other team members who haven't yet finished. The first team to get all five members standing is the winner, *unless* someone's information in incorrect. Each person's list must be checked for errors.

This game can be played with more players per team, which will make it longer, or it can be played in different arrangements. One alternative is as follows:

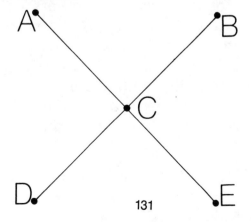

In this game, the time to complete the game is shorter and the player in the center (C) is very busy, while the other players don't participate as much, since they can only communicate with one person. C can communicate with everybody.

Real names can be used instead of letters of the alphabet. A discussion can follow based on related Scripture, such as I Corinthians 12: 12-27. In the Body of Christ, we all have an equally important part as members of the body. (Contributed by Jim Olia, Madelia, Minnesota)

PEOPLE PUZZLE GROUPS

The following is an experiment in communications. First divide your large group up into smaller groups of five. (Pick helpers if there are people left over—the ones you think would get the least out of the experiment.) Each group of five gets an envelope with different shapes of the same color in it for each member. Use construction paper to make shapes out of these colors: Red, Blue, Black, Yellow, Green. Each person's envelope contains shapes in one of these colors. The object is to form five rectangles, all of equal length and width. However, you cannot speak. You will need pieces in the other envelopes and others will need your pieces. There are three steps in putting together the puzzles:

1. No speaking. The only thing you can do is offer one of your pieces of the puzzle to another member. You cannot indicate your need for a particular piece. You may only take a piece if it is offered to you. (5-10 minutes)
2. No speaking. However, you can now indicate your need for a particular puzzle piece. (5-10 minutes)
3. You may speak.
4. (optional) You may help another group finish.

This exercise usually takes from 20-30 minutes for all the different groups to finish. The discussion follow-up must be based on the interaction during the experiment. Discussion takes place in the areas of communication and competition, drawing quickly to human feelings. That's the important thing—how did you feel:
   a. When you couldn't talk? Did others help you? Why was communication in your group hard (or easy)?
   b. About the others in your group? Were they selfish or generous? Do you consider yourself generous or selfish?
   c. When your group finished? Were you proud? When did you start competing with other groups? (This always happens, but never use the word team or competition, always groups and experiment.)
   d. When another group wanted to help you? Did you like the

other groups or feel they were showing off, etc? Which was the best group? The worst group? Why?

e. How did you feel about yourself, your motives? How do you feel about your ability to communicate? Man's ability to communicate?

You can see the different avenues open up, and you must be able to take advantage of them. You could end up in a discussion of God's communication to man, why it is so difficult—why he had to become a man to communicate! Or you could end up in other directions—man's selfishness, pride, competitive nature, etc. Base it on the interaction of your particular group.

HOW TO MAKE THE PUZZLES

When each group has finished, you will have five rectangles made by piecing the colors together as follows:

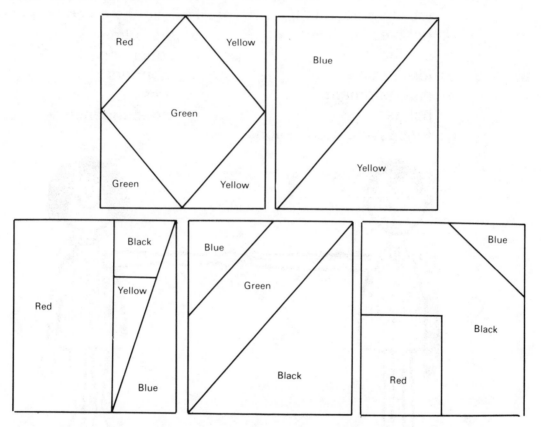

To prepare envelopes, cut the above shapes from the designated colors of construction paper. Make sure they form the five rectangles. Then put all the reds in one envelope, all the blues in another, etc. These five envelopes make up enough for *one* group. If you have five groups, you need 25 envelopes, divided so that each of five groups can complete the puzzle and each of the five people in that group have a different color. (Contributed by Larry Janse, Indianapolis, Indiana)

PERFECT PAIR

For a good discussion on the family, and as a way to discover the values of kids in the group, try this. Simply tell kids that they are to find the world's most perfect couple, that is, the man and woman best suited to create the ideal home and family, and most likely to be happy. Divide into small groups and have them describe their perfect couple. Things to consider:

1. The couple themselves
   a. background
   b. age
   c. education
   d. religious affiliation
   e. race
   f. political views
2. Their lifestyle
   a. jobs (employment)
   b. hobbies
   c. sex life
   d. leisure time
   e. entertainment
   f. habits
   g. friends and associations
3. Their possessions
   a. money
   b. furniture
   c. house and neighborhood
   d. books, magazines
   e. appliances
   f. recreational needs
   g. auto(s)
4. Philosophy on child rearing
   a. discipline
   b. education
   c. manners
   d. dress
   e. independence

The items listed are only suggestions and kids should not be limited to them. After a 20 or 30 minute period of working in their groups, have each describe their perfect couple. Make lists on the blackboard or on an overhead projector. Compare each group's description of their couple. Discuss the differences and similarities and ask *why* certain characteristics were selected. Talk about prejudices and relate to scripture. How does God describe His perfect family? What matters and what doesn't? Also discuss the interaction that took place in each small group. The disputes, differences of opinion, prejudices, etc. You can get hours of healthy discussion out of this exercise. (Contributed by Arthur Mees, Tucson, Arizona)

PERSONAL CHECK LIST

For a night of self examination and serious thought, have your kids go through the check list copy below. Ask them first to check off those things which they feel they really have done without reading any passages of scripture. Then go back over and after reading the passages of scripture, see which one he can check and where he needs improvement. Be careful not to use this to make kids feel inadequate or guilty. Emphasize that God loves us and can still use us in spite of our failures to live in Christian "perfection." You might want to close this meeting with a challenge that as Christians, if society is going to improve and change, it is they who will be doing it as Christ's servants.

_____My relationship to God is my first priority!
(Matt. 13:44-46, 16:24-27, Lk. 9:57-62, 14:25-33)

_____I love others as I love myself.
(Matt. 22:34-40, Lk. 6:27-36, John 14:15-17)

_____I use my talents for God's Kingdom.
(Matt. 25:14-30)

_____I play the role of the servant.
(Matt. 20:20-28, 23:1-12, Mk. 10:13-16, Lk. 14: 7-11, John 13:1-20)

_____I help those in need.
(Matt. 25:31-46, Lk. 10:29-37)

_____I do not give in to lust, even in my mind.
(Matt. 5:3, 27-30)

_____I go the extra mile asked.
(Matt. 5:38-48)

_____I always tell the truth.
(Matt. 5:21-26)

_____I am not angry with my brother.
(Matt. 5:21-26)

_____I do not worry.
(Matt. 6:25-34)

_____I do not seek security in material things.
(Matt. 6:19-21, Lk. 12:13-21)

_____I forgive those who wrong me.
(Matt. 6:7-15, I Cor. 13)

_____I am not judgemental in my attitude toward others.
(Matt. 7:1-5, I Cor. 13)

_____I have complete faith that God will answer my prayers.
(Matt. 7:7-12, Lk. 11:1-13, 18:1-8, John 14:12-14)

_____I am learning to overcome temptation.
(Matt. 18:7-9, John 8:31-38)

_____I give generously of my means.
(Mark 12:41-44)

_____I believe God will redeem His creation through Christ.
(Ephesians, Colossians)

(Contributed by Daniel Unrath, Parkesburg, Pennsylvania

PERSONAL ENCOUNTER

This is a good experience for young people to help them learn more about human relationships. Have everyone sit in two rows of chairs, facing toward each other, positioned in the following manner:

Side A   X X X X X X X X

Side B   X X X X _ X X X X

There should be one empty chair. If there are an even number of participants, then the leader should participate so there will be one chair vacant. After everyone is seated, give the following instructions to the group:

1. When the leader gives the signal, everyone move one chair to the right.
2. After you have moved, you will have one minute to ask the following questions:
   (a) (Person on Side A) "Right now while talking to you, I feel (Finish the sentence)."
   (b) (Person on Side B) "Why?"
   (c) (Person on Side A) "Because . . ."
   (d) (Person on Side B) "What can I do that would improve our relationship as members of the Christian family?"
   (e) (Person on Side A) Responds to above question.

After the group has reached the starting position (their original chairs), meet together for a group discussion period. The following questions can be raised:

1. How did you feel talking to different people?
2. How did you feel talking to an empty chair?
3. Were there certain people you didn't want to talk to? Why?
4. Were there certain people you wanted to talk to but didn't get the chance? (You will notice that because of the way of rotating there will be opportunity to talk to some more than once and others not at all. Youth usually catch this.)
5. Was it hard to express your feeling to certain people?

A common response to this experience is fear on the part of some, to talk with others in the group. This can be channeled into a discussion on the love of God and how it casts away fear. Some appropriate Scriptures would be I John 2:5 and 4:18. (Contributed by Gary Casady, Klamath Falls, Oregon)

PERSONALIZED PASSAGES

A great way to get kids more involved in Bible passages is to "personalize" them. Prepare questions ahead of time, such as the ones below, that each person must answer either by writing them out individually (like a quiz) or by sharing in small groups. The following is a sample from Proverbs, Chapter 10:

1. (10:13) My friends think I'm a good listener because . . .
2. (10:14) I get into trouble when I talk too much about . . .
3. (10:15) One good thing about having lots of money is . . .
4. (10:15) One good thing about having very little money is . . .
5. (10:16) If someone gave me $100.00, I would . . .
6. (10:16) If I had $10.00 to spend at the shopping center, I would . . .
7. (10:19) I feel I have important things to say about . . .
8. (10:20) People don't listen when I . . .
9. (10:23) I think it's *real* fun to . . .
10. (10:23) Something that some people consider fun but I don't, is . . .
11. (10:24) I am afraid of . . .
12. (10:24) My greatest hope is that . . .

By using questions like these, you'll find people responding to verses which might otherwise have held no meaning for them. Base the questions on modern translations for added meaning (those above are from the "Living Bible"). (Contributed by Bob Steir, Loves Park, Illinois)

PICTURE THAT

Hang various pictures on the wall and have each youth pick a picture and think of a one word description for that picture. In turn, have each youth present his word and let the youth guess which picture the word describes. With a good imagination interesting discussions can be generated by asking the youth why they chose their word. (Contributed by James Brown, Rochester, Pennsylvania)

POOR MAN'S HOLY LAND TOUR

You can have a "Poor Man's Holy Land Tour" by taking kids and/or adults on a tour of places within walking or riding distance inside your city. This includes taking them to the tallest building and having a Bible study there about Satan's temptation for Jesus to jump from the high mountain. It also includes a trip to an over-grown old cemetery where we would study about the man from Godara. The options are endless: a city jail, a motel bedroom (David's sin), Jewish Synagogue, mountainside (for Sermon on the Mount), garden (for Garden of Gethsemane), upstairs room in some home (for the last supper), old boiler room (for the story of the Jewish children in the firey furnace), on the roadside (for the story of the good Samaritan or Paul's conversion experience), a lakefront or a wilderness area (depending on where you live). The possibilities are endless and the impression made in the study usually beats most other audio visual techniques combined. (Contributed by Marion D. Aldridge, Columbia, South Carolina)

PRAYER SURVEY

The following survey should be printed up and passed out to the entire group. Each person simply marks an "X" on each line to show their relative position on the issues presented. Encourage kids to be as honest as possible. There are no correct answers in this test. The idea is to see just where you stand on the various questions that come up regarding prayer.

POSITIVE	1 2 3 4 5 6 7 8 9 10	NEGATIVE
I believe beyond a shadow of a doubt that God answers prayer.	— — — — — — — — — —	I believe there is a God but I question whether He is personally interested in man.
I don't always know how God answers prayers but I always have faith He will.	— — — — — — — — — —	I don't see an obvious answer I begin to wonder if God answers at all.
I often praise and thank God as well as petition Him.	— — — — — — — — — —	I treat God like a Santa Claus. Give me this, give me that.

When God says "No" I feel it is for my own good.	— — — — — — — — — —	I can't hardly accept a no answer.
When God answers a prayer my faith is strengthened.	— — — — — — — — — —	"Answered prayer" in book is just a coincidence.
If God says "Wait awhile," I accept His timing without reservation.	— — — — — — — — — —	I prayed once and God never answered, so I don't pray anymore.
I find myself praying all during the day.	— — — — — — — — — —	Days go by and I never pray.
When I don't feel like praying that's when I pray the hardest.	— — — — — — — — — —	If I don't feel like praying then I don't.
I feel as comfortable praying in public as I do alone.	— — — — — — — — — —	I won't pray in public.
I feel my prayer life is really growing.	— — — — — — — — — —	I've almost buried my prayer life.

The survey can be followed up by having all those consistently on the "positive" side of the continuum get together in one group and the "negatives" get into another group. Then have the two groups discuss the following statements as to their validity. One group tries to convince the other, offering examples, personal experience, scripture and other proof.

1. God does answer prayer.
2. God answers prayer in one of three ways. Yes, no, or wait.
3. There are conditions to a yes answer.
4. A mature Christian needs to pray without ceasing.
5. Prayer shouldn't be governed by feelings.
6. The importance of public prayer.

(Contributed by Bob Gleason, Roseburg, Oregon)

PRIORITY AUCTION

Following is a delightful way of enabling a youth group to set priorities in their plans for future programs, without having to first overcome the usual resistence to the work that this task entails. This procedure could also be used for any process of "rank ordering" or "priority setting."'

1. Create some paper "money" for the group to use, or else borrow some from a board game (or print various numerical values on 3 X 5 cards with a check writing machine to make the "money" you want).
2. Distribute the "money" in equal proportions to the group members.

3. Distribute a list of the tasks, programs, or whatever is to be ranked according to priorities to the group members.
4. Explain that the list is like a catalogue issued before an art auction, and that the members are going to bid on each item listed. The members can bid individually or pool their "money" and bid as small groups, but they can spend during the auction only as much money as they have been given. This will mean that each member must rank in his own mind which items are most valuable to him, and bid accordingly.
5 Make sure that each member understands each item listed, and then proceed with the auction, item by item. Make sure to collect the money from the top bidder as each item is sold, and list the selling price. This list, giving relative amounts in dollar value, can then be a means of ranking the items according to the group's sense of priorities.

(Contributed by John Bristow, Seattle, Washington)

PROBLEM LETTER

Most youth leaders who have any rapport at all with kids receive numerous requests for help. These requests are a valuable resource for intragroup, youth to youth ministry. Take such a request, or any of your own choosing and put it in the form of a letter. Ditto it and present it to the youth group for their answers.

If the case is an actual one, then take care to fictionalize it just enough to hide the identity of the person seeking help. You don't want kids playing a guessing game as to who the "mystery person" is. That kind of thing could be disastrous. You should make every effort to protect against revealing the identity of any actual person(s) involved.

After the letter is presented to the group, it can be read aloud and the problems discussed, seeking some answers to resolve the issues presented. One approach might be to break into small groups to work on answers. The leader must take care to insure the answers that arise apply to the problems and also that the group is not just swapping ignorance—not just a lot of head knowledge or advice-giving. The key is the type of questions the leader may ask. For example, "Why do you think that," or "How would Christ respond." Also emphasize the practical by asking, "What things have you found to work in such situations." Be careful to stimulate up-to-date and down-to-earth, meaningful responses.

The following letter is a sample of one used before. You may use it as a guide for writing your own, or you might choose to use this letter as it stands. Of course, such a letter can deal with many other problems than the ones contained in this sample. It should appear to be as ''real'' as possible. That way kids are more serious about helping out with some good advice. You might even want to give some background information on the person the letter is from, again without revealing anything that would tip off kids as to ''who'' it is.

Dear Alvie,

How are you doing? You know I have been having problems at home and I value your opinion more than anyone else's that I know. I know that if I give you a problem to solve or whatever, I know you can take it and look at it objectively. I think that is real good.

Well first of all, my parents tend to put their beliefs, convictions, or whatever on me. Now I realize that they have experienced some things that I haven't and that I never may, but I feel that they are sheltering me too much. For example, no guy is allowed over here if they aren't here at home. This right here insults me and also hurts me (let alone annoys me.) It insults me because it infers they don't have faith in the type of people I choose for friends. Whenever I ask them about it, they always say, ''What will people say,'' or ''What will the neighbors think,'' or else ''We are only trying to protect you from a bad situation.'' Those are exact quotes.

Now, I understand I am their daughter and that they are responsible for me but why do they have to carry it so far? I'd like to know what they are going to do in a year when I have my own apartment and I can do whatever I please (to a certain extent).

People tell me to grin and bear it a year longer but I live right now, not in the future and I don't care to live under such tight circumstances. I'm not saying I don't have freedom because I have some—like I drive the car to school every day, but Dad uses that as a string to get me to do what he wants. It's like a threat every time I don't comply with what he wants.

I guess what I am asking for is advice on how I can think for myself and not have to be protected. One of the latest things that happened was this Sunday. I told them that they didn't have to worry about trusting me, because I didn't ever try to cover up anything from them. I told them that I have smoked and drank and smoked dope. Then they thought I was some sinner and that I needed to become closer to God. They kept me up 'till about twelve preaching at me and telling me how bad and how wrong I was.

First of all, I'll tell you my feeling on smoking, etc. I think smoking cigarettes is bad for a person and it is a habit I hope I never have and, no, I don't smoke. I've tried it and I didn't think it was too cool.

I drink every now and then and I don't feel it is wrong for me. What I think would be wrong is for me to get drunk. That is one thing I just don't dig and I can't see it—having a hangover and everything else that goes along with it.

I guess you could call me a social drinker. I'll have a beer or whatever if I am out with kids but I very seldom do—like maybe one or two times a month. In essence, I feel drinking is fine with moderation. But what about reputation?

Smoking dope is a constant front to me. Kids are always doing it and I say no. I've smoked it more than once but it didn't affect me. It was just like smoking hot air. The last time I did was last summer and I haven't since. I don't know if grass is right or wrong. That is just one thing I can't decide on. I don't really care, because if I want to smoke it I can and if I don't want to, then I won't. I'm not planning on it. It doesn't turn me on—neither does it turn me off.

Alvie, what I wish you would do is give me your views on the three previous things and also give me some advice on how I can get along better with my parents.

You are probably wondering about my Christian life. Well, I know God is there and if I want Him I can get Him. I try to read my Bible in the morning and at night sometimes. I fail because I am tired or hurried. Praying is a struggle for me, because I have not found any effective way to communicate with God and Christ. Sometimes I wonder if I love

God. I know the Bible says, "If you love me, you will keep my commandments," but what are they? I really would like to have a personal relationship with God but I am not sure how and if I did know how, I don't know if I would be willing to put out the effort. Maybe you could advise on this also. I would appreciate it greatly.

Well, I guess the last topic of discussion is Steve. He comes and sees me every Saturday. This weekend he is taking me down to Junction City to meet his parents. I really like him a lot, possibly love more than just a friend. I don't want to end this relationship ever and neither does he. It's a type of agreement between Steve and I. I *someday* want to marry him if things work out the way they have been. Both of us feel the same way about it and we are willing to wait for things to work out the way that is best, which wouldn't be until after we both graduate this year. If you would, please pray that I can be open minded about this and will do what is best from God's point of view.

I hope this letter hasn't been too exhausting. If you could, please answer me promptly. I realize you have other things to do besides answer letters but I would be happy if you could just show this some special thought and consideration. However, I will understand if you can't because you are so busy. Thanks for your time and trouble. Hope to hear from you soon.

Your friend,

Jan

(Contributed by Alvie Robbins, Fairbanks, Alaska)

PUMPKIN CARVING

Next Halloween, have your youth group carve messages in Jack-O-Lanterns, rather than the traditional pumpkin face. A few suggestions: "Peace," "Love," "God is Love," "Smile," etc. (Contributed by Kim Huffman, Converse, Indiana)

QUESTION BOX

Construct a box with a slit in the top that can be used to receive questions that the kids in your group would like answered. Place the box in a conspicuous place in the meeting room and allow kids to drop their questions (on any subject) into the box each week. Allow time each week during the meeting to answer questions that were submitted the week before. This is a very good way to keep your finger on the pulse of the group. (Contributed by Karen Shager, Stephen, Minnesota)

REAL WORLD GAME

The following simulation game can be used effectively prior to a discussion on poverty in the world, selfishness, war, international relations, or any number of relevant subjects. The game requires about an hour and a half and involves a somewhat realistic situation of survival centering around the grain production and needs of various countries. The game involves 7 groups of 6 to 10 persons (it can be adapted to a different number of groups) with each group becoming a country with designated grain production and grain needs per month and also a monthly income.

Materials needed:

a) 15 plus cups grain (unpopped popcorn or whatever can be conveniently measured and handled).

b) 3 rolls of pennies (the income could be changed to dollars so play money could be used).

c) 8 plastic measuring cups with graduations to ⅛th cup. The leader gets a cup and each country gets one cup.

d) 7, 3 x 5 "weather" cards with three of them having instructions (see 3-c on World Situation Fact Sheet).

e) 8 copies of the World Situation Fact Sheet—one for the leader and one for each country.

Procedure:

Most of the instructions are included on the World Situation Fact Sheet. However, the leader needs to keep a few other things in mind:

a) Have all the supplies distributed to each team before the "preparation" period begins in order to save confusion.

b) Make sure all the taking of the monthly consumptions and giving of monthly production and income is fully completed between each monthly time period before another time period is begun.

c) Between each time period collect the "weather" cards and re-shuffle them and have the presidents pick them randomly. This too, should be done before a new time period is begun.

d) It is important that the leader refrain as much as possible from giving additional instructions or answering questions, etc., once the game is in process. This will allow for more initiative by the players in tackling the task without constantly depending on the leader to guide towards a successful conclusion.

If your situation calls for a different number of countries than 7, then you will need to make a new World Situation Fact Sheet. In setting up a different situation, make sure the total production of all the countries is slightly more than the total needed. This will allow (at least theoretically) survival of every country.

INSTRUCTIONS

1. GOAL: Your purpose is to survive as a nation in whatever way you choose: beg (foreign aid), borrow, buy, (or steal!)

2. PREPARATION: You will have 10 minutes in which to study the fact sheet and elect the following officers:

a) President—to lead in deciding his country's policy and to negotiate with other countries that come to him. He MAY NOT

World Situation Fact Sheet				
Country	*Direct Trading Countries	Monthly Grain Production	Monthly Grain Needs	Monthly Gross National Income
Canada	All Countries	2 Cups	½ Cup	3¢
China	Japan, Great Britain, Canada ONLY	2½ Cups	3 Cups	1¢
Great Britain	all but Russia	½ Cup	¾ Cup	3¢
India	all but China	¾ Cup	2 Cups	1¢
Japan	all but Russia	¼ Cup	1 Cup	4¢
Russia	India, Canada, United States ONLY	2½ Cups	1½ Cups	2¢
United States	all but China	2½ Cups	1¼ Cups	5¢

*Trading with countries that you're not allowed to trade with DIRECTLY, MAY be traded with through a neutral country acting as an intermediary. A neutral country is one that can trade directly with the countries that want to negotiate.

leave his own country.

b) Ambassador—to negotiate for his country in other countries. You may elect more than one ambassador if you feel the need.

c) Treasurer—to keep track of and guard the grain and money.

3. METHOD OF PLAY:

a) The game is played in time periods of one month, 6 months total, of 10 minutes each month. Eath month you will receive your monthly income and grain quotas. At the end of each month, you will have taken away from your monthly consumption of grain. Your job is to see that, in the 10 minutes allotted, you have enough grain at the end of the month to equal the consumption that will be taken away.

b) When time is called at the end of each month, all play must stop; and all inter-country communication must cease; and all players must return to their respective countries.

c) At the beginning of each month, except the first, each country's president will draw a weather card; a clear card indicates good weather and no change in grain production; "FLOODS" and "DROUGHT" cards mean your grain production is cut in half that month; "BUMPER CROP" means you have 1 cup extra (large grain producers) or ½ cup extra (small grain producers) that month.

4. STARVATION:

If you haven't enough grain at the end of any monthly time period to meet your needs, your country starves and is out of the game.

(Contributed by W. Clarence Schitt, Bradford, Pennsylvania)

REALIZING OUR NEED FOR GOD

As each person comes into class, have their hands taped together with athletic adhesive tape. Have some activities in which they must use their hands and it is inconvenient for them (arranging chairs for discussion groups, reading scripture, etc.). Read the story of the cripple at the pool of Bethesda in John 5. Tell them that if they can draw a parallel between their situation and the cripple's, they will be set free. Have one person with a tape cutter. The correct answer would be that he was trapped or hindered and needed help outside himself to set him free, as do they. Some will want to know if they can tell others the correct answer. You tell them, "It's up to you."

When everyone is set free, relate a modern day story of someone trapped in a certain situation, possibly drugs, sex, hypocrisy at church, etc. and how they were set free by Jesus Christ.

Draw the analogy now that everyone is bound by something and needs to be set free. There is only one who can set men free (the tape cutter). Christians have the answer that will set men free, but will we share the solution with others? (It's up to you.) (Contributed by Steven E. Robinson, Lubbock, Texas)

RECORD SESSION

Have kids bring their favorite records or tapes. Have equipment ready to go, so that one song can be played for each person. As everyone listens to the song, then try to guess whose favorite it is. After the song, the person then tells why it is his or her favorite. Discussion of the record may follow if it is appropriate. After going through and discussing each record, close with the following meditation experience: Have kids relax and close their eyes . . . then as they listen to one last song they are to fantasize . . . along with the music . . . about the first thing that comes into their minds. A selection with several contrasting musical experiences can really carry a fantasy a long way. When the music ends, everyone shares their fantasy. Be sure that the kids understand the directions. As your record begins, they are to take the first scene that pops into their mind and then let the music set the background as they fantasize about their scene. Their fantasy may develop into a story or the original scene may change or several scenes may shift back and forth. The important thing is to let the fantasy flow with the music. (Contributed by Jim Hudson, North Platte, Nebraska)

RELAY DISCUSSION

Set up two, three, or four chairs (no more) in front of your group. Select a person to sit in each chair and explain that you are going to have a relay discussion. You, as the leader, will read out agree-disagree statements or statements that beg debate or discussion. Only the people in the chairs up front can speak, everyone else listens. Once the statement has been read, the leader can turn the discussion over to those people or he can stimulate and encourage by asking each their opinion. If a person in the front chairs does not want to speak about an issue, he or she may go out into the audience and tap anyone on the shoulder to take his/her place. The chosen person then must go up front and join in the discussion. Also, if any person in the audience has something to say at any time, he or she may run up front and replace any person there. ONLY THE PEOPLE IN THE FRONT CHAIRS CAN SPEAK! Once you see the discussion slowing down, throw out a new statement. Also to stimulate give and take, people can be assigned one point of view or the other, or certain chairs can be labeled "agree" and "disagree." Here are some sample discussion statements:

1. Jesus identified more with the lifestyle of the poor than the rich; therefore, poor people make better Christians.
2. The reason a church runs a youth program is to prove to itself that it is doing something for young people.
3. A Christian should obey his government even if it violates the authority of Scripture.
4. Abortion should be a decision left to the parents or parent of the fetus.
5. Bad language is cultural and is thus not un-Christian.
6. Physical violence can be justified by a Christian if it is in self-defense.
7. It is wrong for a Christian to drink an alcoholic beverage.
8. Christianity is the only religion through which a person can get to heaven.
9. Our parents discipline us because they are trying to do what is best for us.

(Contributed by Dick Davis, Minneapolis, Minnesota)

RESURRECTION NEWS SPECIAL

A fascinating study can be set up in the form of a TV/radio news special, supposedly produced on Easter Sunday. Each member of the group is given the identity of someone involved with the resurrection and asked to read the relevant passages in the Gospel records. They are then interviewed and asked to tell the "listeners"/"viewers" what they know of the disappearance of the body of Jesus during the previous night. People to be interviewed can include: Simon Peter, John, Mary, Thomas, a soldier who guarded the tomb, a Jewish leader, Pontius Pilate Press Secretary, a late news flash from the two on the Emmaus road, etc. (Contributed by David Scott. Riverside, California)

ROLE REVERSAL

This is a good way to help kids solve some of their problems when they are hesitant to talk about them. Have everyone write down their biggest problem on a sheet of paper. Then collect them, redistribute them and have each person assume that the problem on the paper is his. Then each person comes to the front, shares his problem (the one on the paper) and the kids and sponsors try to help him work through the problem by asking questions, suggesting solutions, etc. The person in the group who really has that problem is able to help solve it and gain new insights from others without revealing that the problem is his. (Contributed by Roger Paige, Columbia, Missouri)

SHARE AN ADULT

As part of your weekly program, have an adult share his or her testimony. This is a good way for teenagers to see that adults also have Christian experiences. (Contributed by Paul Cox, Downey, California)

SHOW AND TELL

From time to time, plan a "Show and Tell Time for the Big Kids." Have each person come prepared to "show" or "tell" the group something of their choosing. Anything from a magazine article, a gift, or a poem to an exciting experience or an answered prayer can be shared. (Contributed by Nido Qubein, High Point, North Carolina)

SILENT WORSHIP SERVICE

The creative service below can be a totally different approach to the worship experience. It is completely silent, that is, no one speaks, sings, or makes any verbal utterances during any part of the service. The congregation should be aware ahead of time of what will happen, and how they are to respond. The youth can be in charge of conducting the service and preparing the church for the worship experience.

The following introduction can be printed in the program, passed out to each person on entering.

"Are you afraid of silence? Do you become uneasy when all the talk

stops in a group and people only sit and look away or at each other? Yes, silence can be frustrating in this world of noise and mass media, but it also can be a meaningful time. Silence gives us the chance to digest ideas and analyze feelings. It can be a time of struggle or relaxation.

Our silence today does not approximate deafness, but muteness. Even without anyone speaking, listen to all the other sounds you hear. Have you been aware of all of them? The deaf person cannot even hear these "background" sounds.

This is why we are having a silent service:
1. *There is more to worship than listening to the words of a sermon.*
2. *We should be aware of all sounds.*
3. *Maybe we do not realize the value of speech and singing.*
4. *Maybe we don't realize the value of silence as an equal to sound.*
5. *It's a real chance to talk and listen to God.*
6. *Communication is possible in silence.*

The "Order of Worship" may include the following kinds of things:
1. MEDITATIVE PRAYER WHILE WAITING. (No organ "prelude," etc.)
2. GREETING. (Two or more youth come out, shake hands, wave to congregation, get the congregation involved in shaking hands, also.)
3. CALL TO WORSHIP. (Youth light candles, open Bible, dramatize the coming of the Spirit to the service.)
4. HYMNS. (Congregation is instructed in the bulletin or program to turn to this hymn, read and meditate on its message. Give them plenty of time for this.)
5. MEDITATION ON CURRENT EVENTS. (A slide presentation can be used to show areas of concern for the church in today's world, followed by silent prayer.)
6. THE LORD'S PRAYER. (The words may also be creatively shown on a screen with other slides to illustrate and give added meaning to the prayer.)
7. SCRIPTURE READING. (Provide Bibles. Read silently.)
8. SERMON. (The sermon can take many forms. It can be a printed article that everyone can read. It can be a dramatic presentation done by the youth using only actions, not words. It can be painted signs held up by the youth combined with a slide presentation, etc.)
9. COMMUNION. (The youth can feed each other and motion to the congregation to do likewise with elements provided.)
10. DOXOLOGY. (This can be used at the conclusion to break the silence with everyone singing together acapella.)

(Contributed by Steve Burgener, Cincinnati, Ohio)

SNOWFLAKES

Have everyone cut out a "snowflake" (like they did in the first grade) and write their name on it. Then, using the snowflakes as examples, talk about the unique beauty of everyone in the group. Close this program by having everyone pass the snowflakes around and write an affirming statement or perhaps a Christian wish on them. (Contributed by Dicks McKell, Asheville, North Carolina)

SOME GOOD NEWS AND SOME BAD NEWS

Have the kids cut out all the news in one copy of the local paper and divide it up into good news and bad news. Hang all the good news up in one place and all the bad news in another. Compare the results and discuss. (Contributed by Nido Qubein, High Point, North Carolina)

SPOTLIGHT MEETING

In a darkened room, have kids sitting in a large circle. One person has a "spotlight" (flashlight) that he shines on someone's face. Only the person whom the light is on may speak. The first round is usually word association or some non-threatening kind of game just to get kids loosened up and into the spirit of things. In the second round, the "spotlighter" (usually the youth director or sponsor) can ask each person he shines the light on one question, which they are to answer as honestly as possible. The spotlight draws everyone's attention to t' one person and can be a very effective way for kids to share with each other. Questions can be as deep or shallow as the leader feels he wants to go without embarrassing anyone, but the questions should be designed to allow kids to honestly express themselves and their faith without fear. Allow anyone to "pass" if they are unable to answer the question. (Contributed by Jim Hudson, North Platte, Nebraska)

STRING STORIES

Here's a way to make the stories and parables from the Bible take on a new, fresh meaning and to allow all the members of the group to participate. Form a circle and supply each person with paper, string, and a pen. Have each drop his/her string on to the paper and trace its outline. Now, have each individual draw from his "string design" a creature, person, animal—any living thing. Divide the kids into small groups of three or four, and give them the assignment of utilizing all of their group pictures in portraying a story or parable from the Bible. For variation, have them make up any story, but conclude with a lesson learned from the scriptures. (Contributed by Gary Liddle, Camarillo, California)

SUICIDE ROLE PLAY

The following role play is excellent as a way to make young people aware of the feelings of people contemplating suicide, and to help them develop counseling skills as well.

Select a group of kids from your youth group and divide them in half. One half of the group is to individually research and develop a character who is suicidal. They should do this thoroughly, so that they can answer any question put to them. Each person in this "suicidal" group should have a different motivation for wanting to take his own life, if possible.

The second half of the group is to research various counseling techniques that could be used in dealing with a person considering suicide. When the two groups come together at the meeting, set up some toy telephones, one for each group, and have the two groups send a person in, one at a time. The suicidal person calls the "Help Line," where a counselor is ready to answer. The two carry on a dialogue until either the problem is resolved, or a point is reached where the conversation cannot go any further (no progress is being made). Then have the group discuss and evaluate techniques used in counseling, whether or not such a conversation could have ever taken place, and make suggestions as to approaches they might have taken. (Contributed by Thomas Rietveld, Mundelia, Illinois)

THE THANKFUL LEPER

Use this exercise as a way to point kids toward recognizing the need for expressing thanks to God, rather than constantly bombarding Him with requests. Give each person a mimeographed copy of Luke 17:11-19, the account of Jesus healing the ten lepers. A modern translation of the passage is most effective for the purpose. Another sheet with the following questions and instructions is then handed to each person:

Read the account of Jesus healing the 10 lepers carefully. As you read it, attempt to identify yourself with the feelings of the lepers who did not return to Christ, with the leper who returned to express thanks and with the feelings of Christ in this situation. Then answer the following questions:
1. How do you think Christ felt when only one individual out of ten returned to give thanks?
2. Describe what you think the grateful leper must have felt and thought during his healing encounter with Christ?
3. What excuses can you think of for the nine healed lepers who did not return to give thanks to Christ?

Now attempt to apply this passage of scripture to your life by reacting to the following:
1. With whom in this story do you most identify, the 9 who did not return or the one who came back?
2. What excuses do you usually think of for not thanking Christ for what He has done in your life?
3. What was the last thing Christ did for you or provided for you that you wish to thank Him for?
4. Using the paper and colors provided for you, construct a colorful thank you card addressed to Christ. The outside of the card should express through symbolic colors and expressive symbols, the event or object for which you are thankful. In the inside of the card, write a short letter, poem or prayer that expresses your thankfulness.

After completing this assignment, divide the kids into small groups to share their answers and explain the meanings of the cards they made. Close the meeting with prayer, emphasizing thanksgiving. (Contributed by Ron Carlson, Bloomington, Minnesota)

THIS IS YOUR LIFE

A good way to get to know members in your group is to have a THIS IS YOUR LIFE program each time you get together. Have an adult be prepared each week to give the life history of one teenager. Parents, friends or past teachers can be brought in to share during the presentation . . . leave any pictures used during the program on a bulletin board for one week. (Contributed by Paul Cox, Downey, Calif.)

TIME MACHINE

The following story and exercise can be used most effectively with kids to help them to determine the worth of man and his values. It also forces a group to work something out together and come to a group decision. To begin, tell the following story:

"There is about to be a nuclear holocaust. The human race as we know it will be totally wiped out. However, ten people have discovered a way to survive by getting into a time machine, which will take them into the future and they may at that time start the human race all over again. The ten people are:
1. An accountant
2. His pregnant wife
3. A liberal arts coed
4. A pro-basketball player
5. An intelligent female movie star
6. A black medical student
7. A famous novelist
8. A bio-chemist
9. A 70 year old clergyman
10. An armed policeman

Unfortunately, at the last minute, it is discovered that the machine will only take six people instead of the original ten. Your job, as a group, is to decide which six will be saved and which four must die. You have 30 minutes in which to decide."

Have the kids work this out in small groups of four or five, then at the end of the time period, share their conclusions with the entire group. Have the kids disregard the technicalities of the story, but to concentrate on the process of arriving at a decision based on the facts given. After each group shares its selections, ask questions for further discussion, like: How did your group get along during the process of making a decision? Did you listen to each other or were you so stubborn that no progress was made? Do you feel that no one would listen to you? Did you feel that you had the right answers? Are there in fact any right answers? What do your selections teach you about your values? (Contributed by Daniel Unrath, Parkesburg, Pennsylvania)
Editor's note: Similar exercises can be found in the book Values Clarification *by Sidney Simon, published by Hart Publishing, New York.*

TO SHARE OR NOT TO SHARE

This simple idea is great with Junior Highs. Place a stack of pennies (100 to 200, depending on the size of the group) on a table. Tell the kids that they can come by the table and take all the pennies they want . . . to keep. Have them line up and take turns taking the pennies. After all the kids have had a chance or as soon as all the pennies are gone, discuss what happened and why it happened. (Contributed by Jim Hudson, North Platte, Nebraska)

TWO-DIMENSIONAL PRAYER

Most prayer is somewhat one-sided, that is, we do all the talking. We rarely listen to what God has to say to us. In an effort to do something about this in a symbolic way, one youth group composed a "dialogue with God" at a retreat by asking God questions they wanted some answers to. They then wrote what they thought God's "answers" might be based on scripture and their understanding of the nature of God. The finished product, printed below, was then presented to the church in a contemporary worship service. Each young person would step forward and "pray" one question, which was then "answered" by a tape recording of the responses, recorded with much echo and played back to have a mysterious, awesome quality. Perhaps your group can compose a similar "prayer" as a worship experience:

"A DIALOGUE WITH GOD"

God, are You really there? I need to talk to Someone who knows the truth about life and can give me some real answers.

I AM HERE AND I AM THE ANSWER TO ALL QUESTIONS. THE WORDS YOU HEAR COME FROM YOUR OWN HEART. I SPEAK NOT WORDS BUT THE WORD.

Where are You, God? Are You in Heaven or everywhere? Am I talking to You "long distance" or are You right here?

I AM WHERE YOU ARE AND THERE IS NO PLACE THAT I AM NOT. THERE IS NO DISTANCE! I AM BESIDE YOU, ABOVE YOU, AROUND YOU AND WITHIN YOU.

Do You always hear us when we pray? Or is this time a special deal?

I HEAR ALL YOU SAY OR THINK OR DREAM OR IMAGINE AND I CARE.

While I'm hearing You in words, there are lots of things I've always wondered about. Would You tell me what I want to know?

I AM WHAT YOU WANT TO KNOW. ASK AND LISTEN AND HEAR!

God, why did You make man, anyway?

I MADE YOU FOR MYSELF AND FOR YOURSELF. YOU WERE MADE TO BELONG TO ME. APART FROM ME, YOU HAVE NO MEANING, LIKE A SHIP WITHOUT A SEA.

Were we created by evolution, from cells in the ocean or did You make us from the dust of the earth, personally, like Genesis says?

YOU, AND THE DUST, AND THE SEA, I MAKE FROM NOTH-ING AND THEY STILL ARE NOTHING, APART FROM ME. ALL THINGS YOU KNOW ARE BUT AN ECHO OF MY WORD.

Now, God, I don't understand that; Just answer simply; How did You create me?

I CREATE YOU ETERNALLY, ABOVE AND BEYOND ALL YOU KNOW OF SPACE AND TIME. ON EARTH, YOU ARE NOT YET CREATED. I AM STILL BUILDING WHAT YOU SHALL BE.

Lord, will there ever be peace on earth? When will it be?

THE WORLD CAN NEVER BE AT PEACE. I MADE THE EARTH FOR CHANGE AND UNREST AND TRIAL.

You mean that there's no cure for the world's problems and troubles?

FEAR NOT: TIMES CURES MOST PROBLEMS AND ETER-NITY CURES THEM ALL!

Why do You let men sin? Why don't You make men live as You planned?

SIN IS PART OF MY PLAN. TO CHOOSE ME FREELY, A MAN MUST BE ABLE TO CHOOSE AGAINST ME.

Is the Church doing what You want it to?

ALL THINGS DO MY WILL. THE CHURCH IS THOSE WHO SERVE ME BECAUSE THEY KNOW ME AND LOVE ME. THE REST OF THE WORLD SERVES ME IN SPITE OF THEMSELVES.

Do people really still respond to Your call today, like in Bible times?

I AM IRRESISTIBLE. ALL MEN OBEY MY COMMANDS. SOME MEN ALSO CHOOSE TO OBEY MY LOVE.

God, what does it mean—to love?

I AM ONENESS. I AM LOVE. TO LOVE IS TO BECOME A PART OF ME.

So there really are some true Christians in the world today?

THERE ARE MANY IN THIS PLACE WHO LOVE ME MORE THAN LIFE AND WHO SHALL GIVE ME THEIR LIVES WHEN I ASK.

Is the Judgment Day near?

JUDGMENT DAY IS ALWAYS NEAR: IT IS TODAY!

So be it, then, Lord; We'll be seeing You! God be with us!

I AM . . . (echoing off into the distance.)

(Contributed by Bruce Brigden, Wellington, Kansas)

UPPER ROOM COMMUNION

To add an extra dimension to a youth communion service, use an upstairs room (if you have one available), with a long table and chairs arrangement similar to the upper room description in the

New Testament. There should be thirteen chairs (one left vacant to symbolize Christ's presence in the room). Kids should be brought in 12 at a time, to pass the common cup and loaf of bread. Use candlelight and allow time for individual prayer and meditation. (Contributed by Joe Conarroe, Indianapolis, Indiana)

VALUES IN THE CHURCH

The following exercise will help young people (or adults) to set priorities concerning certain values that they have and also to see the inconsistencies that often exist within the church community, regarding priorities and values. Print up a twelve-square page, such as the one below and give one to each person. Each square on the page should contain a state of concern. Have each person cut the twelve squares apart so that they have twelve individual concerns on separate slips of paper. Then follow the steps :

A Raising Money and Spending it.	B Developing the music program of the church.	C Getting workers to fill all the jobs in the church.
D Spiritual Growth of church members enabling them to become mature disciples of Christ.	E Winning local people to Christ.	F Building and maintaining larger and more attractive church buildings.
G Maintaining or building church attendance.	H Helping to relieve starvation and suffering in the famine-stricken areas of the world.	I Foreign Missionary Work.
J Helping to relieve poverty and / or racial prejudice in the local community.	K Keeping the existing weekly programs of the church going.	L Developing a sense of fellowship, love, and mutual concern.

1. Rank them in order of their importance. Put the most urgent or necessary item on top and the least urgent on the bottom. Now, make a list on another sheet from 1 to 12, showing the order that you decided on. Put the *letter* of the most important item next to the number 1 and so on through number 12.

2. Now, rank them again, only this time according to the amount of attention they receive in your local church. Put the one receiving the most attention on top, the one receiving the least attention on the bottom. List their letter sequence along side the first list.

3. Now, compare the two lists. How are they different from each other and why are they different? Should they be the same? What changes need to be made and on which list? Discuss these and other questions you may have with the entire group.

(Contributed by Bob Gleason, Roseburg, Oregon)

WALLS

This experience has been designed to illustrate how ''walls'' are often erected between man and God and between members of the Body of Christ. It is best with smaller groups (25 or so) but can be adapted for larger ones. It is described here for use in a typical church sanctuary, but it can be done in any room with theater-style seating and a middle aisle.

The auditorium should be prepared with a butcher-paper ''wall'' running down the middle of the center aisle. Perhaps the simplest way to do this is to string some cord from the front (the pulpit, if in a church) to another object (like a coat rack) towards the back of the aisle. Then drape two long sheets of butcher paper, which have been taped together at the top, over the line. The result should be a sort of paper volleyball net that is at least six feet high and as long as half the number of rows as you have participants. Thus, if you have twenty people, the wall needs to run the length of the front ten rows of seats. In the songbook racks, (if you have them) closest to the center aisle, hide a pair of labeled scissors in each. Write on each label a different Christian attribute such as the ''fruits of the Spirit'' in Galatians 5 or the characteristics of love from I Corinthians 13. Then, in the foyer (or at the entry to the building you are meeting in) place chairs for everyone, spacing them as far apart as possible. On the door to the auditorium tape a large piece of butcher paper. Now you are ready to begin.

Have the participants sit in the chairs provided and then explain that the foyer (or the area outside the auditorium where they are seated) represents the world with its cold alienation. (This could be even more graphic if they are seated outside in cold weather.) The paper on the door leading into the auditorium represents the wall between the sinful world and God. Have a discussion on what kind of ''bricks'' a wall like that is made of. Write their answers on the paper with a large felt pen. If no one volunteers it, lead them to finally say that all these add up to one thing: sin. Then ask them how the wall can be removed. The answer should eventually be given as the "Cross of Christ," "the blood of Christ," etc. Draw a large red cross on the paper and then pull the wall down and discard it. Now you are ready to take the group inside.

Before opening the door say something like this, "But before we enter in to the presence of God, I must ask if you REALLY want to. The only way you can enter is to admit your own spiritual bankruptcy, die to self and trust only in Christ to bring you in . . . So . . . count the cost, then when you are ready, come in."

Have them enter one at a time (some will probably hesitate for some time; if possible a helper might be prepared to stay back with them in case they need to talk about it) alternating sides of the paper wall they go on. Have each one sit on the end of a pew alone so that when everyone is in you have people paired off on opposite sides of the wall.

At this point, if your line is tied to the pulpit, walk up there and give the following explanation: "From where I am, I can see all of you but you can't see each other. Now the view from up here is kind of like God's but the view from down there is what it's still like between a lot of brothers and sisters. Now maybe that's you; if so, tell us about it. What are the bricks of YOUR wall made of?" Have each one think of one thing, fear, pride, whatever, that is part of his wall. Beginning with the two people on the front pews, give them markers and have each write down what his brick is and tell the rest about it, then pass the marker back, again, alternating sides. When they've done this, say something like "Now that wall doesn't have to stay there, but some of us feel more secure walled in . . . some church people are content to just sit in their pew and wait for someone else to reach out first. But if you really want that wall down, God's got a gift for you in— of all places—that song book rack in front of you! See if you can find it."

After everyone has discovered the scissors, start at the front again asking each one to tell why his particular pair (trust, patience, etc.) is important in the task of tearing down the wall. "How can THAT help?" Then, before you call on them to destroy the wall with their scissors, point out that it can go down only by God's power—the fruit of the Spirit—but at the same time, we have to co-operate.

Then allow them to attack the wall with all the joyous abandon they deserve to express after all that. But when they're through, close with remarks something like these: "Now . . . there's one more wall to tear down, but we can't illustrate it so easily. You see, it's the wall inside you—between you and the real you—between where you are now and where Jesus is calling you to be. And, after all, aren't all the walls really inside? God wants that wall—all the walls DOWN. He wants you to know peace, with Him, with your brothers and sisters, and even with yourself." Here you may wish to encourage everyone to inwardly make that commitment; you may even afford them the opportunity to do so publicly, especially if there are some non-Christians there. In any case, a song would be a most appropriate ending. (Contributed by Larry Hall, Glendale, California)

WISHING WELL

With the youth group seated in a circle, give each person two or three pennies. In the center, place a tub of water, which becomes your "wishing well." Various puns can then be employed, such as, "You can put in your two cents worth," or, "A penny for your thoughts," etc. One group used this during a lesson on "Spiritual Dryness." Then, any person in the group who wants to speak, sharing some concern, a wish, something they are thankful for, a special blessing, etc., throws a penny into the well and speaks. Note: Have your "well" small enough so that it will take a little aim to sink the penny. This adds a little comic relief when some kids miss. Most kids will enjoy the experience and improvise as they go along, sharing pennies, pretending to throw a penny and making a "ker-plunk" sound, throwing nickels for "longer thoughts," etc. Pennies can then be saved and used again or given away or whatever the kids decide. (Contributed by Gregg Selander, Whittier, California)

WITH-IT

Make cards for each person present. On one side of the card write "With-It." On the other side of the card, write "Cop-Out." After cards are distributed, each person writes two questions on separate sheets of paper. Questions are put into a basket or not if you prefer. Then one person draws out a question and answers it. Then depending on the answer, everyone votes with their card whether the answer was "with-it" or a "cop-out." If there is disagreement, discussion follows. The person can change his answer or kids can change their votes. Scores can be kept by giving plus one and minus one for each "cop-out." After the final vote, proceed to the next kid, who draws out another question, etc. Questions can be as informational or as personal as the group wants. After the first rounds, kids make up two more questions . . . then two, until they are ready for the game to end. Discussion can follow the game. (Contributed by Jim Hudson, North Platte, Nebraska)

YOUTH-LED FAMILY NIGHT

The aim of this event is to utilize youth leadership and talent for a family get-together at the church, emphasizing family life in the home and in the family of Christ. With the instructions in Exodus 37:1-9 (The Living Bible has modern dimensions), the group assigns various tasks required to construct an actual size replica of the "Ark of the Covenant," using plywood, jig-sawed cherubim, ring-type drawer pulls to hold the handles as rings, and all painted gold.

At the family night event an informal drama is improvised (better than written and memorized) by the kids themselves to depict a family altar or family worship time. Families enjoy their kids "acting out" what a Christian home can be like. For balance, the drama can include an exasperating marital experience that could actually stretch the unity of the marriage and home, letting "Act Two" be the family experience of worship in which healing is begun. Capsule cures for family problems should be avoided.

Preferably one of the youth, but possibly the pastor, explains the significance of the Ark on display. Application is made to the practical way in which God's presence is to be understood in a Christian home and church today. The drama points to the experience side. (Contributed by Sid Macaulay, Decatur, Georgia)

Chapter Four

Special Events

ADVENT TREASURE HUNT

This is a treasure hunt in which the goal is to find a sentence having to do with Advent. For example, the mystery sentence might be "The lion will lie down with the lamb." Any sentence will do. The clues are hidden in local merchants' shops. Since there are eight words in the sentence, eight stores are used. At each store, a new word in the sentence plus a new clue is found. There can be a different set of stores per team, though the sentence is the same for all. The clues and the sentence should be difficult enough to cause considerable brain-work. For example, the clue for the post office might be "Help stamp out hard clues." A clue for the plant store might be "This game will grow on you." When the kids find the right store, the teams find a card which the obliging merchant places in a plain-sight position. The word in the sentence and the next clue are on the card. The first team to finish completing the sentence by obtaining all eight words and arranging them in the correct order is the winner, and they phone in to "hunt headquarters" and their time is recorded. The phone number to call can be on the last card (eliminating "cheating" by guessing the sentence).

This can be used anytime of the year, obviously, by simply changing the content of the sentence. It should be done during the day (so that stores will be open) and can be done on bikes or in a shopping mall. The benefits are many: cooperation and contact with the merchants, free advertising for them, the teamwork, the thoughts on Advent, plus a lot of fun. (Contributed by Father David Baumann, Garden Grove, California)

BANANA NIGHT

Here's a party idea that will cause your group to really "go bananas." The theme is bananas and many events can be planned using the popular yellow fruit:

1. *Banana Stories:* Give a prize for the best story or poem about bananas.

2. *Banana Costumes:* Give a prize for the best banana costume. Have everyone wear yellow and suggest that the kids make good use of those little stickers that come on bunches of bananas.

3. *Banana Prizes:* Award banana splits, "Bic Bananas" (the ballpoint pen), etc.

4. *Banana Relay:* A wild team game (see *Ideas Number Six*).

5. *Un-Banana:* A great crowd breaker from *Ideas Number One.*

6. *Banana Race:* Each team gets a bunch of bananas with the same number of bananas in each. Teams line up with their bananas about 50 feet away. Each team member then runs to their team's bananas and eats one, returns, tags the next player and so on. The team that finishes first wins.

7. *Banana Games:* Many other games can be played substituting a banana for a ball, baton, etc.

(Contributed by Harl Pike, Show Low, Arizona)

BICYCLE PEDDLEMONIUM DAY

This is a fun event that can involve the entire youth department in an exciting day full of bike activities. Divide the action into three separate parts: (1) A Bicycle Olympics (2) A Bike Road Rally and (3) A Bike Tour. Begin around noon on a Saturday (or a Holiday) and run all the activities during the afternoon.

The Bicycle Olympics:

Divide the group into four competing groups if you have junior high through college age involved: (a) Junior high boys (b) Junior high girls (c) Senior high and college boys (d) Senior high and college girls. Points and prizes can be awarded the winners in each division. Some sample events:

1. *100 Yard Dash:* A race for time. Use a stopwatch.
2. *20 Lap Endurance Race:* Should be about five miles on a regular quarter-mile track. Award points to first through fifth places.
3. *Backward Race:* Should be optional. Kids ride with their backs to the front tire.
4. *Figure Eight Race:* Set up a figure eight track and contestants ride it, one at a time, for best clocked time.
5. *Obstacle Race:* Set up a track with obstacles, mud, trees, or whatever, to make riding difficult.
6. *Bike Jousting:* Bike riders ride toward each other in parallel lanes. Each rider gets a water balloon. The object is to ride by your opponent and hit him with the balloon, without getting hit yourself. Winners advance.

Bike Road Rally:

This is a simple "treasure hunt" event in which teams of three to four bike riders must follow clues to reach a final destination. By arranging for the teams to go different routes, yet ending up at the same place, they won't be able to follow each other. The first team to finish the course is declared the winner. This should take about an hour.

Bike Tour:

Last on the activity list is a bike ride to a not-too-distant park or beach for a hamburger or hot-dog feed. (Contributed by Ken Etley, Fort Worth, Texas)

BICYCLE RODEO

Here is another collection of bike games which can be included in an all day bicycle outing for your youth group:

1. *Calf-Roping:* Have one kid stand in the center of an open area

and each contestant tries to "rope the calf" as he rides by on a bicycle. After a rider successfully "lassos" the person in the middle, he should immediately drop the rope to avoid injury to himself or the "calf." The calf may duck, but he must keep his hands at his side and stay on his feet. Fastest time wins.

2. *Bull Dogging:* This is rough. Have some big guys play the bulls. (Have them use football gear if they have it). The cowboys and bulls line up about 10 feet apart. When the whistle blows, the bull runs straight out. The cowboy goes after him. Cowboy jumps from bike and tries to bring the bull down. The bull tries to keep going on his feet as long as he can. Use old bikes, as they could possibly be damaged. This game should not be played on pavement or hard ground. Fastest time wins.

3. *The 100-Yard Crawl:* Bikes must travel in a straight line to a finish line 100 yards away. The idea is to go as *slow* as possible. If a rider touches a foot or any part of his body to the ground (trying to maintain his balance) or goes off course, he is disqualified. The last person to finish wins.

4. *Bike Cross Country:* This is an obstacle course race that can include anything you want. The rougher the better. From a starting point, bikes compete for time. On the trail have a "long jump" (4 inch log that the bike must jump over). "Tight rope" (a 2x6, 12 ft. long about 6 inches off the ground). A "Limbo Branch" (low tree branch or board about 10 inches above the handle bars). "Tire Weave" (8 or 10 old tires set up in a row about 6 ft. apart). The one to complete the course in the fastest time wins. You can make penalties for those who mess up on some of the obstacles.

5. *100 Yard Sprint:* This is a regular 100 yard dash from a standstill with bikes.

6. *Bike Pack:* See how many can fit on a bike and still go 10 feet.

7. *Bicycle Demolition:* Have all bike riders form a large circle. Need

about 100 feet diameter. They may each have all the water balloons they can carry. (Stuffed in shirts, pockets, etc.). When the whistle blows, they all interweave in the circle and let each other have it!
(Contributed by Roger Disque, Chicago, Illinois)

BIKE SIT

Since many people don't like to ride their bikes (only sit on them), this activity is designed to enable even the sitters to have fun. Most areas of the country have an extended downgrade of road. Simply truck all the bikes to the top of this downgrade and let them sit on their bikes all the way to the bottom. Some downgrades last for twenty miles! There can be variations too: for those select boys who have a lot of energy, let them try to ride up the downgrade; or see who can coast the furthest without peddling. (Contributed by Tim Doty, Tigard, Oregon)

CARHOP FRY OUT

As a fund raiser and special event, have the youth group grill hamburgers, hot dogs, etc., in the parking lot and invite the community to come and eat. The kids serve as "carhops" and wait on people in their cars, taking their orders and bringing the food. Desserts, drinks and other items should be on the "menu" as well. (Contributed by Roger Voskuil, Brandon, Wisconsin)

COBBLER GOBBLER

This is a baking contest combined with a scavenger hunt. Divide the group into teams of five, with boys and girls on each team. Each team is given a list of ingredients that they must find (such as sugar, flour, fruit, etc.) When the team collects all it's ingredients, it reports back to the church (or wherever you have the use of large ovens) and a recipe for fruit cobbler is given to the team. Each team gets the same recipe, except maybe for different fruit in each. After the cobbler is prepared, it goes into the oven. (While the cobbler is cooking, table games can be played by the team members.) After all the cobblers are done, have judges taste each one and award points for the best tasting, first finished, neatest job, etc. The team with the best score gets ice-cream to eat with their cobbler. Everybody else gets whipped cream. (Contributed by Roger Disque, Chicago, Illinois)

COLUMBO SLEUTH NIGHT

This is a type of "treasure hunt" named after the T.V. detective series, "Columbo," starring Peter Falk. By naming an event such as this after a popular show, it adds a great deal to the fun. (Kids can come dressed up Falk-style, with wrinkled raincoats, messed up hair, etc.) You may, of course, call this event anything you want. The rules are the same, however, no matter who the game is named after.

Each team (or carload) of kids gets an instruction sheet which includes a "briefing," the clues, and the rules. The first team to fill in all the blanks (correctly) is the winner. The clues below were used by one youth group, and they are shown here to give you an idea of how to design your own. You will need to come up with clues (and answers to the clues) that fit your own particular situation.

The Briefing:

"Lt. Columbo, a hideous crime has been committed right here in our city under our very noses. I called you in because I know that you are the only person who could solve such a complex and baffling case. You see, Columbo, in this case, not only do we not know who the murderer is, but we don't know the weapon, the place, the time, the day, the accomplice, the get-away method, or even the identity of the victim! In fact, all we have is this senseless batch of clues which nobody can decipher. I'm counting on you to solve this case as quickly as possible. And, by the way, Columbo, could you comb your hair once in a while, while you're working on this case???"

The Clues:

The Dane with this name was known to brood.
The place with this name serves burgers for food.
Leave off the first word and write down the name
Of the culprit we know whom Shakespeare brought fame.

The murderer *Hamlet (Hamburger Hamlet, a restaurant)*

A giant eye will greet you there
Upon a wall beyond compare.
Above the eye, a yellow ad
Bears the name the victim had.

The victim *Alice (Alice's Restaurant)*

There is a store that bears the name
Of a man of great wealth and fame.
Three paces from its door you'll see
The murder weapons surrounding a tree.

Murder Weapon *Bricks (at Hughes Stationers)*

Where Indian food is next to Chinese,
There is a place that's sure to please.
For it is right across the street,

Where our poor victim met defeat.

Place of Murder *Foyer de France*

Now you need to go real high
To a steak house with health club nearby.
The first hour on Sunday you get fed,
Is when the victim was made dead.

Time of Murder *5:00 (Opening time for the steak house)*

The name of our church you'll find on this store
Full of bright-colored objects which Mom Nature bore.
The address upon it tells the month, day, and year,
When blood on our victim began to appear.

Date of Murder *10-9-32 (Florist shop address)*

On a chromium sign is written the name
Of the beast that you need to help bring you fame.
He's close to some pants, some jewels, and a bank.
For helping with murder, he'll be thrown in the tank.

Accomplice *Hungry Tiger (Restaurant)*

This place never closes, no matter the hour.
On a corner of Wilshire you'll find its sign tower.
The name on the sign is all you need know,
Of the way the murderer decided to go.

Get-Away Method *Ships (Restaurant)*

The Rules:

Solve the clues in any order, go to the location and fill in the corresponding blank. When you have solved all eight parts, return to the designated starting place as quickly as possible. If you are not finished by 8:15, go there anyway, because the game is over. Good Luck and may you "always get your man!"

(Contributed by Jim Berkley, Los Angeles, Calif.)

CRAZY BUS

Divide your busload of kids into teams of no more than ten (boys and girls). Each team should select a captain who is in charge of organizing the team. Everyone rides on the same bus. Prepare a list of activities that each team is going to accomplish. Do not give out the list in advance. Drive to the desired location and then announce what must be done. Points are totaled after each activity.

SOME SUGGESTED ACTIVITIES:
1. BOY DRESS—Go into a neighborhood in your city. Each team is assigned a particular street (or part of a street). Each team will dress

a boy as a girl by obtaining different items from homes on their street. Only one item can be received from any one home. The boy best dressed as a girl gains 10 points for his team. The boy then has to wear the costume for the remainder of the evening.

2. BOWLING—Prearrange to use a bowling alley for a short time. Allow each member of the team to bowl one frame. The team having the highest number of pins wins 10 points for the team.

3. EATING CONTEST—Go to a nearby McDonalds. Each team selects a good eater. Buy for each representative of the team two Big Macs, a large order of fries, a chocolate malt and an apple turnover. The one finishing first gains 10 points for his team.

4. FOLLOW THE LEADER—Go to a nearby park. Each team is timed over a course through a kiddie play area (down slide, over sandbox, across monkey bars, etc.) Winning team gets 10 points. (Contributed by Paul Cox, Downey, Calif.)

CRAZY CREATIVE SCAVENGER HUNT

Here's a fun variation of the old scavenger hunt. Give each team a list of crazy names (such as the following sample list) and the kids have to go out and collect items that they think *best fits* the names on the list. For example:

1. A P B J
2. Zipper zapping shoestring fuse
3. Idaho
4. Tweed
5. Snail Egg
6. Chicken Lips
7. Will be
8. Pine Needle Bushing Brush
9. Snipe
10. Piano Key Mustache Waxer
11. G-Branded Breast Boxers
12. Yellow Grot Grabber
13. Portable Electric Door Knob Kneeler
14. Thumb Twiddly Dummer
15. Thingamabob
16. An Inflatable Deflater
17. Galvanized Goul Gooser

A panel of judges can determine the winners based on each team's explanation of how their "items" fit the various descriptions on the list. (Contributed by Cathy Crone, Newport Beach, California)

DESTINATION UNKNOWN

Have kids meet at the church or some other location on Sunday morning around 6:30 a.m. to leave for a day of activities which are known only by the youth sponsors. It will include church as usual, but the other events make the day very different from the normal Sunday experience. A bus or car caravan can be used for transportation. Here is a sample schedule for a day such as this:

6:30 a.m. Meet
6:45   Go to nearby park
7:15   Breakfast in park (prepared ahead of time by sponsors)
7:50   Leave park
8:00   Bowling (You can get it cheap at this hour.)
9:30   Sunday School and morning worship at church.
12:30 p.m. Leave church
1:30   Lunch at restaurant
2:30   Go to amusement park, beach, zoo, etc.
5:30   Head for home or church for evening service

(Contributed by Jim Landrum, Anaheim, California)

FOOT PARTY

This is an evening of fun built around the "foot." The group is divided into teams, and the following games can be played:

1. Each group is given newsprint and paper plates with poster paint, and then must paint a mural using their bare feet only on the paper. Best job wins.
2. Each group selects the biggest, smallest, and most unusual (or ugliest) foot in the group and prizes are awarded for the winners in each category. Special "toe-rings" can be made to designate the winning feet.
3. Each team can make up a song about feet and perform it for the whole group.

4. Other "foot games" from earlier volumes of IDEAS can be played, such as "Foot Painting," "Foot Signing," "Foot Wrestling," "Marble Fish" and "Lemon Pass" (All in IDEAS NUMBER ONE). There are quite a few others throughout the IDEAS series.

At the end of the evening, serve hot dogs, and award cans of "Foot Guard" to the winning team. (Contributed by Richard Boyd, New Orleans, Lousiana)

FUN FAIR

This activity is good for a whole night's fun and involves creativity, skill and competition. Everybody coming to the evening is told to bring various items such as hammers, nails, string, paper, buckets, etc. They are not told what they are going to do with them. Each person must also bring $.50. As players arrive, they exchange their $.50 for fifty pennies. They are then told to group themselves in teams of two to four people. They are then told that they have one hour in which to think up and build a games booth for their team.

Various items such as balloons, paper, tacks, etc. can be provided for and the participants are allowed to return home for any needed items. At the end of the hour, the Fun Fair is opened and everybody is free (except the ones left minding the booth) to go round and try the other booths, using up your fifty pennies. Any team is not allowed to try their own booth. The winning team is the one, who after, say an hour and a half, has gained the most money. Examples of booths are a simple penny toss into an ash tray, a dart throwing at a water balloon, a horror house, a water balloon tossed at an individual, a ball in the bucket, a penny shove, a jail (where you pay one cent to have a friend captured and held in jail for one minute), and even a kissing booth! At one city, this consisted of a series of tables covered with blankets, with an entrance at one end and a voluptuous kisser at the other. Unsuspecting souls paid their money and climbed underneath the tables to find that it was their fate to be kissed by the minister's Labrador Retriever! (Contributed by Brett Cane, Montreal, Quebec, Canada)

THE GREAT RACE

Carloads of kids (the same number in each car), leave at the same time, with a list of tasks that they must perform. The first team to finish the entire list and return wins the race. Create a list based on your local area and the possibilities it provides. A sample list:
1. Go to the Union Bank Building. Park on the fourth level of their parking lot (if full, wait until a space is available). Everyone go in the bank. One at a time, each member of your team

must ride the elevator from the first floor to the 21st floor and back down again.

2. Next, go to Central Park. Everyone take the free tour of the science museum, which is every half hour. The tour lasts 15 minutes. If you just miss it, wait until the next one.

3. Go to Mayor Smith's home at 4352 Birch Street. Every one sing any Christmas carol you wish, standing on his front porch.

4. Go to Highway 41. Use the trash bag provided and fill it full of litter from along the highway. Do not take cans from any litter cans along the highway and do not pick up rocks, leaves, etc. Only paper, cans, bottles and other trash.

You can make up other tasks, set a time limit, etc. A sponsor should ride with each group to protect against cheating. The group that finishes most of the tasks in the time limit wins or the first to finish them all wins.

GUINNESS GAMES

Here's a great idea that can become an annual event for your youth group. Have a day of contests in which kids may try to set a "world's record" a la *The Guinness Book of World Records*. However, kids do not compete against the Guinness book, but against themselves. The first year, "records" are set and the following year kids try to break them with new records established which last for another year. Here are a few sample contests:

Eating Contests (Amount of food eaten within time limit)
1. Hamburgers
2. Tacos
3. Sloppy Joes
4. Marshmallows
5. Lemon Wedges
6. Onions
7. Bananas

Endurance Contests (Time)
1. Standing on your head
2. Running in place
3. Talking
4. Stare down
5. Pogo Stick jumping
6. Dribbling a basketball
7. Keeping eyes open without blinking

Skill Contests
1. Free throw shooting (percentage of shots)
2. Frisbee throwing (distance)

3. Marshmallow throwing (distance)
4. Burping (number in succession)
5. Bubble blowing (number in succession)
6. Various games (highest score)

Other Contests
1. Volkswagen Stuff (number of kids inside)
2. Hula Hoop Pack
3. Marshmallows stuffed in mouth (number)

There should be a separate boys and girls category in the athletic contests. Kids can pay an "entry" fee, and sign up for whichever events they would like to try. "Trophies" can be presented to the new record holders. (Contributed by Robert Brown, Benton Harbor, Michigan)

HALLOWEEN SCAVENGER HUNT

If you can locate an old-out-of-the-way (deserted) cemetary, here's a spooky Halloween Party idea. Get permission from the cemetary custodians or director to have a "scavenger hunt." Make a list of names found on tombstones and have the kids try to locate them and write in the dates found on the tombstone on the list. The most complete list of names and dates wins. Do it at night, and provide flashlights. Be sure and let the police and neighbors know what's going on. (Contributed by Tom Galovich, Chico, California)

HILLBILLY NIGHT

Have a "Hillbilly Night with the Hills Brothers." Select four guys (sponsors) to be the Hills Brothers: "Mole" Hill, "Boot" Hill, "Aunt" Hill, and "Bunker" Hill. They should dress up hillbilly style and they can be creatively introduced to the crowd. Then divide up into four teams for competition in various games from the IDEAS series. Team names: The Mole Hills, Boot Hills, Aunt Hills, and Bunker Hills, with each corresponding sponsor leading his team. (Contributed by Gary Tangeman, Santa Ana, California)

JELLO RIOT

Have an evening of "Jello" games such as the ones listed below. With a little imagination, you should be able to create many more.

Jello Ad Relay: Get hold of several newspapers that are all the same issue, and preferably one with plenty of grocery store advertising in it. (Usually one night a week the local papers feature lots of big food ads.) Go through the paper ahead of time and try to find all the ads for Jello you can. Cut them out and put them on display. Then have the teams line up and a copy of the paper is placed ten to twenty feet away. On go, the team members run one at a time to the paper, find the ad, rip it out of the paper, and return with it. The first team to get them all, wins. (There should be at least as many jello ads as there are members on a team.)

Jello Pie Race: Fill pie tins with Jello, cover with whipped cream, and have a pie eating race.

Nailing Jello to a Tree: Make Jello in 8" x 8" cake pans, about ½ inch thick. Let it cool. About a half an hour before using, take out of refrigerator and place in freezer. When ready to use take out and cut in one inch squares. Give the teams nails and let them nail up their Jello. Use a log for the tree. The team with the most pieces up in a minute wins.

Jello Feed: Teams pick two couples for contestants. They are seated in a chair facing each other. Blind fold them and place a towel around their necks. Give each a dish of Jello with cream, and let them feed each other. First couple to finish wins.

Jello Pail Fill: Line each team up for a relay race. First person is given a spoon. On a dish in front of them is a square of Jello about one inch square. Each person must put his square of Jello on spoon and run down to his pail, then return and give spoon to next guy. First team with all squares down wins. If Jello is dropped, person must start over again.

Jello Flash Cards: Have four sets of alphabet cards with letters not needed excluded. Have each team line up around the room forming a square. When a Jello flavor is called out (e.g. Cherry) those on each team with the letters that spell that word must run out five feet in front of his team and spell it out. First team to do so gets points. After all flavors are spelled out, the team with the most points wins.

The Jello Gauntlet: The losing team gets this one. Lay out a sheet of plastic on the floor. The other teams line up on either side forming a path. Losers must be blindfolded and barefooted. They must walk the path with other teams guiding them by shouting directions as to where to step. On the plastic path, place spoonfuls of Jello in various places. Give prize to the person who makes it without stepping in anything. (Contributed by Roger Disque, Chicago, Illinois)

MISSING PERSON'S PARTY

This event can be done on foot or by using cars. It takes place in a shopping center or business district on a late shopping night when the stores are open. Select 10 to 20 kids to be "missing" in the shopping area. The "victims" have pictures of them taken in normal dress, that are given to the groups looking for them.

The people who are going to be missing, meet together ahead of time and make up riddles or clues as to the location they'll be in. They also select a disguise appropriate to themselves and the surroundings they'll be in. For example, kids can disguise themselves as bus drivers, cab drivers, old men, blind men, nuns, pregnant young wives, a man in a wheelchair, repairmen, store clerk, or anything that they think they can pull off.

The rest of the group are the "manhunters." They meet at some central location in the shopping area and divide up into groups of from 6 to 10 per group. Each group gets pictures of the victims and the set of riddles and clues in numerical order. Each group is to stick together for the duration of the hunt. When a hunter thinks he has spotted a victim, he approaches the suspected person and says some sort of password like "BEEP BEEP!" If the person is a victim, then he must admit that he has been found. He then tells whether or not there is another missing person with him. If there is another, the hunter informs his group and they continue the hunt. If not, the group goes on after the next victim. The first group to find all its "missing people" wins.

This game works best when you can go in with another youth group and have one group be the "victims" and one group be the "hunters." That way, the kids don't know each other very well, which means they will be harder to find. Also, it gives you more people to participate in the hunt, which makes it more fun. If you have, say, 30 missing people and 30 hunters, then give each hunting group (of six per group) six missing people to find. Each group hunts for a different bunch of victims. That way you only need one picture of each victim, rather than several (one for each hunting group.) Preparation is an obvious requirement of this game. Pictures and disguises must be taken care of well in advance.

You can add another twist to this game by having the hunters "kill" the victims rather than just find them. At the same time, the victims can "kill" the hunters. The killing is done by getting a sticker or piece of tape off the back of the other person. If the victims can kill off more than half the hunting group, then the group has to call off its hunt and is out of the game. However, the hunters have the advantage, so they must "kill" all their victims.

This basic idea can be changed or adapted to meet your own local requirements. It can be called a "Manhunt" or any other name that you choose. After the event, meet together to share experiences, have some refreshments and a time for fellowship. (Contributed by Neil Graham, Edmonton, Alberta, Canada)

NEWSPAPER NIGHT

The following is a good special event, centered around newspapers. To prepare for it, get a huge pile of old newspapers, the more the better. The following list of games can be played with two or more teams.

1. *Newspaper Costume Race:* Teams have five minutes (or so) to dress kids up with newspaper to look like certain things. For example, Santa and his reindeer, Butch Cassidy and the Sundance Kid, Snow White and the seven Dwarfs, etc. Tape can be provided each team to help them construct the costumes. Judge for the best job.

2. *Newspaper Treasure Hunt:* Put in each team's pile of papers several specially colored pages and the team to find the most of them in the time limit wins.

3. *Newspaper Scavenger Hunt:* Call out certain items from the papers and the first team to find them wins. For example, a Honda ad, a want-ad for a 1956 Chevy, a news item about a murder, etc.

4. *Wad and Pile:* Teams get ten minutes to wad up all their paper into a big pile. The highest pile wins.

5. *Hide and Seek:* Hide as many kids as possible under the pile of wadded-up papers. The team with the most kids out-of-sight wins. Set a time limit.

6. *Compact Newspapers:* Teams try to compact the paper on their side into the smallest pile possible.

7. *Snow Fight:* Make a line of chairs between the two teams. On a signal, the teams throw all their paper on the other teams side. When time is up (2 or 3 minutes), the team with the least amount of paper on their side wins.

8. *Disposal Event:* Give each team plastic trash bags. The team to get all of the paper in the bags in the fastest time wins. (Contributed by Greg Kinloch, Bellingham, Washington)

PERSONALIZED PIZZA PARTY

Provide kids with pizza dough and all the goodies that go on top and let them create their own "personal pizzas." Each person gets a lump of dough and shapes it into a creative design. The only stipulation is that there must be a "lip" so the sauce won't run off. The pizza can be decorated with olives, mushrooms, cheese, pepperoni, anchovies and the like. While these creations are being baked, other games can be played. When they are ready, judge them and award a prize to the most creative pizza. Then eat up! (Contributed by Shirley Smithtro, Camarillo, California)

PERSONALIZED T-SHIRTS

T-shirts with designs, words, and symbols printed on them are getting more popular all the time. As a special event, have a get-together in which each person brings a plain white or colored T-shirt; you provide liquid embroidery pens, lettering stencils and cardboard to make other patterns from, and then create "personalized" custom T-shirts. Kids can design a statement of their faith, or an emblem for their youth group, or simply a crazy design with their names. They can be done large or small. It's easy, fun to do, and fun to wear. (Contributed by Ellen Sautter, Lancaster, Pennsylvania)

PROGRESSIVE PANDEMONIUM PARTY

This event is similar to a "treasure hunt" in that the object is to reach a final destination by following certain clues in a certain order. The difference is that the "Progressive Pandemonium Party" uses a map and rather complicated instructions rather than clues.

Print up a "map" for each team similar in style to the sample below. Of course, the map should be of actual streets, buildings, and landmarks in your area. The map should be to scale.

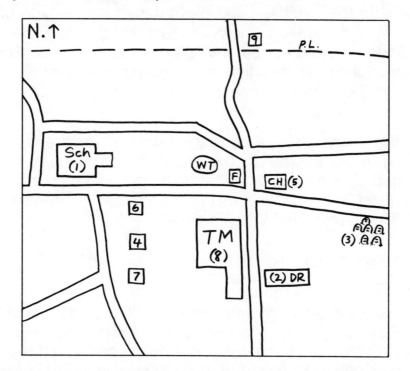

The map is accompanied by a list of instructions which pinpoint the various locations where each team must go. For example, the following list was used for the preceding map:

175

1. Extend the east wall of building 8 straight north to the edge of map. Draw a line from the S.E. corner of building 1 to the N.W. corner of building 5. Meet where the two lines intersect.

2. Draw a radius of 3 inches from the S.E. corner of 7. From the center of 5 draw a 4 inch radius. Then from the N.E. corner of 4, draw a line to the tip of the "N" marker arrow. Meet where the three lines intersect.

3. From the N.W. corner of 4 draw a line to the S.W. corner of 2. Draw a line from the northern most grave-marker to the S.W. corner of the map. Then draw a line from the west side of WT to the extreme S.W. corner of 8. Meet where the triangle is formed.

4. From the N.W. corner of 1, draw a line to the center point of the northern edge of the map. From the S.W. corner of 1, draw a line to the N.W. corner of 9. Then from the S.W. corner of 5, draw a line to the western tip of the second PL dash line west of the northern most road. Then from the N.E. corner of 5, draw a line to intersect the first line drawn for this stop. Meet where these four lines form a square.

Each team should receive the same list of instructions, but in a different order. With a little imagination, you can create your own "instructions," making them as easy or as difficult as you wish.

To add to the fun, this can be combined with a type of scavenger hunt. At each location, the team must find a certain item which may be hidden, buried, or otherwise concealed. Before the team may continue, the specified item must be found. You may also hand out the next "instruction"' at each location rather than passing them out all at once.

This event can also be combined with a "Progressive Dinner" by serving each course of the meal at the various locations designated by the map. The first team to finish all the courses of the meal (and end with dessert) is the winner. (Contributed by Terry Ketchum, Vancouver, Washington)

PUNCHBOWL PARTY

For an unusual swimming party, pour half a quart of red *food coloring* into your pool, stir well, add ice blocks and warm bodies and you have the "world's largest punch bowl." You can use the ice blocks for ice sitting contests, or "ice soccer" (both teams try to get the ice block to their end of the pool). Food coloring does not stain tile and comes out with regular chemicals in about 3-5 minutes. (Contributed by Rich Bundschuh, Palm Springs, California)

ROAST THE PASTOR

Here's a fun idea for the next church banquet or potluck. Have a "roast" (like the Friar's Roasts seen on T.V.) in which various people tell all kinds of jokes and "secrets" in the life of the pastor (who then has a chance at a rebuttal). This means, of course, that you will need a "game" pastor. This theme can be worked around a dinner featuring "roast" beef, "roasted' corn, etc. By charging for the meal, it can be a very effective fund-raiser. (Contributed by Keith Geckeler, Escondido, California)

SCRIPTURE SCAVENGER HUNT

This is a great way to combine a fun special event with some solid learning about the Bible. Teams go out and attempt to bring back items which can be found in the Bible. For example, they might bring back a stick (Moses' rod) or a rock (the stoning of Stephen) or a loaf of bread (the last supper), etc. Every item must be accompanied by a Bible verse to prove that it can be found somewhere in the Bible. The team that returns with the most items is the winner. Each team makes its presentation of all its items to the entire group. (Adapted from an idea contributed by Clifford Asay, Hacienda Heights, California)

SHOPPING CENTER GAME

Take the kids to a local shopping center or downtown area where there are plenty of stores within walking distance. Then divide into small groups and give each group a list similar to the one below. The kids are to fill in the blanks by "comparison shopping", that is — trying to find the best bargains available. The groups with the most blanks filled in and the best prices (within the time limit) wins. Think up twenty or thirty questions such as these:

1. The cheapest pair of size 12 snow boots.
   Store _____ Price _____

2. A one-pound box of candy "turtles."
   Store _____ Price _____

3. An "afro" wig.
   Store _____ Price _____

4. One pair of size 16 boys shorts.
   Store _____ Price _____

5. The best laxative available (recommended by a druggist).
   Store _____ Brand _____ Price _____

6. A "head gasket."
   Store _____ Price _____

7. Twenty-five wedding invitations.
   Store _____ Price _____

8. A heart-shaped locket.
   Store _____ Price _____

9. Five pound sack of "Puppy Chow."
   Store _____ Price _____

10. Ten party balloons.
    Store _____ Price _____

(Contributed by Maynard Johnson, Hutchinson, Minnesota)

STIFF ARM PROGRESSIVE DINNER

As Christians it's imperative that we interact with and minister to each other. An excellent way to exemplify this need and have an enjoyable evening also is to have a "Stiff Arm Progressive Dinner." Arrangements are made for the progressive dinner in the usual manner (a different house or meeting place for each course of the evening's meal). However, when the people gather at a predetermined meeting place before going to the first house (for the first course of the meal), each person is fitted with removable cardboard bands that fit over their elbows. Before entering each house for the meal, they must slide this band over their elbows (each arm). This inhibits all bending of the elbow joint and therefore makes it rather difficult to feed yourself. If the individual wants to eat any food, he must depend on the rest of the people (who also depend on him) to feed him. When leaving the house, the arm bands can be removed, but must be put on before entering the next house. At the end of the night, you can draw your own applications as to how we must depend on each other for our spiritual food and fellowship. (Contributed by Larry Shelton, Covina, California)

TIME CAPSULE

Have a special overnight meeting and have as the last activity before bedding down for the night, a time to write notes about what that particular age group thinks about the world situation...their church...where they think the church will be in the next ten years, etc. Seal these along with a newspaper, personal items, and other such items in a plastic garbage bag and bury it at least three feet deep somewhere on church property. One could carefully remove the grass and dig a hole or a bare spot in the back. Be as secretive as possible (maybe let an elder or pastor know) and just plan to leave it. Maybe ten years from now some member of the group will remember and try to recover the items or you could call the evening "2 Million A.D." and just let it stay and hope some archaeologist finds it a jillion years from now. (Contributed by Don Maddox, Newport Beach, California)

TRIKE OLYMPICS

Find a location with smooth pavement and good lighting. (Tennis courts and drive ways are great, or a parking lot will do.) Pick a captain to ride in the time trials for *pole* position. Divide up by classes or schools, etc. Then get *one tiny* tricycle. Each captain rides the tricycle down straightaway and is timed. Announce that next week will be the races. Each class or team must bring their own tricycle. Set a maximum wheel size. (Rubber tires — not the new plastic ones.) Also, plan to bring two or three spare tricycles yourself as well and some pliers and crescent wrenches to tighten them. Make trophies from dime store tricycles and hondas.

Events: (Use your imagination!)
1. Grand Prix (alternate boys and girls around oval track)
2. Egg Pass (just like a relay baton)
3. Blindfold (spin rider three times and make him go across to where next contestant is waiting)
4. Tandem (boy and girl with boy blindfolded)
5. Backwards Race

(Contributed by Ron Wilburn, El Paso, Texas)

TURTLE TOURNAMENT

For this special event, you will need to obtain a number of live turtles. Large turtles are best, but the smaller miniature turtles can be used, if the large ones are unavailable. You should have one turtle for every four kids. That constitutes a "turtle team." Turtle events can include the following:

1. *Turtle Decorating Contest:* Provide paint, dye, paper, ribbon, or whatever and have each team decorate their turtle within a given time limit. Judge for the best job and award points.
2. *Turtle Races:* Draw concentric circles on the ground with the largest at about 15 feet in diameter. Place the turtles in the center (the smallest circle) and they may "run" in any direction. The

turtle which travels the farthest from the center in the time limit is the winner.

3. *Turtle Tricks:* Each team is given ten minutes to teach, train, or force their turtle to do a ''trick.'' Props may be used and judges give points for creativity, ingenuity, and whether or not the turtle accomplishes the trick.

4. *Turtle Chariot Races:* Each team is given cardboard, paper, tape, wheels, etc., and they must construct a ''chariot'' and hook it up to their turtle. Judge for the best chariots and then have a race on a ''track'' of your choosing.

Keep a tote board with the team names (have each team name their turtles) and their running point total. Have a starting gun, checkered flag, judges with clip-boards, etc. Provide trophies for the winners and try to create a ''derby-day'' atmosphere. (Contributed by Dave Gilliam, Henryette, Oklahoma)

WANDERLUST

The following can be used as a special event *or* as a way to open up a good discussion on ''purpose and direction in life.'' Simply follow the instructions below:

1. Have the kids meet at the church, house, etc., at a pre-advertised time, say 2:00 P.M.

2. Divide the kids into cars, 4 or 5 kids per car. (Make sure you've arranged to have enough cars!)

3. Supply each car with a die (one ''dice'') and a coin (penny).

4. Announce that this will be a ''Wanderlust'' experience involving driving around the countryside. Set a finish time (time to stop driving), say 2:45 P.M. Announce that the goal is to see who gets the furthest away from the church, house, etc. in 45 minutes (obeying all traffic rules and regulations), WITH THE FOLLOWING CONDITIONS:

5. *Give* the directions (printed on pieces of paper) to each car: ''When the signal is given, begin driving your car. You must make a decision at any of these 3 points along the road: (1) 4-way stop sign; (2) traffic light, (3) cloverleaf (interchange). If you come to one of the above points, throw the die. If the die reads 1 or 2, go left; 3 or 4, go straight; 5 or 6, go right. If you come to a dead-end, turn around. If you come to a place where you can't go straight (such as a ''T''), then roll the die again. If it comes up an even number go left; if it comes up an odd number, go right. Proceed, driving the car in this fashion until 2:45 P.M. STOP. Record that location as your furthest point.''

6. Everyone returns to the originating location at that time and the car that got the farthest is the winner. Some will return earlier than others, so have games, refreshments, music or what-

ever for everyone until the entire group returns.

7. To tie in with a learning experience, the event can be likened to life and how many people do everything by chance. Many just go around in circles, hit dead ends or have no idea what the future holds. Discuss the feelings the group had while on the road and tie in with scripture relating to how Christians receive direction for their lives from God. (Contributed by Bob Stier, Loves Park, Illinois)

WAY OUT WEIGH IN

Divide kids into teams (car loads) and have them draw for street names or areas of town. They then have one hour to try and collect as much canned goods or other non-perishable foods as they can from residents of the area which they drew. The teams report back and weigh-in the food they collected. The team that has the most (by weight) wins a prize of some kind, and all the food is then given to the needy. You may want to restrict this to church members only, rather than soliciting food from strangers, however, if done during the Thanksgiving season, most people are willing to share with others. (Contributed by Nat Burns, Palmetto, Florida)

WHAT THE FAT

Here's an idea for a social or party. Give a prize to the person (or group) who comes to the event weighing the most. They can come dressed with rocks and things in their pockets, but must wear what they have on *throughout* the event. Each person is weighed in and (in case of teams) totaled. (Contributed by Ron Wilburn, El Paso, Texas)

WHITE TREASURE ELEPHANT HUNT AUCTION

This idea combines a treasure hunt, a white elephant sale and an auction. The "treasure" consists of poker chips which are placed in caches, perhaps 100 locations, in an area around the church property. The area could be much larger, say an entire town, if the group is large and there is enough time and transportation. Each cache may consist of from one to ten chips. A map is made showing the location of the treasure(s) by marking "X." The map may be posted in a prominent location where all can see before the hunt begins. If there are many people involved or if the area is large, make copies of the map for each team. The treasure hunters should work in teams from 3 to 6 persons. At night flashlights are required. At the start, the hunters rush out to the nearest locations, with some crafty ones going to the further ones to avoid the crowd. A return time should be set, within 1 to 3 hours, depending on distances. A penalty of 5 white chips per minute late can be assessed. Upon return, the teams can look over the white elephant gifts and other items, which each person brought beforehand. The team members can decide what they wish to bid on, knowing only what the total value of all the chips are. The whites are one, the reds are five and the blues are ten. Then, the auction begins! By offering small items first (then putting them back if there are insufficient bidders at the start) and interspersing them with the more valuable gifts, the excitement can really grow. Having more than one auctioneer is a good idea, too. The auction should last between 15 and 30 minutes. This can be done by offering more than one gift at a time, if necessary. (Contributed by Robert C. Hockaday, Kailua, Hawaii)

YAK SHAK

One youth group ran a want-ad in the local newspaper, asking for donations of used furniture for the church youth center. Those who gave furniture received receipts for tax purposes and now the group has a big comfortable, casual "living room" to hold its meetings in. Kids and visitors are much more relaxed in this informal atmosphere and the room has been named the "Yak Shak." Try it if your youth meeting room needs redecorating. (Contributed by Loren Reynolds, Buena Park, California)

Chapter Five

Camping

BIRTHDAYS AT CAMP

Most junior high kids enjoy celebrating their birthdays and this idea will make it possible for *every* kid to celebrate their birthday at camp instead of only a select few. Designate each day as representing two months of the year (such as Monday-January and February: Tuesday-March and April; etc.) A six-day camp would cover the whole year. Then each day, celebrate the birthdays of the kids whose birthdays fall in the corresponding two months! Sing the "happy birthday" song, give small novelty gifts for presents and grant each day's birthday kids certain special privileges. (Contributed by William Moore, Brainerd, Minnesota)

BUCKING BARREL BRONCO

This is a great idea for camps with a "western" theme. It does, however, require some work and preparation. Obtain a 55 gallon drum (barrel) and attach (weld, if possible) four eye hooks to it, two on each end. Then attach heavy ropes or cable to each hook which can be tied to four trees or poles, suspending the barrel about four or five feet in the air. A saddle is then fastened to the barrel and a "rider" can sit in the saddle. Four big guys then grab the four ropes and pull on them (in an up and down manner) and the rider tries to hang on. Time each rider to see how long he can keep from falling off. Note: It is a good idea to place a mattress under the barrel if the ground is hard. (Contributed by Roger Disque, Chicago, Illinois)

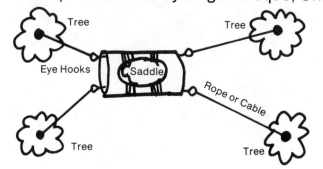

CAMP "SPECIAL DAYS"

To give a Junior High camp some distinctiveness, designate each day as a "special day." Activities and dress can be geared to that special day. Here are some suggestions for special days with appropriate ideas:

1. *Nature Day:* Hike, nature scavenger hunt, picnic, night walk.

2. *Backwards Day:* Reverse schedule for the day, reverse the meals, wear clothes backwards, walk backwards to all activities.
3. *Western Day:* Stage a hold-up with counselors dressed up as bandits, follow by counselor hunt by campers, then gold hunt (rocks sprayed with gold paint).
4. *Skit Day:* Have skits by counselors, by campers, by other staff.
5. *Christmas in June (July, August):* Celebrate by exchanging names, making crafts to give as presents, Christmas drama, Christmas carols.
6. *Indian Day:* Dress up with home made head bands, horseback riding, Thanksgiving drama, archery, tracking through the woods, nature crafts.

(Contributed by William Moore, Brainerd, Minnesota)

CAMP TIME

Most teens complain about having to go to bed *so early* and get up *so early*. By establishing CAMP TIME, you can let them go to bed at 2 am and get up at 9 am! Make the first matter of camp business the establishment of CAMP TIME. Have everyone move their watches *ahead* 2 hours (maybe more or less). All activities will be held according to Camp Time. Even though the teens know about the time change, they really respond to the "new hours." This works most effectively at a week resident camp. (Contributed by Ron Wells, Oregon City, Oregon)

CONCENTRATION CAMP

Have a weekend study retreat with a maximum of teaching, Bible study, discussion, and planning and a minimum of fun and games. Call it a "Concentration Camp" and invite any kid who really wants to dig in for a couple days. This is particularly good at the beginning of the school year. (Contributed by Richard McPherson, Portland, Oregon)

GROUP HUNT

This is a tracking game in which groups try to elude other groups for a period of time in a wooded area, such as at a camp. The groups can be tied together with rope so that they must stick together. The idea is for the groups to move quickly and quietly and to work together as a unit. The game can be made as simple or as complex as you want it to be and may be followed with a discussion relating to cooperation and unity. (Contributed by Dick Babington, Ontario, California)

MARBLE MYSTERY

Next camp, give each kid a marble when he registers and tell him that at the end of camp, whoever has the most marbles will win a prize. As the week progresses, many will lose them, forget about them, but some will work hard all week buying them off of other kids to get quite a collection. The prize: a marble bag. (Contributed by Harl Pike, Show Low, Arizona)

MUD SLIDE

Why let rain ruin camp? Grass is very slick when it's wet. Pick the steepest convenient and acceptable grassy slope and let the kids slide down with or without plastic toboggans or cardboard. Presently the grass will give out and you'll have a nice mudslide. (Contributed by Rogers E. George III, Oak Lawn, Illinois)

NO COUNSELOR-NO BREAKFAST

During a week long camp, it is often a lot of fun to have an early morning "counselor hunt." Have each counselor wake up before his campers and then find a place to hide within a specified area. The campers are then awakened to the announcement that they must first find their counselor before they can have breakfast. (Contributed by William Moore, Brainerd, Minnesota)

PARENT-TEEN CAMP

The following retreat idea has been used with great success in establishing a family ministry in the youth program. In order to attend, there must be at least one teenager and one parent from the same family. The camp begins on Friday, at 9:00 p.m. and ends on Saturday, at 8:30 p.m. This short schedule allows parents to get away and also keeps the cost down.

SCHEDULE

Friday:
9:00 p.m.—All together, Guest Speaker, crowd breakers and surf film.
10:00–10:30 p.m.—Snack time

Saturday:
8:00 a.m.—Breakfast
9:00 a.m.—Parents—Guest Speaker—Kids—Youth Leader
10:00 a.m.—Break
10:30 a.m.—Meet together, Guest Speaker
11:30 a.m.—Recreation
12:15 p.m.—Lunch
1:30 p.m.—Film
2:00 p.m.—Discussions in groups
3:00 p.m.—Free time
5:00 p.m.—Dinner
6:00 p.m.—Leave for home

The first night, some crowd breakers and a surfing film will help loosen everyone up, especially the parents. You can bring a guest speaker along, who is good with families, to share a short message and spend the rest of the evening just in fellowship. Have fathers room with sons, mothers with daughters, etc. You can work this any way you want. The next day, two meetings are scheduled. The first can be with parents and kids, separated and talked to as individual groups, then everyone meets together in one group for a rap session with the guest speaker. Recreation can include volleyball (Parents must hold hands with their kids—really wild). Basketball can also be a good family game: fathers and guys vs. mothers and gals, but fellows could use only one hand. Other games from *Ideas* work well, but include everyone in them. During the afternoon, show the film "Parents, Pressures, and Kids" put out by BFA Educational Media, 2211 Michigan Street, Santa Monica, California. After this, families meet and discuss pressures in their families. It usually takes a while for these to get going, but the results are great. After 45 minutes, the families join together in the large group to share what they felt had been accomplished. Then, discuss ways that the families can do things to understand each other better. Kids can share what they like to do with their parents or what they like about their parents and vice-versa. For a short but effective retreat, the long range results of this type of thing can be very good. (Contributed by Jim Grindle, Van Nuys, California)

SPIRITUAL EMPHASIS CAMPOUT

The following are great ideas for spiritual emphasis campout, or a weekend retreat in a rustic area away from civilization with plenty of natural surroundings:

1. TRUST THE LEADER. Props: Clothesline with knots equally spaced on it. Blindfold everyone except the leader who takes the front of the line. Have EVERYONE take a knot and hold on to it. Complete silence is expected. The leader leads around trees, under bushes, through the swamp, under fences, etc. Object: DISCIPLINE and TRUST THE LEADER TO GUIDE YOU.

2. TREETOP HYMNSING. Pick a big tree with big limbs. The entire group climbs up the tree and has a treetop hymnsing. Have small chorus books or sheets. Anyone afraid of heights, of course, can sing from the ground underneath the tree.

3. NATURE HIKE. (Purpose: to appreciate God's creation.) Set rules—1. Everyone remain silent and serious (discipline.) 2. Everyone walk in a line following one another. When one person sees something that is significant about God's creation he shouts "STOP." Everyone huddles around the person while he shares his thought about this thing in God's creation. Others won't have any thoughts to share while others will share more than once. (Contributed by Ronald Allchin, Gary, Indiana)

Chapter Six

Skits

"AND THE LAMP WENT OUT"

CAST OF CHARACTERS
1. The Reader . . . . Narration
2. Evelyn DeVere . . . . The Heroine
3. Ralph Grayson . . . . The Hero
4. Mrs. DeVere . . . . Evelyn's Mother
5. Herbert Vanderslice . . . . The Villain

SETTING
The library of the DeVere Home.

PROPS
1. False arm to fit under Mother's sweater or dress sleeve.
2. A small pail.
3. A small sponge filled with water concealed in handkerchief.
4. A whisk broom.
5. A traveling bag or briefcase.
6. Large clock.
7. Calendar.
8. Thermometer.
9. Photograph
10. Needlework for Mother.
11. Lamp to "go out."

PROPS OFF STAGE
1. Broom.
2. Pans or drums for thunder.
3. Branches of tree to wave.
4. Moon made of tin or cardboard covered with foil.
5. Comic book for Evelyn.
6. Strong flashlight.
7. Red paper heart for Ralph.
8. Chains.
9. Sign with "time" written on it.

INSTRUCTIONS
The following script is to be read by the Reader. At each numbered place in the script, the characters or stagehands perform the "actions" as listed after the script. "Ham" acting is essential in order to make the skit as ridiculous as possible.

SCRIPT
(The story read by the Reader)

Fiercely the storm raged — the rain fell in torrents, the trees were lashed by the fury of the elements (1); the thunder crashed and roared. (2) But within the softly lighted library, silence reigned. Presently the door opened and Evelyn DeVere tripped into the room. (3) Gracefully sinking into a chair, she was soon engrossed in the latest novel of the day. (4)

Footsteps were heard (5) and tossing her book aside, (6) Evelyn sprang to meet the newcomer. (7) But disappointment was written plainly on her face when Herbert Vanderslice stepped over the threshold. (8) Although it was not he whom she had expected, she greeted him pleasantly. (9)

The young Vanderslice's nervousness was evident. (10) He paced the floor rapidly for a moment (11), then dropped on his knees at Evelyn's side (12) and clasping her hand in his, cried, "Evelyn, pride of my heart, I love you. I cannot live without you. Say that you will be mine and make me the happiest man in the world." (13)

Evelyn answered, "Herbert, I cannot. I am sorry for your sake that it cannot be, but I do not love you." Withdrawing her hand from his, she rose and, walking over to the table gazed lovingly at the framed photograph there. (14)

Springing to his feet, (15) Herbert cried, "Ah ha! I see it all now. You love Ralph Grayson — but I swear it now you shall never be his."

Evelyn was greatly frightened by his manner, and her tears fell fast. (16) Herbert turning, saw Mrs. DeVere standing in the doorway. Giving him a look of scorn, she swept into the room. (17)

"So, you would threaten my child — you cad, you scoundrel!" she cried. "Leave this house and never darken our doors again." (18) Bewildered at her great wrath, he stood, nailed to the spot. (19) Time passed rapidly (20), still he did not move. Then Evelyn, with never a glance in his direction, took her mother's arm and left the room. (21)

"Go!" said Mrs. DeVere. Herbert attempted to speak, but she silenced him with a gesture. Just then the clock struck. (22) Vanderslice staggered through the doorway.

Weeks flew by. (23)

It was a beautiful night; the moon rose (24) and its silvery beams played about the room. (25) Mrs. DeVere was sitting in the library, doing a dainty bit of Punchwork, (26) the picture of placid industry, when a hearty laugh was heard, and Ralph Grayson slid into the room. (27)

Dropping her work (28) with a glad cry of welcome, she rose to meet him with outstretched arms. (29) "Ralph, my dear boy, I am so glad to see you! When did you return? We have missed you sorely during your travels."

Mrs. DeVere pointed to the conservatory and smiling, said, "You will find her there." (31)

Evelyn's mother, memories crowding, sat thoughtfully, but was startled by the sounds of someone creeping softly into the room. (32) Startled to see that it was Herbert Vanderslice, she rose from her chair, and drawing herself to her full majestic height, said in a haughty manner, "Pray, to what do I owe this unexpected intrusion? Have I not forbidden you in the house?" (33)

"Mrs. DeVere, I must and shall see Evelyn, and naught can . . ." Just then the door opened and Eveyln and Ralph danced gaily in (34), smiling and happy. When Evelyn saw Herbert there, she turned a little pale. (35) "Did you wish to see me?" she asked.

In the midst of the warmth and light, he shivered, chilled by the frosty tones of her voice, (36) then frowned blackly, and striding toward her, attempted to pass Ralph. But Grayson quickly stepped forward and placed himself as a barrier between them, while Mrs. DeVere whisked her daughter from the room. (37)

Herbert in his great anger strode back and forth tearing his hair. (38) The room seemed intensely hot, and the thermometer rose rapidly. (39) Evelyn, watching the scene from the doorway, caught her breath with fear. (40) Ralph emitted a low whistle (41) as he gazed upon the insane fury of Herbert. Then, hoping to soothe the man, placed his hand on his shoulder (42), but Herbert turned upon Ralph suddenly and the two grappled in fierce embrace.

Evelyn stood chained to the spot (43), watching the terrific combat, but finally as Ralph threw Herbert to the floor, with a piercing scream (44), she ran to him and fell fainting at his feet. (45)

Herbert slowly picked himself up from the floor and stood quiet and subdued, while they tenderly placed Evelyn in a chair. (46) Mrs. DeVere glared at him and said, "Now, young man, the tables are turned." (47) Evelyn soon revived and gazed scornfully at her rejected suitor. (48) Ralph walked to Herbert with outstretched hands and said, "Vanderslice, take your defeat like a man. I have won Evelyn, and you have lost her, but won't you wish us well?" Herbert stood motionless for a moment, then slowly extended his hand, which Ralph clasped with a hearty grip. (49) Walking to Evelyn, Herbert took her hand, pressed it to his lips, and then, with his face drawn with pain (50), walked haltingly from the room. (51)

Ralph held out his arms, and Evelyn ran into them. Mrs. DeVere laughingly gathered both in her embrace. Presently the lovers sauntered out toward the conservatory. (52) Mrs. DeVere resumed her dainty work, but — affected by the peace and quiet — soon dropped into gentle slumber. (53)

The clock ticked on. The lamp went out. (54)

ACTIONS
1. Branches are waved from behind stage so as to be seen by the audience.
2. Noise made by pan or drums.
3. Actually trips and stumbles.
4. Sprawls in chair and reads comic book.
5. Loud footsteps in uneven time.
6. Throws book high in air over shoulder.
7. Actually jumps.
8. Steps as if over high obstacle.
9. They shake hands. Evelyn goes back to chair.
10. Jerks and acts nervous.
11. Walking as if measuring floor.
12. Drops on knees and acts dramatically.
13. Acts as if talking.
14. Herbert follows Evelyn still on his knees.
15. Jumps up.
16. Squeezed sponge in handkerchief held to her eyes.
17. Sweeps in with broom, places it behind sofa.
18. Points dramatically to door.
19. Hammering offstage.
20. Kid with "TIME" sign runs across stage.
21. Mother holds false arm under real one, Evelyn takes it.
22. Mrs. DeVere strikes Herbert with clock.
23. Mother tears three or four leaves from calendar.
24. Moon (cardboard) is on floor at back. String attached goes over back curtain. Stage hand back of curtain pulls it up.
25. Flashlight.
26. Punches with great force into White Cloth.
27. Slides as if on ice.
28. Drops work, makes noise.
29. Ralph and Mrs. DeVere shake hands.
30. Use red paper heart. Have in back pocket. Look for it first.
31. Mother sits; Ralph exits.
32. Creep in on hands and knees.
33. Both stand up.
34. Evelyn and Ralph waltz in together to center stage.
35. Lifts pails concealed behind sofa, turns it, replaces it.
36. Shivers and blows on hands to warm them.
37. Use whiskbroom.

38. Pulls out locks of false hair.
39. Thermometer (large cardboard) pulled up same as moon.
40. Catches with hands.
41. Shrill whistle offstage.
42. Takes left hand with right, places it on Herbert's shoulder.
43. Chains clank. Ralph assists Herbert to lie down on floor.
44. Make any hideous noise offstage.
45. Evelyn slowly and carefully seats herself at Ralph's feet, arranges her dress, fixes hair, then lies on floor.
46. Ralph and Mrs. DeVere lead her to a chair.
47. Ralph and Mother turn end table completely around.
48. Very dramatic!
49 Use briefcase concealed behind sofa.
50. Makes hideous face.
51. Two steps, halt, repeat.
52. Done extravagantly.
53. Loud snores from behind stage.
54. Lamp should be securely fastened to small table on which a long cover, under which a person is concealed. OR table and lamp can be pulled off by means of strong string.

(Contributed by Dave Treat, Durham, North Carolina)

CHANNEL CHANGERS

Here's a new version of an old idea, which is simply to show what might happen if you flipped back and forth between five different channels on your TV set.

To pull it off successfully, here are a few suggestions:
1. Assign the five speaking parts to five very good readers who can put some life into the lines. The lines aren't funny enough to carry themselves.
2. Rehearse it many times. *Timing* is very, very important. Each person should come in at the precise moment to get maximum laughs.
3. Have the kids memorize the lines if possible. They shouldn't be too dependent on the written script.
4. For the best visual effect, construct a false-front "TV set" out of a big box or something and have it set up so that each speaker can get behind it at the right time to say his lines. Cut a hole out for the TV screen and put some knobs on to "change channels" with. (This is optional, of course. You can simply have each speaker run on and off the stage area each time a channel is "changed.")
5. Each speaker can wear appropriate costumes and use whatever "props" will add to the humor.

THE SCRIPT (Each *"click"* is a channel change.)

Story Lady: Today, boys and girls, our story is about Little Red Riding Hood. Once upon a time there was a little girl named Little Red Riding Hood. One day her mother asked her to go through the woods to visit her grandmother. And on her way who should jump out from behind a tree but . . . *(click)*

Boy Scout: The Boy Scouts of America! Yes sir, fellas, the Boy Scouts are just the group for you. Why for just a dollar . . . *(click)*

Gangster: You can shove it down your throat! Try and steal my gal, will ya. Why for two cents I'd . . . *(click)*

Recipe Lady: Set carefully in a quart of prune juice. And when the mixture is settled, ladies, just pop it into the . . . *(click)*

Football Announcer: End zone for a touchdown! Wow! Did you see that last play ladies and gentlemen? Terrific! And now a word from our sponsor, Shavo. With Shavo, the sharpest razor in the world . . . *(click)*

Gangster: You can cut your own throat for all I care, you slob! Who do you think you are anyway??? . . . *(click)*

Story Lady: Little Red Riding Hood . . . *(click)*

Recipe Lady: What a smell! Doesn't that just make your mouth water, ladies? Now for the vegetables. Ladies, this next recipe is very unique. It calls for one . . . *(click)*

Football Announcer: Broken leg! The star is definitely out of the game. The wildcats really need help. Guess they'll have to call in the . . . *(click)*

Boy Scout: Boy Scouts of America! Each year, fellas, we make a camping trip. Boy, there's nothing like it. You're out there all alone with no one but the wind, the stars and . . . *(click)*

Story Lady: Little Red Riding Hood. As she entered the cottage she said . . . *(click)*

Gangster: This is the dumbest thing I've ever done! How

	could I have ever called you a friend when you turn on me and steal my girl. You slob! You're nothing but a . . . *(click)*
Recipe Lady:	Hot dog! Slice it carefully and then cook the casserole on top of the . . . *(click)*
Football Announcer:	Football field. That should do it for the Wild-cats, folks. With Brooks out of the game, it doesn't look like they have a chance. Now they line up. The snap. Draw play! What a hand-off. There goes Johnson! Look at him go. He's going all the way to the . . . *(click)*
Boy Scout:	Outhouse. We don't have running water either. You will learn how to make Mulligan Stew though. You'd be surprised how it tastes in the fresh air and woods. After a hearty meal, you can't help but say . . . *(click)*
Gangster:	I think I'll shoot myself! That gal meant more to me than . . . *(click)*
Recipe Lady:	A handful of chopped nuts. Chop them fine and fold into the flour mixture. Next beat the eggs until they look like . . . *(click)*
Football Announcer:	Mud in your face. What a pile up. The Pan-thers didn't even get past the line of scrim-mage! Boy, these Wildcats have really worked hard this half. With the score at 10-10 and five minutes to go, who will win??? . . . *(click)*
Boy Scout:	The Boy Scouts of America! Boy, fellas, you can't pass up this opportunity to join now. Right now you're probably saying to yourself . . . *(click)*
Story Lady:	What a big mouth you have! And the wolf said . . . *(click)*
Gangster:	Listen, honey. You're coming with me. I'm tired of all this fooling around. And you, ya dirty yeal-low rat, you're nothing but a . . . *(click)*
Football Announcer:	Hound Dog running down the field! Oh-oh. It looks like he's heading right for the . . . *(click)*
Recipe Lady:	Garbage. There's no need to keep it. After this dinner, ladies, you'll sigh with satisfaction. Your husband will tell you it's delicious and you'll say, "Oh, you . . . *(click)*

| Story Lady: | Dirty old wolf! Little Red Riding Hood ran out of the house screaming, "Save me! Save me! Who will save me??" . . . *(click)* |
| Boy Scout: | The Boy Scouts of America! |

(Contributed by Dennis Dressler, Pasadena, California)

HUNG-UP ANNOUNCEMENTS

For a "change of pace" at announcement time, try this little skit. Have a piece of rope strung across the front of the room and at the appropriate time, have a guy (dressed up like an old lady) walk in with a clothes basket. He (She) proceeds to hang up her laundry on the clothesline, with announcements written on each article of clothing. The idea is to take the audience by total surprise. The guy should really "ham it up" and act like a sloppy old lady, dropping the clothes, blowing her nose on them, etc. (Contributed by Steve Morgan, Los Angeles, California)

MASHED POTATO SKIT

A man comes into a restaurant *(table and chair)* and sits down. Waitress comes in and asks for order.

Man:	I'll have a big pot of mashed potatoes.
Waitress:	Is that all?
Man:	Yup.
Waitress:	No beverage?
Man:	Nope. Just a big pot of mashed potatoes.
Waitress:	No salad or soup or dessert or anything?
Man:	Listen! All I want is a big pot of mashed potatoes.
Waitress:	Well, ok. I'll tell the cook.

Waitress goes back into a wing off stage and in a voice which everyone can hear, tells the cook that there's a weirdo out there that wants a big pot of mashed potatoes.

Cook:	Is that all?
Waitress:	Yup. That's all he wants.
Cook:	No salad?
Waitress:	Nope.
Cook:	No beverage or anything?

Waitress: Nope, just a big pot of mashed potatoes.

Argument goes on for a while. Finally the cook condescends and gives the waitress a huge pot of mashed potatoes *(get the biggest pot you can)*. Waitress brings the pot of potatoes out to the customer. He looks around suspiciously, lowers pot to floor and sticks his head as far into the potatoes as he can—up to his neck. Then he proceeds to jam them into his mouth, ears, pockets, down his shirt, etc. Finally, waitress, standing there all this time, asks the man what the heck he's doing with all those mashed potatoes. Man slowly looks up at waitress with question mark on his face . . .

Man: Mashed potatoes??? I thought this was spinach!!!

Man stands up, turns, and walks out.

At this point everyone is confused, including the Waitress. Suddenly she turns . . .

Waitress: Spinach—oh, I get it.

Waitress dives into the pot of potatoes head first, mushing them all over the place, in her hair, her mouth, etc. Then she gets up and leaves. Finally the cook who has been watching the whole thing from a little distance yells . . .

Cook: Spinach—I get it! Is that ever funny!

Goes through same procedure as Man and Waitress.

Now everyone is thoroughly confused. At this point, someone comes through with a sign saying, "What is SPINACH spelled backwards?" A plant in the audience then jumps up yelling that he gets it too, and dives into the pot, mushing it all over himself.

You can end the skit here by having the announcer come out and suggest to the crowd that if they think about it for a while, they'll get it. If this is to be the last skit in the evening the announcer might even come out and apologize for trying to put over such a crummy skit on the crowd. Then he pauses, and reflectingly says, "Spinach spelled backwards . . . Oh, I get it, and he dives into the pot too. Curtains close. (Contributed by John Splinter, Winnipeg, Manitoba, Canada)

STATUE IN THE PARK

One person poses as a statue with a park bench or seat in front of him. Two people come along to eat lunch—the statue takes some of their lunch whenever it is left on the seat. The eaters look more and more suspiciously at each other until they finally leave in disgust. A couple then approaches and sits down at one end of the seat. They are in the early stages of courtship and sit rather shyly next to each other, with no physical contact. After a while, the statue puts an arm around the girl, who reacts sharply, slapping the face of the boy and leaving in disgust. Then comes one of the gardeners with a bucket, mop and feather duster. He first of all cleans the seat, then looks up at the statue. He dusts the statue with the feather duster, while the person posing tries not to move, sneeze, laugh, etc. He is about to put the mop into the bucket when there is a voice calling him off-stage. He looks at his watch, yells out "I'm coming," picks up the bucket and throws the contents over the statue. (Contributed by David Scott, Riverside, California)

THREE AGAINST A THOUSAND

Three guys walk in all bandaged up, smeared with dirt and blood, limping, moaning, and shaking their heads in disbelief over the fantastic battle they just went through. "What a battle, what fantastic odds! We should never have attempted it in the first place. Three guys against 1000! Unbelievable!" Finally one guy says, "Yeah, they were the toughest three guys I've ever seen." (Contributed by Ron Wilburn, El Paso, Texas)

TUG-O-WAR SKIT

You'll need a room with two doors up front or a room divider, which will block out the view of the audience. This skit should take place while someone else is talking, so that it distracts the attention of the audience. A boy will come out of one of the doors tugging for all he's worth on a heavy rope. He struggles with this while pulling it across the stage and out the other door. A second or two later, as soon as he's disappeared from sight, and while the rope is still moving across the stage, he reappears in the first door on the other end of the same rope, except this time he's pulling vainly against the

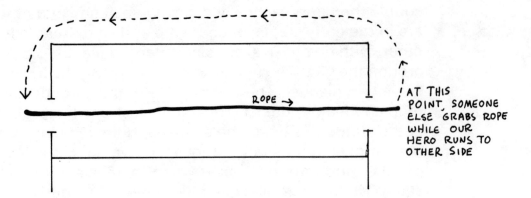

ROPE →

AT THIS POINT, SOMEONE ELSE GRABS ROPE WHILE OUR HERO RUNS TO OTHER SIDE

tugging as he is dragged across the stage and out the second door. (Contributed by Pete Steveson, Greenville, South Carolina)

Chapter Seven

Publicity

BAG INVITATION

Next time you want to invite your group to a ''sack lunch'' meeting, here's a great way to do it: Use an ordinary lunch bag as an envelope. Put the invitation inside the bag, staple it shut, address it, and mail it. The invitation can read: ''Bring your lunch in this bag to . . .'' (Contributed by Paul Lewis, Julian, California)

BLOW-UP ANNOUNCEMENT

Next time you need a clever handout idea, try this. Print up a card which folds in half (like a greeting card). On the front of the card print this message:

Inside the card, tape a *balloon* and print your announcement. (Contributed by Larry Rice, San Jose, California)

BULLETIN BOARD PHOTOS

If you have trouble getting kids to read the news and announcements hung on the youth group bulletin board, try this. Have someone shoot photos of all your youth activities and each week hang a new batch of pictures on the board. Kids love to see themselves and others in their group and they'll make it a point to check out the bulletin board every week. Appropriate humorous captions can be placed under each photo for added fun. (Contributed by Ray Peterson, St. Paul, Minnesota)

REASONS WHY PASSOUT

Here's a publicity idea that you may want to try out sometime. Print up a handout that folds in half. On the outside of the card (front) the words are printed "Good Reasons Why You Should NOT Attend (such and such meeting):"

When you open it up, the inside is blank. The details of the meeting are then printed on the back. (Contributed by Dave Gallagher, Pomona, California)

SCHIZOPHRENIC PORTRAITS

Take everyone's picture with a Polaroid "Big Shot" camera. Use a plain background and make sure each subject is the same distance from the camera and centered (not off to the right or left) looking straight forward. Cut each picture in half, right under the eyes, straight across. Then match every person's top half to someone else's bottom half and mount on the stiff paper that comes with the film. Hang the finished photos on your youth bulletin board. They'll be quite an attraction. (Contributed by Kathryn Lindskoog, Orange, California)

PRESS COVERAGE

You can get hundreds of dollars worth of free publicity if you can learn to think like a newspaper editor. These people are always on the lookout for pictures with seasonal themes. If your group is going to have a Hallowe'en party, the black and white picture you take while the gang is doing the decorating, might be usable as a theme picture in your local paper. The picture is valuable only before the event, there isn't great demand for a patriotic theme on July 5th. You don't even have to develop the film; the paper can do it easily. Just take the film to the editor (in smaller places) or the city desk (in larger ones) and tell them what pictures you took. They will carry on from there and of course, the decision as to whether the picture is usable is theirs alone. They may want you to provide a cut line describing the scene or they may take down the facts and write their own. Why not give it a try? (Contributed by Marion Hostetler, Montpelier, Ohio)

Chapter Eight

Service Projects

ADOPT-A-GARDEN

Here's an idea that can really "grow" on you: Invite your group to adopt the gardens of shut-ins, chronically ill, hospitalized, or aged people. Supply the seeds and encourage the youth to supply the tools and muscle-power. They can prepare the soil, plant, cultivate, and ultimately harvest the crops of vegetables, all for the people who own the gardens, and who, of course, are unable to do the work. It makes for great interaction between the generations! Especially helpful are youth who are into farming, biology, and the "back-to-the-earth" movement. Novices can learn fast, too.

An adaptation of this idea involves others in the congregation. While publicizing "Adopt-A-Garden," invite others who already have gardens to set aside one or two rows for giving away to the hungry. Again, youth can supply the seeds, and after the harvest, can deliver the food to the needy. This can fit well into a long-range hunger-awareness program. (Contributed by Jeremy Pera and Nate Castens, Glencoe, Minnesota)

AIRPLANE WASH

As a possible fund raiser, contact your local private plane airport and inquire into the possibility of having a "plane wash." Most airplane owners will usually pay plenty to have their plane washed. All it requires is plenty of hose, buckets, rags, towels, soap, and kids to do the work. All it takes is a few airplanes to make the effort very worthwhile.

BANDAGE ROLLING

Bandages are always needed by hospitals overseas in mission fields. By collecting old sheets (clean), kids can cut them into strips (from 2 to 4 inches wide) and roll them into bandages for distribution to missionaries and hospitals. One group held a "Roll-a-thon" and secured sponsors who gave 10 cents to one dollar (or as much as they could) per bandage rolled by the youth group in one day. The group wound up with over 600 bandages. (Contributed by Tom Sykes, Princeton, Florida)

BABYSITTING CO-OP

If your church Sunday School facilities are vacant during the summer, look into the possibility of a babysitting co-op for service or for fund raising. Arrange to have babysitting available for a few hours each day by appointment and sign up members of the youth group to sit one day a week or less depending on the size of the group. You'll be surprised at how many grateful mothers will leave their youngsters for babysitting while they go shopping or to meetings or to the pool. However, you must be careful about which ages you'll be able to accept and that there will always be enough teens or adults on hand for good child supervision. (Contributed by Ellen Sautter, Lancaster, Pennsylvania)

BUCK-A-BASKET BALL GAME

Here's a fund raiser that is both effective and a lot of fun. Have a basketball game which pits two rival teams against each other. Take pledges from people to give a "buck a basket" scored by their favorite team. The game can be regulation time and open to the public.

A variation of this would be to make it a "marathon" game, lasting as long as the players can continue. Donors may pledge a "penny a point," based on the total number of points scored by both teams. The more points scored, the more money will be raised. In other words, if the teams were able to play a game continuously for eight hours, scoring a total of 1250 points, then each donor would pay $12.50. Of course, pledges can be more (like the buck-a-basket), but each person may give as much as they feel they are able. The funds raised can then be used for a worthy project. If people know ahead of time what the money is being raised for, the response will normally be greater. (Contributed by Robin Williams, Roseville, California)

A CUP OF COOL WATER IN HIS NAME

This is both a service project and an opportunity to witness for Christ! Any church that is near beaches or other recreational areas where large groups of people gather can do this. Materials needed are a five-gallon cooler (filled with ice water) and paper cups. The cooler can be pulled in a wagon or at the beach, may be carried by a guy on a back-pack frame. The water is usually appreciated by people on a hot summer day, when offered at no charge, with a smile and perhaps a word about "Living Water" (John 4), it can be a positive way to share Christ with people. (Contributed by Mike Weaver, Panama City, Florida)

ECOLOGICAL SCAVENGER HUNT

The following is a good activity for get togethers at the beach or at a picnic and park area. Give the kids a list of the following items which must be found *on the ground.* No taking from garbage cans allowed!! Give points for each item found (no limit per item, that is, someone can bring back 25 aluminum cans and collect 25 points). Also, award bonus points for the most different items on the list, for example, if anyone brings in at least one of every item on the list, he might get a bonus of 100 points. If he brings back 7 different items, 70 bonus points could be awarded, etc. Below is a sample list:

1. Candy wrapper
2. Aluminum beverage can
3. Plastic fork
4. Paper cup
5. Plastic spoon
6. Gum wrapper
7. Paper plate
8. Pop or Beer bottle
9. Napkin
10. Article of clothing

All items must be brought in complete. No tearing things in half and counting them twice. You may add items to the list about as you see fit, depending on where you do it. Give everyone a plastic trash bag to collect their stuff in, and have a prize for the winner. (Contributed by Phil Miglioratti, Chicago, Illinois)

ECOLOGY WALK

This takes in two ideas and can be very successful if you have a large group of over 25. First of all, as in a regular walk-a-thon, you get sponsors for your kids. Then, as the kids walk, they pick up all the aluminum cans which litter the highways. Have some one follow along and pick up full containers in a truck. Divide the kids in groups of 5 or 6 and send them each in a different direction with plastic bags which they can leave filled at the side of the road. If you have a good day, you can easily pick up between 500 and 1,000 pounds of aluminum which can be recycled. Cost at present for the cans is somewhere around $200.00 a ton. (Contributed by Daniel Unrath, Parkesburg, Pennsylvania)

FREE CAR WASH

Set up a youth car wash at a local shopping center or filling station as you normally would. However, instead of charging for the wash tickets, *give them away.* Advertise it as a "FREE CAR WASH." Make it clear that there are "no strings attached." Anyone may get their car washed free by the youth of your church simply because it is a gesture of Christian love and friendship.

However, those who care to may make a contribution of any

amount they choose. This money can then be used by the youth for a missionary project, a relief agency providing food for famine stricken countries, or other worthy projects.

A sign may be posted at the car wash site similar to this one:

> Your car is being washed by the youth of _____ church for free with no strings attached. It's just one small way for us to demonstrate to you the love of Jesus Christ.
> Another way we are attempting to share Christ's love is by collecting funds to help purchase food for the hungry. If you would like to help us with this project, your contribution would be greatly appreciated. Thank you and God bless you.

Of course, your version of this sign would depend on what you were raising money for, but it is suggested that you avoid using this to simply increase the coffers of the church building fund or the youth group's social activities fund. You can print this information on the tickets as well, and many people will come prepared to give.

One youth group did this twice and raised a total of $800.00, strictly through contributions received at their free car washes. Pick a good (busy) location, make sure you have plenty of hard-working, friendly kids, and the experience can be very rewarding. (Contributed by Gary Close, Sharon, Pennsylvania)

GIFT OF LOVE

An effective way for young people to exercise their faith is through helping others without regard for getting anything in return. Try mailing a letter such as the one below to homes in your community and see what develops.

> Dear friend,
>
> The members of the church Youth Fellowship want to show appreciation for our special friends by a work day. Can we help you in some way? Does your lawn need mowing? Do you need help getting groceries? Would you want windows washed? Would you like us to read to you? Just visit you?
>
> Just mark on the enclosed card how we can be of some help. If we receive a reply from you, we will come on ____. Please indicate whether you prefer morning or afternoon.

Of course, there is no charge. This is a gift of love.

(Contributed by Alyce Redwine, Phoenix, Arizona)

HIGH-RISE HAYRIDE

Hayrides still can be done even if you live in the city! Use trucks and fill them with hay and kids. A flat-bed "semi" truck and trailer can hold fifty to one hundred kids. Plan a route on not-so-busy streets and keep the speed down to 20 m.p.h. or less for safety. At Christmas, you can go "caroling" at high-rise apartments or condominiums, and people will come out on their balconies to hear. It's a great way to spread a little "Christmas cheer." (Contributed by Bill Serjak, Hollywood, Florida)

INVENTORY

Call large retail stores in your city and volunteer for "group inventory." Every store has to take a periodic inventory and usually needs temporary help to do it. They'll pay at least minimum wage, which can be a good fund raiser for the youth group, if the kids agree to kick in their pay. (Contributed by Richard McPherson, Portland, Oregon)

RAKE AND RUN

Here's a way to involve kids in a ministry to the community which is great if you live in an area where neighborhood trees shed their

Be sure to join us in our "Rake & Run" Party this Saturday afternoon from 1:00 until 4:00.

Bring a leaf rake (If you have one) Wear old clothes. We'll ride the bus to various deserving homes and rake their leaves and then run to the next one.

We'll eat too!

Lots of fun while we do something worthwhile for others.

leaves each fall. Load up all the kids in a bus and "arm" each with a lawn rake. You just go up and down streets and whenever you see a lawn that needs raking, everyone jumps out and rakes all the leaves up. No pay is accepted for any of the work. It is all done in the name of Christ. You might find out the names of shut-ins who cannot rake their own lawns as specific homes to visit. It can be a fun and rewarding for the kids. Note: During the Winter, kids can shovel snow in the same way. You can call it "SNOW AND BLOW." (Contributed by Arthur Merkle, Wilmington, Ohio)

THIRD WORLD BANQUET

This idea has been used successfully as one way to demonstrate the severe problem of hunger and famine in much of the world. Have a banquet for the youth and serve half the group steak with all the trimmings, and the other half rice and water. Do it without any explanation at first and watch the hostilities develop among the "underprivileged" half of the group. Explain that this is the way it is in the real world (you can give statistics) with only half of the world's population controlling much of the earth's resources. If you give the "privileged" half enough on their plates, many of them will undoubtedly share part of their food with the others who received only rice. Some will even offer to trade meals. Others will remain "selfish" and enjoy their steak by themselves. Obviously, this experience can lead to a very revealing discussion on world hunger and our response to it and can be tied in with a film, speaker or fund raising even relating to this subject.

TEN STEPS TO ACTION

It is often easy to see problems in the world and something else to do something about them. As an exercise to help kids to see what they can do, give the following instructions, one at a time and give enough time for kids to think through each point. Discussion can follow.

1. List 5 social problems in your community.
2. Circle 3 for church.
3. Underline 2 of those you can do.
4. Rewrite one of these 2.
5. List 5 things to be done to deal with this problem.
6. Circle 2 you can do.
7. Underline 1 you will do.
8. What will hinder you from accomplishing the task?
9. What will help you to do it?
10. Will you do it?

(Contributed by Homer Erekson, Fort Worth, Texas)

WORKATHON

Here's a service project that gets both kids and adults involved, plus helps fill needs at home and abroad. Have the kids in the youth group work for various people in the community who can't afford to pay for it or who are unable to do it themselves. This could include painting, gardening, housekeeping, shopping, or any other service that the kids could perform. Each kid gets one or more sponsoring adults to pay their ''wage'' (so much per hour) for each hour that they work. The money collected (which can be a considerable amount) can then be given to feed hungry people in famine-stricken areas or to support missionaries in other lands. This way you get twice the mileage out of one act of service. (Contributed by David Self, Irving, Texas)